PRAISE FOR JAMES CHACE'S 1912

"James Chace has served up a rich, irresistible slice of Americana in recounting the storied 1912 presidential campaign. He gives us red-blooded American politics as it was once practiced, complete with bunting and brass bands, whistle-stop tours and frenzied, whooping crowds, shady bosses and spirited reformers deadlocked in sweltering conventions. So many major themes of the coming century were first enunciated here. Best of all, Chace supplies sharply etched portraits of the four leather-lunged, barnstorming giants—Teddy Roosevelt, William Howard Taft, Woodrow Wilson, and Eugene Debs—who waged this most memorable contest. *1912* seems like the perfect home companion for this or any other presidential election year."

—Ron Chernow, author of *Alexander Hamilton*

"A brisk tale of how a bruising presidential race changed the major U.S. political parties f............ .... fficiently and with an ear for good quotes ......

—*Time*

"Engrossing. . . . T.. t of the 20th century is particularly pertinent today. . . . It's hard to recall another American presidential drama with such compelling characters."

—*BusinessWeek*

"Roosevelt, Wilson, Taft, Debs—four of America's political giants in the decades when the 20th century was young—each commanded the enthusiastic faith of millions. The country's two-party system, unable to contain the clashing ambitions of all four, broke down in the presidential election of 1912. This is the riveting story that James Chace tells in his important new book, *1912,* which is peopled with outsized, colorful characters, and punctuated by wonderful anecdotes. It has much to tell us that is of value today, and it abounds in 'what ifs': moments when, but for some minor accident, American, and even world, history might have turned around and gone the other way."

—David Fromkin, author of Europe's Last Summer

"Chace has created in *1912* a lively, riveting story of a presidential election that has all the necessary elements for an absorbing film. Chace does an outstanding job in recounting one of America's most fascinating presidential election campaigns with surprising twists and turns. . . . *1912* is a well-done, fascinating book that should be must reading for any student of American politics."

—Buffalo News

"Chace shows with clarity and insight that a little-remembered political season 92 years ago has echoed mightily throughout the 20th century and on into the 21st. . . . In *1912,* Chace has sketched an engrossing political horse race that is at once familiar and strange. In revealing both aspects, the book makes for engaging historical reading during our own election season."

—Christian Science Monitor

"Chace has ably captured the men and issues of the campaign. But this is more than history in a bottle, for he goes beyond the 1912 election to locate its continuing effects on and significance in subsequent American history."

—Los Angeles Times Book Review

"For sheer drama—or melodrama—few elections can approach the four-way donnybrook of 1912, cradle of modern American politics. A ruptured friendship leading to a shattered Republican Party; the meteoric rise of a messianic professor turned reformer; the high-water mark of American Socialism; an assassination attempt on the eve of voting— *1912* reminds us that history is, above all, a great *story.* James Chace is a great storyteller, capturing in prose as vivid as the year itself all the poignancy and egotism, crusading zeal and authentic passion of an electrifying contest for America's soul."

—Richard Norton Smith, author of Patriarch

"The story is a great one, and Mr. Chace tells it well."
—*The Washington Times*

"[The 1912 election] has never been researched more exhaustively or told better. . . . *1912* traces the decline in the relationship of Taft and Roosevelt in vivid detail. . . . Chace's treatment of the determined Socialist [Debs] is expert."
—*The New Leader*

"Some histories interpret new evidence and add to our store of knowledge. Some, relying on other's research, simply tell a known story. Chace's work is the best of the latter kind: a lively, balanced and accurate retelling of an important moment in American history. . . . Chace brings sharply alive the distinctive characters in this fast-paced story. There won't soon be a better-told tale of one of the last century's major elections."
—*Publishers Weekly*

"A lively recounting of this pivotal, bitter contest. . . . With perfectly chosen anecdotes, Chace moves nimbly among the candidates. . . . At the same time, he underscores the race's larger, often enduring, issues. . . . Entertaining, insightful history about a defining moment in 20th-century politics."
—*Kirkus Reviews*

"In 1912, four formidable personalities of mythic proportions clashed in their quest for the presidency. This was a unique event in American history, and James Chace does full justice to a dramatic story."
—Arthur Schlesinger, Jr.

"Chace doesn't need to prove that this election changed the country or even the Republican Party—the story of the 1912 campaign is worth telling because it's one of the great political stories in American history. . . . If I could cover any election in American history, I would direct my time machine to 1912."
—*The Wall Street Journal*

"Chace fills an expansive narration with a sense of drama and excitement."

—*Austin American-Statesman*

"An intimate account that captures the personalities of the four contenders. . . . Scholars, presidential buffs, and the general public will thoroughly enjoy this well-crafted and timely page-turner. Highly recommended."

—*Library Journal*

"Chace's . . . portrayals of the four players are fascinating. This is a valuable look at how and why our current political culture has evolved."

—*Booklist*

"The nation has had only a few elections where it faced a crossroads, where its ideals and understanding of itself were put to the test. The presidential race of 1912, as James Chace shows in his new book, was such an election."

—*The New York Sun*

"For sound, fury and continuing interest over the years, it would be hard to top the presidential election of 1912. Chace's book illuminates the vivid contending personalities and provides lively reading."

—*The News & Observer* (Raleigh, North Carolina)

ALSO BY JAMES CHACE

Acheson:
The Secretary of State Who Created the American World

The Consequences of the Peace:
The New Internationalism and American Foreign Policy

What We Had:
A Memoir

America Invulnerable:
The Quest for Absolute Security from 1812 to Star Wars
(with Caleb Carr)

Endless War:
How We Got Involved in Central America—and What Can Be Done

Solvency:
The Price of Survival

A World Elsewhere:
The New American Foreign Policy

The Rules of the Game
(novel)

Wilson, Roosevelt, Taft & Debs—

the Election That Changed

the Country

1912

JAMES CHACE

Simon & Schuster Paperbacks

New York   London   Toronto   Sydney

For Joan and for Caleb

Simon & Schuster Paperbacks
Rockefeller Center
1230 Avenue of the Americas
New York, NY 10020

First Simon & Schuster paperback edition 2005

SIMON & SCHUSTER PAPERBACKS and colophon are registered trademarks
of Simon & Schuster, Inc.

For information about special discounts for bulk purchases,
please contact Simon & Schuster Special Sales:
1-800-456-6798 or business@simonandschuster.com.

Manufactured in the United States of America

3   5   7   9   10   8   6   4   2

The Library of Congress has cataloged the hardcover edition as follows:

Chace, James.
1912 : Wilson, Roosevelt, Taft & Debs—the election that changed
the country / James Chace.
p.   cm.
Includes bibliographical references and index.

ISBN-13: 978-0-7432-0394-4
ISBN-10:   0-7432-0394-1
ISBN-13: 978-0-7432-7355-8 (Pbk)
ISBN-10:   0-7432-7355-9 (Pbk)

1. Presidents—United States—Election—1912.   2. Presidential candidates—
United States—History—20th century.   3. Wilson, Woodrow, 1856–1924.
4. Roosevelt, Theodore, 1858–1919.   5. Taft, William H. (William Howard),
1857–1930.   6. Debs, Eugene V. (Eugene Victor), 1855–1926.
7. Political parties—United States—History—20th century.   8. United States—
Politics and government—1909–1913.   9. United States—Social conditions—
1865–1918.   I. Title.

E765.C47 2004

324.973'0912—dc22

2004041660

CONTENTS

Prologue   The Defining Moment   I

PART ONE   *America's Destiny*   9

One   "Back from Elba"   II

Two   "The Ruthlessness of the Pure in Heart"   39

Three   The Heirs of Hamilton and Jefferson   55

Four   The Debs Rebellion   67

PART TWO   *Chicago and Baltimore*   91

Five   "Stripped to the Buff"   93

Six   "A Rope of Sand"   107

Seven   Standing at Armageddon   115

Eight   The Fullness of Time   125

Nine   Baltimore   143

Ten   The Indispensable Man   161

Eleven   To Make a Revolution: Debs and Haywood   169

PART THREE   *The Contenders*   189

Twelve   The New Freedom vs. the New Nationalism   191

Thirteen The Crusader   199

Fourteen   The Moralist   209

Fifteen   The Authentic Conservative and the Red Prophet   219

Sixteen   "To Kill a Bull Moose"   227

PART FOUR   *The Consequences of Victory*   241

Seventeen   The Ironies of Fate   243

Eighteen   Endgames   261

Epilogue   The Inheritors   277

Notes   285

Bibliographical Note   305

Acknowledgments   307

Index   309

PROLOGUE

The Defining Moment

To Woodrow Wilson, it seemed the cheering would never end. The president had sailed to Europe three weeks after the Armistice that had halted the savage killing of the First World War. Now his task was to complete a peace treaty that would bring forth a League of Nations that he believed would prevent a great war from ever happening again.

As the steamship *George Washington* reached the French seacoast of Brittany just before dawn on December 13, 1918, Wilson could see lights on the horizon as a flotilla of American warships sailed out to greet him. Nine battleships came abreast of the warship and the five destroyers that had accompanied the *George Washington* across the Atlantic. Each fired a twenty-one-gun salute to the president of the United States as Wilson's ship sailed toward the harbor at Brest.

There was more to come. Two French cruisers and nine French destroyers came up from the south, firing their own salutes. By the time Wilson entered the harbor, shore batteries from the ten forts on both sides of the cliffs began firing salutes. The military bands on the top of the cliffs blazed forth with renditions of "The Star-Spangled Banner" and "La Marseillaise."

Once the president and his wife were onshore, the mayor of Brest offered Wilson a parchment scroll, festooned with red, white, and blue ribbons, which contained the greetings of the city council. The Americans then climbed into open automobiles that took them up the cliff and on to the railroad station where French President Raymond Poincaré was waiting to escort them to Paris.

Along the route American soldiers were standing at attention. As the train approached the French capital people swarmed the tracks waiting to welcome the American president. The next day, the largest number of Parisians ever to welcome a foreign leader packed the streets and boulevards. Under a clear autumn sky, from the church of the Madeleine to the Bois de Boulogne, they thronged the sidewalks and rooftops. Thirty-six thousand French soldiers formed lines to hold back the crowds.

Flowers floated down on Mrs. Wilson when the entourage passed under a banner stretched across the Champs-Élysées that proclaimed "Honor to Wilson the Just." For the first time in living memory, a carriage passed under the Arc de Triomphe. "No one ever had such cheers," the American journalist William Bolitho wrote, "I, who heard them in the streets of Paris, can never forget them in my life. I saw [Marshall] Foch pass, [Premier] Clemenceau pass, [British Prime Minister] Lloyd George, generals, returning troops, banners, but Wilson heard from this carriage something different, inhuman—or superhuman. Oh, the immovably shining, smiling man!"[1]

For the rest of the month of December, similar scenes were repeated in England, including a trip north to Carlisle near the Scottish border where Wilson's mother was born and his grandfather had been a preacher before immigrating to America. Then back to Paris and on December 31 by the Italian royal train to Rome, where he was met with near hysterical demonstrations. Airplanes roared overhead as he rode with the king and queen through streets covered with golden sand from the Mediterranean, an ancient tradition of honoring heroes come to Rome. Leaving the capital to journey north to Turin and Milan, he blew kisses to the crowd.[2]

Wilson thought he was on the verge of realizing his dream of bringing perpetual peace to a worn-out continent, a Europe whose statesmen believed that maintaining a balance of power among nations was the only way to contain conflict.

Only two months earlier, Wilson had suffered a serious setback. In November 1918, his Democratic Party lost both the House and the Senate to the Republicans. Now the opposition asked what right did he have to go to Europe as a representative of the American people. His greatest antagonist, former president Theodore Roosevelt, had declared: "Our allies and our enemies and Mr. Wilson himself should all understand that Mr. Wilson has no authority whatever to speak for the American people at this time. His leadership has been emphatically repudiated by them . . . and all his utterances every which way have ceased to have any shadow of right to be accepted as expressive of the will of the American people."[3]

It was Roosevelt who had split the Republican Party by running against President William Howard Taft in the presidential election of 1912, and by so doing may well have handed Wilson the presidency. Now Roosevelt, having repaired his relations with the Republicans, was, at sixty, their likely candidate for president in 1920. During the campaign, Wilson had written that Roosevelt appealed to people's imagination; by contrast, "I do not. He is a real, vivid person . . . I am a vague, conjectural personality, more made up of opinions and academic prepossessions than of human traits and red corpuscles."[4]

Of the other two men who had run in the 1912 campaign against Wilson, William Howard Taft was now happily teaching at the Yale Law School, relieved that he had not been re-elected president; by running a second time for an office he had never truly enjoyed, he had achieved his goal of preventing Roosevelt, once his closest friend, from regaining the White House.

As for the Socialist candidate, Eugene V. Debs, he was still fervently committed to an ideology Wilson both feared and despised. Debs had opposed Wilson's war. Now he was awaiting the verdict of the United States Supreme Court on his appeal to overturn a conviction for violating the Espionage and Sedition Acts.

As THE ROYAL TRAIN bore him through the Italian Alps toward France, Wilson and his wife sat alone in the royal coach. He was in high spirits, for those who had opposed him were far away and he was being hailed as the savior of Europe. About nine in the evening, January 6, 1919, the train stopped at Modena for a short time. Wilson remained in his seat while newspaper correspondents strolled along the platform to stretch their legs. They could easily see him through the window as a messenger brought him a telegram.

When he first glanced at the piece of paper, Wilson was clearly surprised at what he was reading. One of the correspondents saw what he thought was a look of pity—then, finally, a smile of triumph. A few moments later, the newspaperman learned that the telegram had informed the president that Theodore Roosevelt was dead.[5]

TR's FUNERAL took place in early January. He had been very sick since the day the Armistice was signed on November 11, 1918, in and out of hospitals, and finally home to Sagamore Hill for Christmas Eve. It was difficult for him to walk, racked as he was with what the doctors believed was inflammatory rheumatism, and doubtless complicated by parasites he may have picked up on his trip to explore the River of Doubt in the Brazilian jungles five years earlier. Dying in his sleep at four in the morning on January 6, of an embolism, Roosevelt was to be buried at Youngs' Cemetery at Oyster Bay, Long Island, a site not far from Sagamore Hill. The service's only ceremony was the Episcopal Church's Burial of the Dead.

It was snowing that morning. The airplanes that had been flying for the past two days in tribute to the former president and his son, Quentin, a pilot who had died over France during the World War, could no longer keep up their vigil. Roosevelt's wife, Edith, stayed in the house, as was then customary, and read through the funeral service, while some five hundred villagers and dignitaries attended the service at Christ Church.

William Howard Taft, when he heard of Roosevelt's death, telegrammed Mrs. Roosevelt, saying that the world had lost "the most commanding personality in our public life since Lincoln."[6] By now, Taft and Roosevelt had been reconciled. Later, he wrote to TR's sister Corinne to say how glad he was "that Theodore and I came together after that long painful interval. Had he died in a hostile state of mind toward me, I would have mourned the fact all my life. I loved him always and cherish his memory."[7]

Arriving at Oyster Bay, Taft found that the arrangements for receiving him at the funeral services had been botched. He was at first put in a pew with the family servants. When Roosevelt's son Archie saw what had happened, he came up and said, "You're a dear personal friend and you must come up farther." He seated Taft just behind Vice President Thomas Marshall, who was there representing Woodrow Wilson, and just in front of the Senate committee headed by TR's closest political ally and Wilson's great enemy, Senator Henry Cabot Lodge of Massachusetts.[8]

As the coffin was borne out of the church, the snow had stopped falling, although the sky was still gray and heavy. Taft and the other mourners made their way to the cemetery, which was about a mile and a half from the church, and then climbed the hill to where the open grave was waiting. The simple burial service came to an end. Others moved away from the graveside. Taft, however, remained longer than anyone, weeping.[9]

EUGENE V. DEBS, the Socialist candidate for the presidency in 1912, was waiting in early 1919 to be spirited off to prison. Debs, who saw the tradition of American liberty as the cornerstone of American socialism, seemed to welcome the prospect of going to jail for his beliefs.

America at that time was in the grip of a Red Scare that Wilson's Attorney General, A. Mitchell Palmer, had inflicted on those whom the government suspected of Bolshevik sympathies and/or being too critical of the war effort. Wilson ordered Palmer "not to let this country see Red,"[10] and in the opening months of 1918, more than two thousand radical unionists were arrested, and two hundred convictions had been secured under the new espionage law.[11]

In defending himself in his address to the jury in September 1918, Debs invoked the memory of George Washington, Tom Paine, and John Adams, "the rebels of their day," and recalled the memory of America's abolitionists. In contesting the specific charges against him, Debs not only defended his right to free speech under the Constitution but also bitterly cited Wilson's 1912 campaign speeches supporting that right.

All was in vain. The jury found him guilty as charged.

Two days later at the sentencing, Debs rose and made a statement to the court. His words have remained as the clearest declaration of his humanist principles. After recognizing his "kinship with all living beings," he famously said, "while there is a lower class, I am in it, while there is a criminal element, I am of it, and where there is a soul in prison, I am not free."[12]

The judge sentenced Debs to ten years' imprisonment.

THE YEAR 1912 constitutes a defining moment in American history. Of the four men who sought the presidency that year—Wilson, Roosevelt, Taft, and Debs—not one of them had definitively decided to run after the congressional elections of 1910.

Wilson, who had just been elected governor of New Jersey, had long hoped that someday the White House would be his, but all his experience had been as a college professor, and later a president of Princeton. He had been a noted theorist of congressional government, never a practitioner.

Debs had run for president on the Socialist ticket twice before. His firm commitment to social and economic justice targeted him once again as the favorite of Socialist voters, but he himself was weary of campaigning, often too sick to do anything but speak. His thrilling oratory, however, made him invaluable in the struggle against the excesses of industrial capitalism.

Taft, the reluctant incumbent, might well have abandoned the field of battle in 1912 and taught happily at Yale Law School while hoping for an appointment to the Supreme Court. Roosevelt, though lusting after the power of the presidency, still expected to support Taft. TR, after all, had shown himself to be a consummate politician during his two terms in office and appreciated the potency of the party organization. If Taft could have approached his former mentor directly, confessed his anxieties about dealing with a Congress so dominated by right-wing Republicans that he was finding it impossible to fulfill the reformist policies of TR, he might then have urged Roosevelt to run for a third term. This would have prevented Roosevelt from challenging him for the presidency that Taft had so often loathed.[13]

Had the charismatic Roosevelt received the Republican nomination, he almost surely would have won. He, far more than Taft, was in tune with the progressive spirit of the time. The Republican Party, in his hands, would likely have become a party of domestic reform and internationalist realism in foreign affairs. With his heroic virtues and condemnation of materialism, Roosevelt represents the road not taken by American conservatism.

THE VOTE POLLED in 1912 by Debs, who garnered the largest share of the popular total ever won by a Socialist candidate, revealed the depth of the reformist forces sweeping the land. Never again would the Socialists show such strength. The Democrats during Wilson's first term quickly picked up many of the social remedies Debs—and a radicalized Roosevelt—had championed.

Like Theodore Roosevelt, Woodrow Wilson embraced change, both men recognizing that their own careers could not flourish if they were to hold back the tide of reform.[14] Neither leader believed that repose was essential to the happiness of mankind. The issues at stake were vital if America was to transform itself into a society that would deal effectively with the problems of the new century without sacrificing the democratic values that the Founders had envisaged. With the recent influx of new immigrants, many of them were condemned to work in squalid sweatshops and live in the deteriorating conditions of the urban poor. Journalists, social workers, ministers, and middle-class Americans were outraged at the widespread corruption of political bossism in the nation's cities.

The threats to the environment by the expansion of industry and population seemed to require a national commitment to conserving the nation's natural resources to avoid further destruction of wildlife and grasslands. The issue of woman suffrage, the safeguarding of the right of black Americans to vote, and the need to end child labor and to regulate factory hours and conditions went to the very heart of the promise of American democracy.

Above all, there was the question of how to curb the excesses of big business, symbolized by the great trusts, which had accompanied the rise of industrial capitalism. For Roosevelt, calling for a "New Nationalism," the role of government was to regulate big business, which was surely here to stay. For Wilson's "New Freedom," the government's task was to restore competition in a world dominated by technology and mass markets that crushed small business. For Debs, America needed federal control of basic industries and a broad-based trade unionism. As for Taft, the White House simply needed to apply laws that were designed to restrain the excesses of industrial capitalism. Indeed, all four men struggled to balance nineteenth-century democratic values with emerging twentieth-century institutions and technologies. For Roosevelt and Wilson, this required the bold use of executive power; between them they created the modern presidency.

In its essence, 1912 introduced a conflict between progressive idealism, later incarnated by Franklin Delano Roosevelt's New Deal—and subsequently by Truman, Kennedy, Johnson, Carter, and Clinton—and conservative values, which reached their fullness with the presidencies of Ronald Reagan and George W. Bush. The broken friendship between Taft and Roosevelt inflicted wounds on the Republican Party that have never been healed. For the rest of the century and even into the next, the Republican Party was riven by the struggle between reform and reaction, and between unilateralism in foreign relations and cosmopolitan internationalism.

Above all, the contest among Roosevelt, Wilson, Taft, and Debs—over reform at home and later over American involvement abroad—recalls the great days of Jefferson and Hamilton,[15] as the 1912 presidential campaign tackled the central question of America's exceptional destiny.

PART ONE

America's Destiny

ONE

"Back from Elba"

AN ASTOUNDING AND dreadfully poignant letter from his successor, William Howard Taft, awaited Theodore Roosevelt a few days before he was to board an ocean liner for his return to America. It was June 10, 1910, and for more than a year Roosevelt had deliberately absented himself from the political scene at home to hunt wild beasts in Africa with his nineteen-year-old son, Kermit. After the safari, TR was joined by his wife, Edith, and their daughter Ethel. The family then toured Europe where thousands hailed the former president of the United States, whose drive, ebullience, and sweeping intellect made him the most sought-after statesman in the world.

Roosevelt read with growing sadness the letter Taft had written in his own hand on May 26, a casting up of the accounts of the Taft administration, and, behind his words, a barely concealed plea for sympathy and forgiveness. "It is now a year and three months since I assumed office and I have had a hard time," Taft wrote:

> I do not know that I have had harder luck than other presidents but I do know that thus far I have succeeded far less than have others. I have been conscientiously trying to carry out your policies, but my method for doing so has not worked smoothly. . . . My year and two [sic] months have been heavier for me to bear

because of Mrs. Taft's condition. A nervous collapse, with apparent symptoms of paralysis . . . made it necessary for me to be as careful as possible to prevent another attack. Mrs. Taft is not an easy patient and an attempt to control her only increased the nervous strain.[1]

In London, a troubled Roosevelt dictated a hasty reply. He admitted that he was "much concerned about some of the things I see and am told; but what I have felt it best to do was to say absolutely nothing—and indeed to keep my mind as open as I kept my mouth shut."[2]

The day after he composed that letter Roosevelt disappeared from London to go walking through the valley of Itchen to hear English songbirds with the British foreign minister, Sir Edward Grey; during this outing a far more alarming description of the ex-president's views emerges. As Grey recalled, "He spoke of Taft and of their work together with very live affection; he had wished Taft to succeed him, had supported him, made way for him. How could he now break with Taft and attack him? Roosevelt spoke of this prospect in a way that left no doubt of sincerity and poignancy of feeling. On the other hand, how could he sit still and see all his own work being undone and the policies in which he believed being ruined? Roosevelt had come to no decision then, but there was evidence of strong internal combustion of spirit. Such spirits as his, however, are not consumed in this process; the result is energy, decision, and action."[3]

DEPARTING A YEAR EARLIER with Kermit for an eleven-month safari to British East Africa (now the Republic of Kenya), along with a team of Smithsonian naturalists and taxidermists, Roosevelt wrote to the journalist William Allen White that he had planned the trip "so that I can get where no one can accuse me of running, nor do Taft the injustice of accusing him of permitting me to run, the job." Already, in the time that had elapsed between the election in November and the inauguration in March, Taft knew that, as he wrote to Roosevelt at the end of February 1909, "People have attempted to represent that you and I were in some way at odds during the last three months, whereas you and I know that there has not been the slightest difference between us." He signed his note, "With love and affection, my dear Theodore."[4]

Roosevelt answered his letter promptly: "Your letter is so nice—nice isn't anything like a strong enough word, but at the moment to use words as strong as I feel would look sloppy."[5] Although Taft was right in declaring that the two friends were not at odds, he could not know of TR's doubts, which Roosevelt had confided to the journalist Mark Sullivan the day before his departure from the White House on March 3, 1909. Roosevelt and Sullivan had walked to the door and were looking out to the lowering sky over Lafayette Park. "How do you really think Taft will make out?" Sullivan asked. "He's all right," the president replied. "He means well and he'll do his best. But he's weak."[6]

Even though it meant that he was away from his wife, whom he both adored and depended on for her sage political judgments, Roosevelt reacted with characteristically boyish excitement as he embraced the African adventure. And, indeed, it went off remarkably well. Neither TR nor Kermit, who had taken time off from Harvard, suffered from any debilitating illness, and his father was justifiably proud of Kermit's courage. Writing to his oldest boy, Ted, he described Kermit as "a perfectly cool and daring fellow. Indeed he is a little too reckless and keeps my heart in my throat: he is not a good shot, not even as good as I am, and Heaven knows I am poor enough; but he is a bold rider, always cool and fearless, and eager to work all day long. He ran down and killed a Giraffe alone . . . and the day before yesterday he stopped a charging Leopard within six yards of him, after it had mauled one of our porters." Roosevelt may have been, as he put it to his sister, "dreadfully homesick for Edie," but he also admitted that he was "absolutely contented," and as he rode along in a special seat built for him over the cowcatcher of the engine, he hardly knew "a thing which is going on in the other world."[7]

He had brought along his "pigskin library" of eighty books, which meant that he read at least two a week, and many of them several times.[8] Roosevelt later wrote in his own book, *African Game Trails,* that he found in Africa much the same thrill he had first experienced when he was much younger and sought solace in the Badlands of the Dakotas from the pain he was feeling after the sudden death of his first wife, Alice Lee. In Africa, he found

> the joy of wandering through lonely lands; the joy of hunting the mighty and terrible lords of the wilderness. . . . But there are no words that can tell the hidden spirit of the wilderness, that can reveal its mystery, its melancholy, and its charm. . . . swamps where the slime oozes and bubbles and festers in the steaming heat; lakes like seas; skies that burn above deserts . . . mighty rivers rushing out of the heart of the continent through the sadness of endless marshes; forests of gorgeous beauty, where death broods in the dark and silent depths.[9]

The "other world" rudely intruded on his African idyll on January 17, 1910, when a native runner brought a cable from the Press Agency with the news that Chief Forester Gifford Pinchot, an ardent conservationist, had been dismissed by President Taft. Roosevelt who was hunting the rare white rhino in the Congo, about two degrees north of the equator, was shocked by what had befallen Pinchot, one of his closest collaborators; but, as he wrote later that day to Senator Henry Cabot Lodge, "Of course I said nothing. I most earnestly hope it is not true."[10]

The African postman—"who runs stark naked with the mail"—later picked up another letter, this one from Roosevelt to Pinchot. "Dear Gifford," TR wrote. "We have just heard by special runner that you have been removed. I cannot believe it. I do not know any man in public life who has rendered quite the service you have rendered."[11] Roosevelt would not receive for another month Gifford's charges that Taft had all but abandoned TR's environmental policies. In an anguished letter Gifford began by declaring, "We have fallen back down the hill you led us up."[12]

Although Pinchot bore the rather lowly title of chief forester, serving under Secretary of the Interior James R. Garfield, he had become vital to Roosevelt's campaign to save the wilderness from rapacious loggers. Moreover, Pinchot had achieved a true friendship with Roosevelt. Like TR, Pinchot was rich and well connected, as well as having a strong social conscience.

Pinchot believed in "scientific management" of the North American forest, and, along with Roosevelt, saw himself as anointed to save and wisely use America's resources. In 1891 Congress had passed a law permitting the president to put certain federally owned properties into "forest reserves." Other presidents had already transferred some fifty million acres of timberland into the reserve system. Roosevelt expanded the practice. To help accomplish this, he chose Gifford Pinchot as a man who combined, as Roosevelt saw it, "entire disinterestedness and sanity" with "great energy and knowledge." Guided by Pinchot, TR placed another 150 million acres as forest reserves.[13]

Taft retained Pinchot after dropping Interior Secretary James R. Garfield and replacing him with Richard Ballinger, a one-time reform mayor of Seattle who now apparently favored exploitation of natural resources. Thus, a struggle between Pinchot and Ballinger was all but inevitable, and Taft concluded that he had to fire Pinchot.

According to Cabot Lodge, who also wrote Roosevelt about the matter, Pinchot had brought the ouster on himself by allowing his disagreements with Ballinger to escalate into virtual insubordination. Lodge, hearing that Pinchot was planning to go abroad to meet TR, warned the ex-president not to be "put in the apparent attitude of upholding Pinchot against the administration." As Lodge put it, "There is a constantly growing thought of you and your return to the Presidency." Above all, "I want you to be entirely aloof from these things, at least until we can meet and discuss the situation."

Upon receiving Lodge's letter when he met a steamer on the Upper White Nile, Roosevelt wrote the senator to assure him that he would "say nothing about politics until I have been home long enough to know the situation." TR would be willing to meet Pinchot if he came abroad, but, he wrote Lodge, they "must renominate" Taft for the presidency in 1912.[14]

Arriving on March 14, 1910, in Khartoum in the Anglo-Egyptian Sudan, TR went directly to the railroad station to join Edith Roosevelt and their eighteen-year-old daughter, Ethel. Together with Kermit, the family made their way by train and steamer down the Nile to Cairo, and thence to Alexandria, where they boarded the steamer *Prinz Heinrich* for Naples. In Rome as in Naples, Roosevelt was greeted with great enthusiasm at state dinners and meetings with mayors and monarchs. Far from being dazzled by royalty, Roosevelt was both amused and distressed by them, writing of their "appallingly dreary life" and speculating that meeting him was "a relief to the tedium, the dull, narrow routine of their lives."

These observations were only reinforced by his travels to other capitals on the continent. Kaiser Wilhelm II flattered him by inviting him to review German troops for five hours. Later, the kaiser sent him a photograph of the two of them on horseback talking earnestly. On this, the kaiser wrote: "The Colonel of the Rough Riders instructing the German Emperor in field tactics." On another, he scribbled: "When we shake hands we shake the world."[15]

WHILE ROOSEVELT was making his stately journey from Egypt to Italy, a tall, lean gentleman with thinning hair and a dark, drooping mustache had boarded the liner *President Grant* for Europe. This was Gifford Pinchot, heading for Porto Maurizio on the Italian Riviera to see his old friend and protector, Theodore Roosevelt.[16]

The Roosevelts, wearied by the round of dinners and receptions they were attending, were hoping to relax at a villa rented by Edith's spinster sister, Emily Carow, in the ancient town of Porto Maurizio on the Ligurian Sea. They arrived on April 10 to encounter once again ecstatic cries of "Viva Roosevelt" from what seemed the entire population of the town of six thousand. After a ceremony during which the mayor made Roosevelt an honorary citizen, they repaired to the villa for the night. That same evening, Gifford Pinchot checked into the Riviera Palace Hotel, and the next morning Roosevelt emerged from his villa at nine o'clock to greet Pinchot with a joyful shout of "Hello, Gifford."

They talked for two hours, which Pinchot recorded in his diary as "one of the best & most satisfactory talks with T.R. I ever had."[17] Not only did Pinchot defend his position in criticizing Taft's new secretary of the interior, but he also brought with him letters from some of TR's closest collaborators, such as Republican Senators Albert J. Beveridge of Indiana and Jonathan P. Dolliver of Iowa, and journalist William Allen White. They provided a rich bill of particulars against the administration and, most especially, criticized the president for cooperating too closely with the reactionary and imperious Nelson W. Aldrich of Rhode Island, so powerful that he was called the "manager of the United States," and the acknowledged boss of the Senate.

The Republican arch-conservatives had always been wary of TR's commitment to political and economic reform: they detested Roosevelt's effort to regulate the great business and financial trusts, his disposition to reduce tariffs, and his environmental policy of protecting and conserving the wilderness.

By signing the Payne-Aldrich tariff bill, Taft seemed to have broken the promises made in the Republican platform of 1908, when the party had pledged tariff revision, which was understood to mean a reduction in the high levels established a decade earlier. Aldrich had worked closely with the equally conservative, whiskey-drinking, poker-playing speaker of the house, "Uncle" Joe Cannon, ostensibly to support the lower tariff that Taft wanted. Although Aldrich, along with Cannon and Sereno Payne, chairman of the House Ways and Means Committee, did produce a bill that reduced the rates on a number of items, most of the changes went upward. In humorist Finley Peter Dunne's newspaper column, his imaginary Irish saloon keeper-philosopher Mr. Dooley observed: "Th' Republican party has been thrue to its promises. Look at th' free list if ye don't believe it. Practically ivrything necessary to existence comes in free. Here it is. Curling stones, teeth, sea moss, newspapers, nux vomica, Palu, canary bird seed."[18] Although Taft was deeply wounded by Aldrich's betrayal, he refused to interfere with the legislative process, as TR had often done, and became therefore even more dependent on Aldrich and Cannon. As Senator Dolliver put it, Taft is a "ponderous and amiable man completely surrounded by men who know exactly what they want."

The meeting between Pinchot and Roosevelt was a turning point in Roosevelt's attitude toward Taft. In the letter TR composed to Lodge immediately after his encounter with Pinchot, responding to the senator's urging that Roosevelt save the party from defeat in the upcoming congressional elections by supporting the Taft administration, Roosevelt replied with some outrage that since the administration had "completely twisted round the policies I advocated and acted upon," supporting Taft was out of the question.[19]

The reform legislation that had been passed during his presidency justified in Roosevelt's eyes his growing disenchantment with his successor.

Had he not begun some forty suits against trusts? Not that he wanted to break them up so much as regulate them; he was not against big business, he was against wickedness. Only too often he had seen that the very rich, those "malefactors of great wealth," were often the very wicked. As he had written to the investment banker Jacob Schiff in 1907, "I wish to do everything in my power to aid every honest businessman, and the dishonest businessman I wish to punish simply as I would punish the dishonest man of any type."[20]

He had ordered the successful antitrust suit against J. P. Morgan's Northern Securities, a giant holding company that controlled the big western railroads. By threatening to intervene in the anthracite coal strike of 1902, he had forced the mine operators to accept arbitration. He had put an end to freight rebates by railroads, and with the Hepburn Act strengthened the Interstate Commerce Commission, which authorized the government to set railroad rates. In 1906, the Pure Food and Drug Act was passed to remedy the scandals of the meatpacking industry. And there were the Employers' Liability and Safety Appliance Laws to limit the hours of employees, and more.

Even when he did not achieve everything he wanted, he had set the agenda for his successor. In his annual message to Congress in 1907, he had called for the imposition of income and inheritance taxes, currency reform, limitation of injunctions in labor disputes, the eight-hour day, and control of campaign contributions.

Taft had certainly carried out part of this agenda: the eight-hour day for government employees and support for a constitutional amendment in favor of an income tax. He brought more antitrust suits in one term than in TR's two terms, one of which broke up Rockefeller's Standard Oil Company. Nonetheless, his failure to achieve meaningful tariff reform, and now his removal of Gifford Pinchot, signaling an abandonment of TR's conservation policies, fixed TR's criticisms against him.

Even though he had no intention of becoming a candidate for the presidency in two years, even while he still believed that Taft had to be renominated, Roosevelt was now beginning to feel more sympathy for the insurgents, those Republican senators who were fed up with the Aldrich-Cannon axis. In defending his choice of Taft as his anointed successor, he wrote Lodge that "the qualities shown by a thoroughly able and trustworthy lieutenant are totally different, or at least may be totally different, from those needed by the leader, the commander. Very possibly if Taft had tried to work in my spirit and along my lines, he would have failed; that he has consciously tried to work for the objects I had in view, so far as he could approve them, I have no doubt."

He went on to castigate the "Cannon-Aldrich type of leadership," which represented, in his view, "not more than ten per cent. of the party's voting strength." But "if the great mass—the ninety per cent. of the party,—the men who stand for it as their father stood for it in the days of Lincoln, get convinced that the ten per cent. are not leading them right, a revolt is sure to ensue." In a postscript, he protested that he was not planning to be the standard bearer of the party in the next presidential election: "I don't think under the Taft-Aldrich-Cannon regime there has been a real appreciation of the needs of the country [but] I very earnestly hope that Taft will retrieve himself, and if, from whatever causes, the present condition of the party is hopeless, I most emphatically desire that I shall not be put in the position of having to run for the Presidency, staggering under a load which I cannot carry, and which has been put on my shoulders through no fault of my own."[21]

Theodore Roosevelt was not being disingenuous. He was fearful that the people would blame him for foisting William Howard Taft on them; but he was not the betrayer, rather he was, as he saw it, the betrayed. At the same time he retained a real measure of affection for Taft—his secretary of war, the man to whom he had twice offered a place on the Supreme Court. Taft, the loyal and able lieutenant, was quite simply *not* the commander that Roosevelt had been.

ON THE NIGHT before Roosevelt wrote his anguished letter to Lodge, the night that Pinchot had arrived in Porto Maurizio, President Taft sat in the Blue Room of the White House with a former Yale classmate, his sister-in-law, and his military aide Archie Butt. They were listening to Enrico Caruso on the Victrola, and Taft, aware that Pinchot was seeing TR in Italy, pondered his helplessness before what Pinchot would say. "I suppose Pinchot will fill his ears with prejudicial tales," he mused, "but that I cannot help and I cannot checkmate." He was asked by his old classmate if he thought Roosevelt would run for the presidency at the next election. "I don't think he will want to," Taft responded, "but the country may demand it of him; and if he does, he will most certainly be elected."[22]

On another occasion at the White House, reflecting on Roosevelt's extraordinary reception in Europe, Taft spoke out with characteristic honesty and generosity: "I don't suppose there ever was such a reception as that being given Theodore in Europe now. It does not surprise me that rulers, potentates, and public men should pay him honor, but what does surprise me is that small villages which one would hardly think had ever heard of the United States should seem to know all about him. . . . It is the force of his personality that has passed beyond his own country and the capitals of the world and seeped into the small crevices of the universe." Asked what would be Roosevelt's chief claim to greatness, Taft's answer was prompt and acute: "His rousing of public conscience. . . . his power over the imagination and his inspiration to the public conscience is his predominant claim to greatness."[23]

IN EUROPE, meanwhile, Roosevelt and his family went on with their grand tour. In Paris on April 23, the former president gave an address at the Sorbonne on "The Duties of the Citizen," in which he talked of the need for sound character, homely virtues, virility, and the desirability of maintaining a high birthrate; the effect of his speech on his audience was, as he put it, "a little difficult for me to understand"; his listeners may have found a beguiling innocence in his advice. Later, he met with Parisians at a salon held by Mrs. Roosevelt's cousin Edith Wharton, at her place on the rue de Varenne. Few of the French could speak English, and TR spoke French "with a rather bewildering pronunciation," according to Mrs. Wharton.[24]

In Norway, on May 5, to receive the Nobel Peace Prize for his mediation of the Russo-Japanese War in 1905, the first to go to an American, TR gave a speech that was especially noteworthy because of his suggestion that a world organization be created to prevent war. In words that foreshadowed Woodrow Wilson's League of Nations, Roosevelt called for the creation by the great powers of "a League of Peace, not only to keep the peace among themselves, but to prevent, by force, if necessary, its being broken by others."[25] TR's League, unlike Wilson's, would have a strong military component to enforce its dictates.

Arriving finally in London before he embarked on the homecoming voyage across the Atlantic, Roosevelt was asked by Taft to represent the United States at the state funeral for King Edward VII, who had died when Roosevelt was in Norway. The late king was related to all the monarchs of Europe, and his funeral was to be the last gathering of continental royalty before the holocaust of the First World War. London was brimming with royals, and most of those who had never met him were eager to do so: at one point while TR was catching up with his mail, a silk-hosed footman announced to him that a king had come to call and was waiting downstairs. "Confound these kings," TR said, "will they never leave me alone?"[26] He was eager to return to America.

ALREADY VAST NUMBERS of New Yorkers were gathering in the early morning of June 18, 1910, at the Battery, and thousands more were lining up along Broadway and Fifth Avenue. Some had stood for hours in the heat and now in the rain. But nothing could quell their spirits. Theodore Roosevelt was back from Africa and that was enough.

As the *Kaiserin Augusta Victoria* dropped anchor and readied itself for the boarding of a health officer at the quarantine station, the clouds lifted and the sun started to break through. Later, out of the fog a launch appeared, circling the liner until the health officer gave permission for those visitors to board if they could scale the ladder. Except for the secretary of the navy's wife, they could, and did: the secretary himself, George Meyer; Secretary of Agriculture James Wilson, who was nearly eighty and almost fell off the ladder; Senator Henry Cabot Lodge; Ohio Congressman Nicholas Longworth, married to Alice, TR's daughter by his first wife; and Captain Archibald Willingham Butt, Roosevelt's former and Taft's current military aide, who was bearing two letters in his boot leg—one for Mr. Roosevelt from Mr. Taft, and the other for TR's wife from Mrs. Taft.

The boarding party found the ex-president in his sitting room, and after greeting everyone, Roosevelt quickly skimmed Taft's letter of welcome and urged Archie Butt to tell his successor that he was "deeply touched that he has chosen to send it through you." He then took Cabot Lodge aside for a confidential talk, doubtless to confirm that he had done what Lodge had asked him to do in those months he had been in Africa, and in Europe dining with kings and queens—say nothing publicly about politics.

Their conversation was interrupted by the arrival of Mrs. Roosevelt, Kermit, and Alice Longworth. Like her husband, Edith Roosevelt greeted Captain Butt with great warmth: "Archie," she said, "come let us see if we can see the children on any of the boats." They went to the railing and did spy their oldest boy, Ted, far below with his bride-to-be, along with his two younger brothers, Archie and Quentin, and TR's two sisters, Corinne Robinson and Anna "Bamie" Cowles.

"Think," said Mrs. Roosevelt, "for the first time in nearly two years I have them all within reach." She went back to the cabin and called to her husband: "Come here, Theodore, and see your children. They are of far greater importance than politics or anything else."

As the boys clambered up, the sounds of the welcome to the ex-president, which some newspapermen dubbed "the back-from-Elba bandwagon," reverberated throughout the New York harbor. A naval parade of six battleships, a torpedo boat, destroyers, and a flotilla of yachts of all sizes accompanied the ship. According to Archie Butt, for the next hour "there was a perfect pandemonium of sound. Every craft which could float was out, and each was yelling its steam whistle hoarse. The fleet went as high as Twenty-fourth Street and then turned back to the Battery." Acknowledging the naval display, the fog whistles, the foghorns, Roosevelt, once assistant secretary of the navy, "crowed with delight." After transferring to a smaller vessel as his party neared the landing, TR mounted the bridge, and when the crowds onshore saw him, the cries were loud enough, wrote Archie Butt, "to waken the stones."[27]

Onshore, after a formal greeting from Mayor William Gaynor, it took half an hour to form the line of fourteen carriages to go up Broadway, with the mayor, the ex-president, and Cornelius Vanderbilt, who headed the welcoming committee, in the lead. Almost every band in the city was allowed to stand on the line of march to play. Accompanying the returning hero was a regiment of Rough Riders—soldiers that Colonel Theodore Roosevelt had led in the Spanish-American War—mounted on sorrel horses; two boys, Bud and Temple Abernathy, aged six and ten, respectively, had traveled on horseback from Oklahoma to New York to see the great man. For five miles, through a densely packed crowd, Roosevelt received, as Archie Butt reported, "one continuous ovation."

No one was more thrilled than Captain Butt, who had become very much a member of the boisterous Roosevelt family during TR's years in the White House. He was immensely loyal to Roosevelt, but he was trying to be equally loyal to the new president and now was beginning to fear that Roosevelt and Taft, once the best of friends, would drift apart. In his letter to his sister-in-law—his "dear Clara"—that Butt wrote the day after the extraordinary reception, he spoke of the Roosevelt he now encountered a little more than a year after TR, at fifty, had quit the White House. "To me," he wrote, "he had ceased to be an American, but had become a world citizen. His horizon seemed to be greater, his mental scope more encompassing." He admitted he could offer no hard evidence of the change. "But it is there. He is bigger, broader, capable of greater good or greater evil, I don't know which, than when he left; and he is in splendid health and has a long time to live."[28]

WILLIAM HOWARD TAFT had never wanted to be president. Had Roosevelt not given a rash promise on election night not to seek a third term after he won the 1904 presidency by an overwhelming majority, Taft might never have sat in the White House; instead, he would doubtless have accepted TR's offer of a seat on the Supreme Court. The law, not politics, was his passion. This had been true ever since he was a very young man growing up in Cincinnati as the son of a judge who was also a member of President Grant's cabinet and a minister to Vienna and Saint Petersburg. When he was an undergraduate at Yale, Will Taft fully expected to go to law school and later became a judge in the Cincinnati Superior Court.

He was a model youth, which might have made him obnoxious were it not for his unfailing good humor; even as he struggled with being fat, he was a good athlete, rugged, and in exceptionally fine health. (When he was a baby, his mother wrote, "He is very large of his age and grows fat every day. . . . He has such a large waist, that he cannot wear any of the dresses that are made with belts. He spreads his hands to anyone who will take him and his face is wreathed in smiles at the slightest provocation."[29])

As a child, so as a man. Taft struggled throughout his life against obesity but with little success. An oft-repeated story in this respect came out of Taft's tenure as governor-general of the Philippines in 1900. Taft had gone on a fact-finding trip to the islands that were to become America's first colony, and on his return he cabled Secretary of War Elihu Root, "Stood trip well. Rode horseback twenty-five miles." To which Root replied, "How is the horse?"[30] A special bathtub, seven feet long and nearly four feet wide, was installed in the White House after Taft had become stuck in an ordinary bathtub. With food as his principal solace, Taft weighed 355 pounds on the eve of the 1912 presidential election.

Both Roosevelt and Taft entered college in 1876, but unlike TR, a hurried young man filled with ideas, who did not conform to the studied style of Harvard indifference, Will Taft fully embraced the Yale ethos of fellowship and achievement. He was a scholar, hardworking and well behaved. Like his father, he was elected to the elitist secret society Skull and Bones, which generally sought out young men who were prominent achievers, and at commencement Taft was salutatorian, graduating second in his class. In 1899, he would be offered the presidency of Yale, but he turned it down because he was a Unitarian rather than a member of the orthodox Congregational church of New England. If the next president of Yale was not to be an ordained minister, he could not in any case be what Taft was, a man who, as he wrote, did not believe "in the Divinity of Christ."[31]

Taft could easily have attended such prestigious law schools as Columbia, Harvard, or Yale itself, where his father had received his law degree. That Taft chose to enter the Cincinnati Law School testifies to his devotion to Ohio (and perhaps to Ohio politics), where the Tafts were becoming one of the most admired families in the state. He was admitted to the Ohio bar even before his 1880 graduation. Appointed assistant prosecutor of Hamilton County, he rose rapidly through the Ohio political machine to become a judge on the Ohio Supreme Court.

Taft's career in politics would owe much to Mark Alonzo Hanna's control of Ohio politics. Hanna, a former grocery clerk in Cleveland, had become a great merchant whose fleets transported tonnages of coal and iron ore along the Great Lakes. He was often portrayed in the press as a bully, smoking a big cigar, drinking whiskey, and stamping on the skeletons of working-class women and children. A big man, he was once described as looking like a "well-fed merchant prince from an old Dutch master-piece."[32] Above all, he was the new man in party politics, the businessman who constructed a well-run machine that forced out the political adven-turers who had come to Ohio after the Civil War and who were often per-sonally corrupt and willing to prey on the rich as well as the poor.

Once Hanna became wealthy, he turned over his business to his brother and concentrated all his efforts on creating the "business state." As he once remarked bluntly to a group of dinner companions, "All ques-tions of government in a democracy [are] questions of money."[33] Eventu-ally he became chairman of the Republican National Committee, and the most powerful boss in Republican politics. His signal triumph was putting Ohio's governor William McKinley into the presidency in 1896, and a year later he himself served as a senator from Ohio until his death in 1904.

Will Taft was not particularly close to Hanna, but after Hanna became the dominant force in Ohio politics after 1888, Taft was responsive to the new order and loyally backed McKinley. A telling factor that connected the Taft family to Hanna was the willingness of Taft's brother Charles to join a "syndicate," organized by Hanna to pay off McKinley's debts when the governor found himself in serious trouble after endorsing large sums of notes owned by a ruined business associate. (Several future cabinet members and ambassadors were also in the "syndicate.")

Under Hanna's direction, political professionalism was allied to finan-cial capitalism, whose mantra was high tariff protectionism for industry coupled with "sound money," tying the dollar to gold. Under these condi-tions, foreign monies soon flowed into the United States, making the country independent of European capital markets and one of the great creditor nations of the world.

IN 1889 when Benjamin Harrison was elected president, thirty-two-year-old William Howard Taft, thanks to the Ohio political attachment as well as his own righteous conservatism, was appointed solicitor general, effectively the U.S. government's lawyer.

The White House under Harrison was a dull place. The president himself was generally described as a cold man, little liked even by his fellow Republicans. Washington society was therefore dominated by the John Hay–Henry Adams set, which included not only Cabot Lodge and the British ambassador, Cecil Spring-Rice, but also the newly arrived Civil Service Commissioner Theodore Roosevelt, who once described Harrison as "a cold-blooded, narrow-minded, prejudiced, obstinate, timid old psalmsinging" politician.[34]

Unlike Roosevelt, Taft was not brought into the clever and worldly Hay–Adams circle. Nonetheless, Roosevelt and Taft, almost the same age, got to know each other well. They lived near each other and frequently walked to work and lunched together.

Passing by the White House on the way to their offices, they surely viewed the seat of executive power quite differently. Restless and ambitious, Roosevelt must have yearned to occupy the president's residence, whereas Taft preferred to dream of a place on the Supreme Court. After a two-year stint in Washington, Taft happily accepted an appointment back in Ohio as United States circuit judge for the Sixth Judicial Circuit, a position that could put him in line for promotion to the Supreme Court.

This was not what his young wife wanted. The daughter of a prominent Cincinnati attorney, Helen Herron—always called Nellie—married Will Taft on June 19, 1886. She was highly intelligent, sharp tongued, and ambitious for her husband and for herself. She often criticized Will, which he claimed he usually welcomed, seeing her words as a necessary spur to achievement and no threat to his love for her, or hers for him. "I know that I am very cross to you," she wrote a few years after their marriage, "but I love you just the same."[35]

Nellie Taft always resented Roosevelt, certain that his offer to appoint her husband to the Supreme Court in 1906 was in order to keep him from the presidency, which she, rather than her husband, craved. At that time, a family friend asked young Charlie Taft if his father was going to become a Supreme Court justice. "Nope," said the boy. "Why not?" "Ma wants him to be president," Charlie answered. Will Taft, shortly after the offer was made, told Roosevelt: "Nellie is bitterly opposed to me accepting the position and . . . she telephoned me this morning to say that if I did, I would make the great mistake of my life."[36]

That same year, when Taft was secretary of war, he and his wife were dinner guests at the White House. After the meal, the president brought them up to the second-floor library, threw his head back in an easy chair and closed his eyes. "I am the seventh son of a seventh daughter and I have clairvoyant powers," he intoned. "I see a man weighing three hundred and fifty pounds. There is something hanging over his head. I cannot make out what it is. . . . At one time it looks like the presidency, then again it looks like the chief justiceship."

"Make it the presidency," said Mrs. Taft.

"Make it the chief justiceship," said Mr. Taft.[37]

WHEN TAFT, with Roosevelt's full backing, won the presidency in 1908, Nellie Taft saw her hopes fulfilled: the Tafts were in the White House, and Theodore Roosevelt would soon be in Africa.

On the eve of the inauguration on March 4, 1909, the Tafts were to dine with the Roosevelts and then spend the night in the White House. It was a mistake. Although the friendship between the two men was undimmed, the shadows of their future break were already evident. Taft's cabinet was not what Roosevelt had expected. Taft had indicated he would keep on anyone who wished to remain in the new administration, but once elected, he decided that he needed his own men who would not owe their highest loyalty to Roosevelt. Nonetheless, TR was determined to reserve his judgment and focused his attention on planning his safari.

Neither wife was happy at the prospect of the small dinner. Edith Carow Roosevelt, who had known Theodore since childhood, had about her an air of detached amusement at the boyish enthusiasms of her husband. After the birth of her fourth son she remarked, "Now I have *five* boys." She has been described as an archetypal patrician, who loved art and poetry, "gracious but disciplined, a great lady but one who always regarded herself in the light of a loving support to a greater man."[38] Archie Butt declared that in all her seven years at the White House she never made a mistake.[39]

The burning logs in the fireplace gave a welcoming tone to the evening, but the relationship between the two women had never been close, and the idea of leaving the White House where her children had played so happily made Mrs. Roosevelt pensive. Even the presence of TR's daughter Alice Longworth, who was accompanied by her husband, Nick, did not enliven the gathering, though Alice was considered a mischievous woman with a clever tongue. (According to one anecdote, a friend once begged Roosevelt to "look after Alice more." "Listen," TR responded, "I can be president of the United States—or I can attend to Alice.") Alice was known in Washington society and by the Roosevelts themselves for her imitations of Mrs. Taft.

Others present included Senator Elihu Root of New York, a sardonic man whom Roosevelt had first hoped would succeed him as president but whose reputation as a corporation lawyer made him unacceptable to western progressive voters, and his austere wife, Clara, who could on occasion be moved to tears; Roosevelt's eldest sister, Bamie, and her husband, Admiral William Cowles; Mabel Boardman, who was devoted to Will Taft and who had accompanied the Taft party to the Philippines in 1905; and Archie Butt, who at Taft's request would remain as his military aide. Except for Captain Butt, Nellie Taft had little use for anyone at that table.[40]

At the end of the evening, Mrs. Roosevelt gently took Mrs. Taft's hand and expressed the hope that her first night in the White House would be one of sweet sleep.[41] That night the snow that had been sparse in the early evening became severe, accompanied by seventy-mile-an-hour winds. In the morning at breakfast, the president-elect said to the president, "Even the elements do protest." And Roosevelt said, "I knew there would be a blizzard when I went out."[42]

Despite the snow the inauguration went on as scheduled, and as Theodore Roosevelt and his family headed for their home at Sagamore Hill in Oyster Bay, Long Island, the Tafts watched the inaugural parade, which went on from three to six o'clock. Then there was a reception held for Taft's Yale classmates, followed by a dinner at the Metropolitan Club given by the class of 1878. Then came the inaugural ball at the Pension Building. It was one o'clock in the morning before the president and his party drove home.

The Tafts were a weary couple by that time, but they had endured without complaint the seemingly endless festivities. For Nellie Taft, the high moment of the day had been the return from the swearing-in shortly after noon, when she paused in the doorway of the White House. "I stood for a moment," she remembered, "over the great brass seal, bearing the national coat of arms, which is sunk in the floor in the middle of the entrance hall. 'The Seal of the President of the United States,' I read around the border, and now—that meant my husband."[43]

For Taft, the need to get away from the onerous duties of the presidency often meant riding horseback with Archie Butt, who was happy to stay on at the White House as Taft's invaluable companion. Again and again Taft would summon Butt to accompany him on his expeditions, sometimes on horseback but increasingly giving way to a motor car. In good weather, Taft took Butt along as a golfing partner. Uneasily Taft tried to get used to his high office and to believe that it was indeed he who held it. Toward the end of his first week in the White House, he was asked how he liked being president. "I hardly know yet," he replied. "When I hear someone say Mr. President, I look around expecting to see Roosevelt." But soon "his dear Theodore" would be sailing for his safari in Africa, and Taft keenly felt his absence, the one person outside of Nellie whom he leaned on for advice and guidance.[44]

On the eve of Roosevelt's departure on March 23, Taft sent Archie Butt with a letter of farewell to be delivered to the ex-president on the deck of the S.S. *Hamburg*. Roosevelt was unable to read it until the vessel turned down the Hudson River, but when he did so, he was deeply touched by Taft's promise to carry on the work they had done together. Above all, Taft wanted to reassure TR that the arch-conservative leaders of the party, Nelson Aldrich and Joe Cannon, would follow his lead. He shared with Roosevelt his distrust of both men, but he had seen Roosevelt determined to work with them, which had especially been the case during the first Congress of TR's administration; Taft fervently hoped to do the same.

Taft also knew that Roosevelt would doubtless read of cordial meetings between him and these two legislative barons, and he wanted to reassure him that he would not fall away "from your ideals." No matter what others might report, Taft reminded Roosevelt, "you know me better and will understand that I am still working away on the same old plan and hope to realize in some measure the results that we both hold valuable and worth striving for." He would "never forget that the power I now exercise was a voluntary transfer from you to me," therefore "the succession shall be vindicated according to the standards which you and I in conversation have always formulated."

In a hastily scribbled telegram sent with the pilot to be dispatched to Washington, TR reassured him: "Everything will surely turn out all right, old man."[45]

BUT THINGS DID not turn out well at all. Even as Taft wearily struggled to persuade Aldrich and Cannon to produce a bill that revised tariff rates downward, tragedy struck so close to home that the new president could hardly believe that things would ever brighten for him again. Nellie Taft was keeping a frenetic pace in her efforts to put the measure of her own taste on the White House. She replaced the heavy brocade of curtains and upholstery with chintz, and she wanted to share the president's political cares; at social gatherings she would quickly join him if she saw that he had been taken aside by a politician for a private conversation. She seemed tireless, giving dinner parties, receptions, and musicales. At one afternoon reception she received visitors with her husband and shook two thousand hands.[46]

On May 17, young Charlie Taft was to be operated on for adenoids at the Episcopal Eye and Ear Hospital. Despite a planned excursion to Mount Vernon on the presidential yacht, the *Sylph,* later that day, the president was to meet Mrs. Taft at the hospital to see how the operation went. Taft was late and found his wife looking quite pale but pleased to report that the operation was successful, even though the poor boy was hysterical when he came out from under the ether. Finally, the presidential party boarded the ship, but before the *Sylph* had reached Alexandria, Attorney General George Wickersham turned to Archie Butt and said, "Mrs. Taft has fainted. See if there is any brandy aboard."

This revived her, but according to Captain Butt, she was "deathly pale" and did not speak. Butt half-carried her into the saloon to rest, and the president, equally pale, rushed to join her. The trip back seemed interminable, and after reaching the dock, Mrs. Taft was put into a limousine and brought to the White House, where a doctor was waiting. As Butt described the scene, "The president looked like a great stricken animal. I have never seen greater suffering or pain shown on a man's face."

That evening a dinner was scheduled, which the president attended, smiling in the "most nonchalant way" in order to keep his wife's condition a secret. No newspaper reported that Mrs. Taft had suffered a stroke, probably a cerebral hemorrhage. Without drugs of any kind she slept sixteen hours, and upon awakening she rose from her bed "without warning" and tried to walk.

Her recuperation proceeded slowly, confined as she was to the second floor, until she slowly recovered her balance and her ability to express herself clearly again. With infinite patience her husband would sit beside her, teaching her to speak. By June, she was well enough to travel to the town of Beverly on the North Shore of Boston, which would henceforth be the site of the Tafts' summer vacations. Never again would the White House be the center of the celebration and revelry that Nellie Taft had intended for it. Her health slowly returned, but she never dared test her stamina to the extent that she had during those first few grueling but satisfying weeks when she had at last occupied 1600 Pennsylvania Avenue.[47]

TAFT, HOWEVER, had to remain in Washington to negotiate with Senator Aldrich and Speaker Cannon, and to try to mediate between the liberal "insurgent Republicans" and those two powerful conservatives who still ruled the party. The handling of tariff revision demonstrated the new president's clumsiness in handling the politics of governing. Roosevelt as well had been sympathetic to a reduction in the high tariff rates on imports that the Republican Party had traditionally favored: he knew that southerners and farmers in the Midwest, both producers of exportable commodities, were eager to lower such tariffs. Small businesses, too, were beginning to suffer from the greater competition of a growing industrialized America while the great trusts benefited under the protection of high tariff rates. Yet Roosevelt, while he spoke in public of lowering the tariff rates, had done nothing about them.

In his first term, TR was willing to enforce the Sherman Anti-Trust Act, which had been on the books for a decade before he became president. But TR was reluctant to fight a pitched battle against Nelson Aldrich over the tariff question, especially during his first term, when there were few Republican progressives in the House and Senate.[48]

By Roosevelt's second term, the wave of reform, starting to gain force throughout the country, elected an ever growing group of Republican senators sympathetic to reform. Roosevelt found new strength to go beyond moralistic generalities and called for the national regulation of corporations and some tribunal to gain power over railroad rates. He did not intend, he remarked in a speech in 1905 to the Pennsylvania industrial and financial leaders, to allow the United States to become a country in which the poor plundered the rich or the rich exploited the poor.

Through the final two years of Roosevelt's second term, the Bureau of Corporations and the attorney general's office began suits against three of the country's biggest combines: the Standard Oil Company, the American Tobacco Company, and the Sugar Trust. In his message to Congress in January 1908, TR concluded with a tirade against corrupt businesses that had made the "name 'high finance' a term of scandal."[49]

Roosevelt, however, knew that he could not afford to wholly alienate the conservative wing of the party. His rhetoric had stirred the country to demand further reform, and in this respect, as historian George Mowry has called him, Roosevelt was "the advance agent of mainstream progressivism." At the same time he needed someone who could bridge the gap between the progressives and the standpatters, and that man, he concluded, was William Howard Taft.

Here was a man with few personal enemies, congenial, seemingly committed to TR's policies, while at the same time distrustful of radicals. Roosevelt had continued to refrain from promoting specific plans to lower tariffs. To Senator Aldrich, high tariffs were good for big business; to farmers and westerners, the tariffs were costly. Nonetheless, the Republican platform in 1908 demanded a revision of tariff rates, and Taft was determined that he would now carry through on the party's promises, despite inheriting a Congress that was still dominated by conservatives.[50]

Roosevelt had also urged Taft to try to find common ground with Aldrich, and Taft took him at his word. Both the progressive and conservative camps therefore thought of Taft as their man. A person of unquestionable integrity, Taft detested radical change. If he could fulfill his predecessor's promises without unduly disturbing the body politic, he would do so. His tragedy was trying to be Rooseveltian without TR's gift for inspiring people.

Taft thought that he could strike a deal with the autocratic though often charming Nelson Aldrich, who had first made his money as a wholesale grocer and gone on to become a millionaire many times over. Determined to tighten the links between business and politics but untainted by scandal, he had an excellent mind and could master the intricacies of tariffs and high finance. As his social, financial, and political status grew (his daughter married John D. Rockefeller Jr.), Aldrich scorned the cries of the progressives. Industry and finance were to rule the United States, and the complaints of the working class were of no account.

This was the man Taft knew he had to lean on to lower tariffs. Yet Aldrich was the man who first betrayed him. "Where did we ever make the statement that we would revise the tariff downward?" Aldrich asked disingenuously. It was true that the Republican Party in its platform had spoken only of revising the tariff—not whether it would be up or down. But everyone, and especially the president, believed that meant downward. Yet when the Payne-Aldrich tariff revision bill finally came out of a conference between the House and Senate, the revisions downward were insignificant.

This was Aldrich's doing. As the powerful chairman of the Senate Finance Committee, it was he who had picked the Senate conferees. In the House, there was also no problem: Uncle Joe Cannon was in full charge. Taft, on the other hand, did not think that the president should use the power he possessed through the patronage he controlled—those thousands of large and small jobs that depended on the appointment power of the chief executive—to pressure recalcitrant legislators to vote as the president demanded.

In this respect, he could not have been more different from Roosevelt. In a book written after he was president, Taft quoted TR's belief that "executive power was limited only by specific restrictions and prohibitions appearing in the Constitution." Under this interpretation, according to Roosevelt, "I did not usurp power, but I did greatly broaden the use of executive power." Taft condemned such an "unsafe doctrine," which assumes the president "is to play the part of a universal providence and set all things right."[51]

Had Taft quietly acquiesced in Payne-Aldrich, he might still have ridden safely through the storm of protest against the new law. After he signed the bill into law on August 5, 1909, however, he felt compelled to go on a speaking trip around the country to defend his policies. It was in the town of Winona, Minnesota, that Taft made a fatal error. After admitting that Payne-Aldrich did not accomplish everything he wanted, he declared: "On the whole . . . I think the Payne bill is the best bill that the Republican party ever passed."[52]

Taft never recovered from this wild overstatement. The Republican Party was now openly split. By the summer of 1910, the Republicans were in such disarray that the congressional elections that fall were likely to heavily favor the progressive Republicans and the Democrats. Soon after his arrival in America, Theodore Roosevelt was condemning his successor not so much for his conservatism as for his ineptness as a politician.

IT WAS IMPORTANT to Roosevelt—and perhaps even more so to Senator Lodge—that if TR would not run for president in 1912, then he must show everyone that his friendship for Taft was not shattered. And Roosevelt, to save the party from serious setbacks in the upcoming 1910 congressional elections, was prepared to demonstrate his continued regard for the president. So that their relationship might not be too badly damaged, Lodge suggested that TR meet with Taft. Roosevelt agreed.

Roosevelt's estimation of Taft on the eve of their encounter is contained in a letter he sent to Gifford Pinchot shortly after his return to America.

> While I very keenly share your disappointment in Taft, and in a way even more deeply than you do, because it was I who made him President, yet it behooves us to realize that . . . two years hence circumstances will be such as make it necessary to renominate Taft. . . . As you know, my judgment is that in all probability Taft has passed his nadir. He is evidently a man who takes color from his surroundings. He was an excellent man

under me, and close to me. For eighteen months after his election he was a rather pitiful failure, because he had no real strong man on whom to lean, and yielded to the advice of his wife, his brother Charley, the different corporation lawyers who had his ear, and various similar men.

Roosevelt reiterated his view that reelecting Taft would be "on the whole the best thing for the country." But then TR concluded with a caveat that allowed Pinchot to hope that the ex-president might yet change his mind and run again. If Taft failed to mend his ways, Roosevelt wrote, "I could see very ugly times ahead for me, as I should certainly not be nominated unless everybody believed that the ship was sinking and thought it a good thing to have me aboard her when she went down." Left unsaid was an alternative scenario in which TR would be nominated in order to save the ship of state from sinking.[53]

To give the meeting between Taft and Roosevelt a casual air, Lodge suggested that it take place at Taft's summer retreat on the North Shore of Massachusetts just after the Harvard graduation exercises that TR was planning to attend. Taft was often happiest in Beverly, where he could play golf almost daily at the Myopia Club. He also used his time there to indulge in physical therapy in a vain effort to keep his weight under control. Usually he would spend an hour exercising with Dr. Charles Barker: then boxing, wrestling, and throwing the enormous medicine ball. In the afternoon he would pass time with Nellie, trying to distract her from her illness and helping her to articulate her words.

Two days after Roosevelt wrote Pinchot, Lodge and he set off in the senator's closed touring car from the Lodge summer home in Nahant for Beverly. Archie Butt was amazed at the reaction of the press to the visit. A great number of reporters, some with cameras, waited outside the gates of the summer White House, known locally as the Evens Cottage, to see what transpired. The next day, the New York Times printed a page-one story headlined "Roosevelt and Taft in Warm Embrace."

"For a full minute, this afternoon," the Times reported, "President Taft and Colonel Roosevelt stood on the veranda of the Evens cottage with hands upon each other's shoulders while evident delight shone in every line of their smile-wreathed countenances. . . . They patted each other affectionately on the shoulder, they laughed in a way that left not a single lingering doubt as to the exuberance of their feelings."[54]

Doubts surely did linger, for both men were determined not to be left alone where they might have discussed embarrassing substantive issues. For that reason, along with Archie Butt and the president's secretary, Charles Norton, Nellie Taft and her daughter, Miss Helen, were invited to join them. When Butt quietly suggested to Lodge that he could delay the arrival of Mrs. Taft and Miss Helen, Lodge told Butt that TR had said that "he did not want to be left alone with the president."

On the surface all was bonhomie. "Ah, Theodore, it is good to see you," said Taft, stretching out his hands to greet him.

"How are you, Mr. President? This is simply bully."

"See here now, drop the 'Mr. President,'" Taft said, hitting Roosevelt on the shoulder. But then the ex-president said, "Not at all. You must be Mr. President and I am Theodore. It must be that way."

Nonetheless, Taft went on calling him Mr. President, and when the latter complained later on, Taft explained: "The force of habit is very strong in me. I can never think of you save as Mr. President."

Roosevelt, when asked what he wanted to drink, showed his anxiety by saying he needed, rather than wanted, a scotch and soda.

Taft began the conversation by bringing up the situation in New York politics, where the Republicans were threatened with the loss of the governorship. This, of course, was merely the ostensible reason for the invitation. In any case, TR showed little interest in having a lively discussion about the outcome of the election. At this point Mrs. Taft and her daughter appeared, and TR, primed not to ask Nellie any questions because of her continued speech impediment, did most of the talking, which seemed to put her at ease.

Roosevelt was highly entertaining in his description of his trip through Europe, with piquant portraits of the rulers he had met. Of Kaiser Wilhelm II, TR reported: "I must say on the whole I was disappointed with him. I found him vain as a peacock. He would rather ride at the head of a procession than govern an empire." When he asked the kaiser if he contemplated war with England, Wilhelm replied that "he loved England next to Germany, and then in a sort of whimsical way, almost leerish, I thought, he told me the British did not treat him kindly when he visited there. That is what hurt him." When Taft suggested that a peace commission be sent to Europe, and that Roosevelt should head it, TR laughed and said, "Why not name [Andrew] Carnegie? He would certainly finance the commission." At that suggestion, Mrs. Taft finally spoke up in her characteristically forward way: "I don't think Carnegie would do at all."

Unwilling to pursue what might have been a delicate question, Roosevelt amused them with a story about the dinner at the king of England's funeral: "I never attended a more hilarious banquet in my life. I never saw quite so many knights. I had them on every side. . . . and each one had some special story of sorrow to pour into my ear. Finally when I met a little bewizened person known as the King of Greece, he fairly wept out his troubles to me."

After more anecdotes, it was time to go and greet the two hundred or so reporters at the gate. Roosevelt told Taft that, if he had no objection, he would stop for a minute and say that he had just had a delightful call on the president. "Which is true as far as I'm concerned," said Roosevelt.

"And more than true as far as I am concerned," said Taft. "This has taken me back to some of those dear old afternoons when I was Will and you were Mr. President."

Even Nellie Taft found something of the old spirit of friendship. As she wrote later, she had even believed TR held her husband "in the highest esteem and reposed in him the utmost confidence, and that the rumors of his antagonism were wholly unfounded."

But then she concluded—"I was not destined to enjoy this faith and assurance for very long."[55]

TWO

"The Ruthlessness of the Pure in Heart"

WHILE ROOSEVELT WAS weighing the possibility, however remote, of running for president again, the man who was destined to become the candidate of the Democrats was being wooed by the party bosses of New Jersey.

Woodrow Wilson, president of Princeton University since 1902, enjoyed among the larger public a reputation as a renowned educator. When he had first assumed that office, he was determined to raise scholarly standards and change the tone of Princeton undergraduate life from its easygoing, somewhat disorderly ways. He saw the college experience for students as one requiring "a certain seclusion of mind preceding the struggle of life, a certain period of withdrawal and abstraction."[1]

To this end, he was remarkably successful. He tightened the curriculum, hiring forty new instructors as "preceptors," modeled after the English college system of tutors. These young academics would live on campus to guide the undergraduates as they worked to achieve a balance between required courses that would provide a general education and elective courses reflecting their particular interests. As Wilson liked to put it, he wanted to "intellectualize" the students in their most formative years.

Although by 1906 Wilson was seen as an innovative and accomplished educator, in late 1904 in a speech before the New York Society of Virgini-

ans he had shown himself to be a conservative Democrat. He distrusted
the often demagogic populism of William Jennings Bryan, the defeated
Democratic Party candidate in the 1896 and 1900 presidential elections.
Wilson's speech, reported in the *New York Sun,* revealed him as someone
who distrusted the radical theorists in the party. What the country
needed was not "a party of discontent and of radical experiment," but
rather "a party of conservative reform, acting in the spirit of law and
ancient institutions," which essentially meant reaffirming states' rights
and limited government. As a born southerner, Wilson believed that
these values could counter the persuasive tenor of Bryan's western populism, and especially Bryan's call for the free coinage of silver, which hor-
rified the banking and industrial interests of the East.

For these reasons, Colonel George Harvey, the editor of *Harper's
Weekly,* was sure that in Woodrow Wilson he had found the man who
could rescue the Democratic Party from Bryanism. So it was that in February 1906, sitting across the table from Wilson at New York's Century
Club, an association that was founded in the nineteenth century for
artists and amateurs of the arts, Harvey evoked for his eager listener a
glittering future.

Harvey was the key to money and the political connections that could
propel Wilson to high political office, a status he had always yearned for.
The colonel had, with the help of utilities magnate Thomas Fortune
Ryan, become rich. He was able to buy the *North American Review,* and
his success with that journal attracted the notice of the publishing house
of Harper and Brothers, then threatened with bankruptcy; the firm's
directors soon asked Harvey to be president. J. Pierpont Morgan, the
company's biggest creditor, enthusiastically consented.

It was also George Harvey who, in 1904, persuaded the expatriate novelist Henry James to revisit his native America after more than two
decades in Europe and to let Harvey publish his account of what he saw
and thought. To James, the "objectionable colonel" was the essence of
the new hustling America that he detested.[2]

Shortly before his meeting with Wilson at the Century Club, Harvey
had given a dinner in Wilson's honor at another New York club, the
Lotus, at which time he said that it was with a sense "almost of rapture"
that he contemplated "even the remotest possibility" of voting for

Woodrow Wilson as president of the United States. Soon newspapers all over the country were discussing his proposal for nominating Wilson for president, and the more conservative editors saw Wilson as the one Democrat who could overcome the progressive policies of Roosevelt. At the follow-up at the Century Club, Wilson carefully queried the colonel about the prominent men who, Harvey had suggested, might support him in a political career.[3]

Throughout the rest of 1906, Wilson's name was bruited about as a significant new man in the Democratic Party, but Wilson knew such talk of a presidential run was far too premature. In addition, rumors of this nature could easily interfere with his plans for further reforms at Princeton. On his behalf, Harvey had wooed such influential figures as Thomas Fortune Ryan, Adolph S. Ochs, publisher of the *New York Times,* and William F. Laffan, publisher of the *New York Sun,* one of the most reactionary papers in the country. By October 1906, rumors were rife that Wilson would seek the Democratic nomination for senator from New Jersey the following year. Harvey had even secured the support of former senator James Smith Jr., the Democratic boss of New Jersey's Essex County. Progressive Democrats had rallied around the candidacy of Edwin S. Stevens of Hoboken, and Wilson decided he would not contest Stevens for the nomination. He feared both antagonizing his Princeton trustees and dividing the party. In January 1907, it was time to call a halt. Wilson wrote to Harvey that he must withdraw. Harvey, in turn, urged Wilson to align himself with no faction of the party.[4]

Although Wilson's political career had been launched, now he could once again turn all his attention to the affairs of the college and continue with the program of educational reform that he believed would make him an even more attractive candidate for high political office—perhaps even the White House itself. The new year marked the high point of Wilson's university presidency, and it was the politics of New Jersey bossism that would later rescue him from disaster at Princeton.

FROM HIS EARLIEST DAYS, Thomas Woodrow Wilson had been trained in the art of performance. His father, Dr. Joseph Ruggles Wilson, was a Presbyterian minister with a stunning gift for oratory and an equally stunning ego that had been inflated through years of success in his calling, first in Virginia, and later in Georgia and South Carolina. His son Tommy, who was born in 1856 in Staunton, Virginia, doted on him, an intense preoccupation that the father returned in an often destructive way. Dr. Wilson had a caustic wit, which he directed at his son, and expected a perfection that Tommy could not possibly fulfill. Yet the boy accepted his father's demands and tried to emulate him; inevitably he failed and interpreted Dr. Wilson's lethal criticisms as humiliating evidence that he would always be inferior to his towering father.

Such an upbringing made Wilson an ideal candidate for manipulation. For the first three decades of his life, his utter dependence on what he called "his incomparable father" apparently satisfied this craving for parental direction. When absent from his father's house for too long, Wilson became racked by blinding headaches and crippling digestive disorders. In early adulthood these symptoms became chronic and could only be eased by a return to his paternal home for a long rest.

Tommy Wilson was a poor student as a boy, and desultory one as an undergraduate at Princeton. He was ignorant of the written alphabet until he was nine and could hardly read until he was eleven. He never did gain much speed at reading, once remarking to his brother-in-law that he was "the slowest reader in the world." He most probably suffered from dyslexia but conquered it by developing a fierce concentration and near-photographic memory; he never became a wide reader. At sixteen he taught himself shorthand, but mostly he composed his writings and talks in his mind. "I write in sentences rather than words," he told a friend in 1897. "They are formed *whole* in my mind before they begin to be put on paper, usually." He preferred to speak from brief outlines, often in shorthand.[5]

His struggle to overcome the odds that had been set against him may have added to his compulsive striving for perfection. His will must prevail if he wished it so. To accomplish this meant that he *must* dominate, perhaps out of fear of being dominated. After Woodrow Wilson's death, his daughter Margaret summed up her grandfather's pedagogical creed: "His idea was that if a lad was of fine-tempered steel, the more he was beaten the better he was."[6]

This is not to say that Wilson's father was always a martinet. On the contrary, he could be fun to be with, and he was affectionate, often greeting his son with a kiss. His letters generally began with a salutation of "My precious Son," and despite Tommy's academic failings, his ambition for him was boundless.[7]

Although the Presbyterian faith in which Wilson was brought up posited a God who offered forgiveness for original sin and eternal life for those who gave unquestioning obedience to his divine law, Joseph Wilson belonged to the more liberal Presbyterian establishment. He embraced the idea of worldly success, and the Calvinist view that material interests could be reconciled to the pursuit of God's will contributed to Woodrow Wilson's political outlook. Nor did Dr. Wilson regard slavery as a betrayal of his church's teachings, and he gladly sided with the Confederacy.

So did his son. Woodrow Wilson was in essence a white supremacist, holding a romantic view of the courtesy and graciousness of the antebellum southern plantation owners, as well as accepting uncritically the post-Reconstruction South that arranged to keep the black Americans in their place. Although he came to embrace the idea that the South's defeat made federal union desirable, he never abandoned his condescending attitude toward people of color; his first presidential administration is forever marked by his allowing segregation in certain government buildings. As late as 1915 he wrote to his second wife, whose niece intended to marry a Panamanian: "It would be bad enough at best to have anyone we love marry into a Central American family, because there is the presumption that the blood is not unmixed."[8] In his racial attitudes, he was more doctrinaire than Roosevelt, who once dined with the African-American leader Booker T. Washington at the White House. (For this transgression, many in Congress roundly criticized TR, who never dared to repeat the invitation.)

Wilson had little tolerance for a war against vice; he was far less of a moralistic crusader against personal failings than was Bryan or, for that matter, Theodore Roosevelt.[9] Shy, thin, betraying vigor only in his dazzling gray eyes, the young Wilson might have had a happy or at least a peaceful life if he had followed his father into the clergy and became a spellbinding preacher; instead, while still a teenager he made the momentous decision to enter politics.

As a young man Wilson had idolized British Prime Minister William Ewart Gladstone, a figure who combined the righteousness of a clergyman with the celebrity of a national leader. Studying Gladstone, Wilson adopted the Briton's crusading zeal, and this fed his ambition to succeed in politics. The way to do it, he concluded after graduating from Princeton in 1879 and unhappily practicing law, was through entering the academic world—which he often referred to as "minor statesmanship." Long, often boring years of teaching at Bryn Mawr, Wesleyan, and even Princeton made him all but despair of his goal. Despite these frustrations, Wilson kept abreast of national politics, and by the 1890s had formulated a system of beliefs that would influence his behavior throughout his career.

Unlike Theodore Roosevelt, Wilson shied away from violence and radical actions in life and in politics, preferring the slow development of orderly, constitutional programs as the only antidote to such dangers. He advocated one goal above all others—social order—and one means of attaining it, representative government. Anyone who threatened that goal and that system—whether from the left or from the right—was anathema to this introverted and driven man.

WILSON MET ELLEN AXSON while practicing law in Atlanta in 1883 after graduating from the University of Virginia Law School. Also the child of a Presbyterian minister, Ellen's literary and artistic bent deeply appealed to Wilson. More important, she gave him a continuous and unqualified flow of affection and approval. "It isn't pleasant or convenient to have strong passions," he once wrote to her during their engagement. "I have the uncomfortable feeling that I am carrying a volcano about with me. My salvation is in being loved. . . . There surely never lived a man with whom love was a more critical matter than it is with me."[10] Never was Wilson more perceptive about his emotional needs than in his letters to women whose support he desperately needed.

Marriage to Ellen was not possible until he had finished a two-year graduate program in political science at the Johns Hopkins University in

Baltimore. For Wilson was bored with the law, which he found "antagonistic to the best interests of the intellectual life." At Johns Hopkins, a fairly new university that was modeled on German methodology in research and scholarship, he felt "merrier and happier than I ever did before."[11]

Nonetheless, as he wrote Ellen in 1884, "I am afraid of being a mere student. I want to be part of the nature around me, not an outside observer of it. . . . Disraeli knew nothing about the principles of politics, but he knew men—especially House of Commons men. . . . You'll never find in a cloister a fulcrum for any lever which can budge the world."[12]

On June 2, 1885, in the parsonage of the Independent Presbyterian Church of Savannah, his bride's childhood home, he married Ellen Axson; she willingly gave up her aspirations for a career as a painter, after studying at New York City's Art Students League. Referring to the artistic path not taken, Ellen wrote to him prior to their wedding day: "As compared with the privilege of loving and serving you and the blessedness of being loved by you, the praise and admiration of all the world and generations yet unborn would be lighter than vanity."[13]

Ellen remained devoted to him, and the marriage produced three children, all girls. But Ellen felt the strain of giving up the intimacy of their house for the Princeton president's mansion in 1902. In addition, Ellen had a hard winter in 1905 in trying to care for her brother Stockton, who was suffering from a severe form of melancholia; it reminded her of her father's mental illness, which had resulted in his being committed to a mental hospital where he committed suicide the year before her marriage. Along with her brother's illness, in 1905 her beloved nephew, Edward Axson, his wife, and his two-year-old son drowned in a freak accident. She found it increasingly hard to entertain, and was often depressed.

Wilson was therefore deprived of his wife's full attention, and there were growing tensions with his university colleagues when he tried to make further reforms in the college. His own health had also been affected by a small stroke in May 1906, which had damaged not only the vision of his left eye but also may have had the permanent effect of exacerbating his irritability and ingrained stubbornness.[14] And so, at Ellen's suggestion he went alone to Bermuda for a winter vacation in January

1907. Wilson was lucky in having a wife who catered to his violent mood swings. At these times he needed absolute rest from the inner tensions that consumed him as he drove himself to fulfill his intellectual ambitions.

On this first trip to Bermuda he met Mary Allen Hulbert Peck, a bright flirtatious woman, six years his junior. Separated from her husband, she had taken a large house on the island in which she entertained notable people. Her vivacity and unquestioned interest in Wilson's work drew him to her. Another solitary holiday to Bermuda in the winter of 1908 brought him once again into contact with her. They walked the broad beaches and island roads, and Wilson spoke to her of his dream of a political career.

Wilson's biographer August Heckscher believed that Wilson and Mary Peck passed from having a romantic friendship to a physical affair at the end of 1909 and early 1910. In 1915 while in the White House, in an unpublished document, Wilson admitted to "a passage of folly and gross impertinence" in his life, during which time he had put aside "standards of honourable behavior." To Edith Bolling Galt, the woman he was courting in 1915 after Ellen Wilson's death the previous year and who later became his wife, he wrote of a "folly long ago loathed and repented of," one bringing him "stained and unworthy" to beg her love. It had been, he told her, "the contemptible error and madness of a few months."

Doubtless the affair began after Mary Peck had decided to definitively break with her husband in November 1909, establishing herself with her mother and son in an apartment in New York just to the north of Madison Square Park. Wilson had long seen New York as a place of dangerous temptations and had written to Ellen in the early years of their marriage that he dared not stay overnight there because he feared what his "mysterious passions" might lead him to do. Yet, with Mrs. Peck officially separated from her husband, he did visit her frequently on East Twenty-seventh Street. It is only when he went to Bermuda in February 1910, without either Mrs. Peck or Ellen, that the affair probably ended, though Wilson continued to write her frequently well into his White House years.

That Ellen almost surely knew what had taken place is evident from what she told their trusted White House physician, Dr. Carey Grayson, in her last years. At that time she said that Mrs. Peck was the only unhappiness her husband had ever given her.[15]

IN HIS EARLY YEARS as president of Princeton, Wilson was energetic in making serious changes in the undergraduates' social environment. Many students may have believed with F. Scott Fitzgerald's Amory Blaine that they were just this side of paradise at Princeton; others did not. The undergraduate system of eating clubs fostered a form of social snobbery that excluded large numbers of young men, and, as Wilson himself described it years later, "Princeton is exactly what they say of it: a fine country club, where many of the alumni make snobs of their boys."[16]

By December 1906, he had produced a scheme to reorganize student social life. In essence, Wilson wanted a quad system, whereby the undergraduates would live and eat together with resident faculty members in a quadrangle of buildings. His model was the English college system as it existed at Oxford and Cambridge. The upper-class eating clubs would either fade away, or become integrated into the quad plan.

Although Wilson argued that the rise of the clubs had resulted in a "decline of the old democratic spirit" of Princeton, his primary reason for wanting the quadrangle system was to further intellectualize the college. First came the preceptors, then the quads, and in this way a new Princeton would arise that would become, he hoped, the intellectual rival of Harvard and Yale.

In no small part, the reformed Princeton curriculum, which deemphasized elective courses, was a challenge to the famed Charles William Eliot, president of Harvard, who had radically reformed the college system by sweeping aside many of the old required courses and trusting the students to follow their instincts. Moreover, the success of his curriculum reform permitted Wilson to think that he could almost surely persuade the board of trustees to support the quad plan; indeed the trustees did approve the plan in principle in June 1907.

But Wilson underestimated the growing hostility to his English-style college. Plans to create a graduate school with its own residential quarters would have to wait until the quad plan was under way. This did not at all please Dean Andrew West of the graduate faculty, who now opposed the quads. More important, the alumni were not prepared for the abolition of the eating clubs.

There is no better description of the atmosphere of the club system than the one provided by the literary critic Edmund Wilson, who came to Princeton in the class of 1916:

> In spite of their heaviness and emptiness, the clubs have inevitably become identified with that peculiar idyllic quality which is one of the endearing features of Princeton. It is difficult to describe this quality in any very concrete way, but it has something to do with the view from Prospect Street, from the comfortable back porches of the clubs . . . and with the singular feeling of freedom which refreshes the alumnus from an American city when he goes back to Prospect Street. . . .
>
> It was commencement, and these institutions were holding their annual banquets. . . . It was at this moment that Wilson chose for communicating to the Princeton clubs a note that had the form of an edict—that seemed brusquely to break the news that they were summarily to be disbanded. . . .
>
> The proud undergraduates and the jolly alumni—many of them, no doubt, drunk—must have felt as if their delightful houses were being snatched from over their very heads, and that at the moment when they loved them most dearly; that their joyfully renewed good fellowship, their love of Princeton itself, were receiving a cold affront from the president.[17]

Many of the alumni showed that they would not consider subsidizing the quad plan, so some of Wilson's strongest supporters on the board of trustees urged him to change his objective to reform rather than abolish the clubs. But Wilson remained adamant. The clubs must go. The quadrangles must be built. In October 1907, the trustees, led by their most influential member, Moses Taylor Pyne, formally requested him to withdraw his plan.

Determined not to lose, Wilson appealed directly to alumni in a series of speeches in the East and Midwest. This availed him nothing. In April 1908, a committee appointed by the trustees defended the clubs, and all was lost. Most cruel of all, John Grier Hibben, Wilson's best friend on the faculty, the man he most often turned to for solace and support, declared he was in favor of reforming rather than abolishing the clubs. Despite Hibben's effort to maintain their friendship, Wilson never forgave him and later unsuccessfully opposed Hibben's appointment as his successor to the presidency of Princeton.

Wilson's unwillingness to settle for reforming the clubs showed poor judgment that had not been evident before. And now he faced a new battle involving the creation of the graduate school, and his antagonists were formidable: Andrew West, dean of the graduate school, teaming up with Moses Taylor Pyne to push through their own version of what the graduate school should look like.

The ostensible controversy was over where to build the residential graduate school. West preferred a site far from the campus, whereas Wilson wanted the residence to be at the very center of university life. As in the quad plan, Wilson's preference probably made more sense. And to allow West to get his way would mean a fatal challenge to Wilson's authority.

West alone might not have been strong enough to carry the day, but Pyne, a far more able man, was determined to curb Wilson's power after the quad episode. Having secured monies to build the graduate school off campus, West appeared to be in a strong position, and had Wilson not insisted that the school be built on campus, a reasonable compromise could have been reached. Even if Wilson had conceded the argument to West, this need not have destroyed his effectiveness as president. But he could no more give in to West and Pyne than he could to Henry Cabot Lodge in the fight over ratification of the League of Nations in 1919. In his conflicts at Princeton as well as during the campaign for the League, Wilson appealed over the heads of his opponents, which only strengthened their determination to beat him. By January 1910, Pyne had lost all confidence in Wilson's presidency.

That spring Wilson appealed to alumni for support—in Baltimore, Brooklyn, Jersey City, St. Louis, and finally New York. The alumni, again, did not rally to Wilson's standard. On April 14, at a meeting of the trustees, Pyne refused to let Wilson put the question of the graduate center to the faculty, who would doubtless have supported the president. Two days later, Wilson spoke to the Princeton alumni in Pittsburgh and went too far. The construction of a graduate college along the lines Dean

West had suggested was a challenge to democracy: "Seclude a man, separate him from the rough and tumble of college life, from all the contacts of every sort and condition of men, and you have done a thing which America will brand with contemptuous disapproval."[18]

The Pittsburgh speech reverberated throughout the country. Pyne and the trustees were infuriated, and Wilson himself realized he had committed a blunder. Nevertheless, the board of trustees remained deadlocked, and a compromise was proposed by the trustees that would require West to resign as dean and yet have the graduate college built away from the undergraduate campus with West as resident master. Wilson refused to give an inch.

The denouement came in May when Isaac Wyman died and left his entire estate, estimated at between $2 million and $4 million, to Princeton with the proviso that the graduate college be built according to West's plan. Wilson was at the end of his tether. He now had no choice but to accept West's victory or resign. On June 9, 1910, Wilson declared that he had withdrawn his objection to the construction of the graduate residence away from the undergraduate campus.[19]

His active role as president of Princeton had now come to an end. Only the political career that Colonel Harvey offered gave him an honorable way out. To seek the nomination in 1910 for the New Jersey governorship seemed the best way to let him resign from Princeton and at the same time seek the political rewards he had always so fervently desired.

EARLY IN JANUARY 1910, Harvey invited James Smith, the leading New Jersey Democratic politician, to lunch at Delmonico's in New York. Given the reputation of the restaurant as New York's finest, and the elaborate menu customers were expected to sample, this was bound to be a lengthy repast, which is exactly what Harvey wanted. Determined to keep the conversation intimate, Harvey made sure that there was enough time for him to make his case. In fact, the two talked for the entire afternoon. Smith, a portly, well-dressed man, poised and dignified, a former United States senator, was delighted at the choice of Delmonico's and soon realized that this was a time for careful deliberation.

Harvey was out to secure the political machine's support for Woodrow Wilson as Democratic candidate for governor. At this early stage, Smith would not commit himself. True, he admitted, Wilson would make a strong candidate, but was Wilson himself ready to embrace the hurly-burly of political life? Harvey had to reassure Smith that Wilson was aligned with them as a conservative Democrat. Certainly, Wilson was against labor unionism and the closed shop, which he had documented in a "Credo" written in 1907 for possible use by the *New York Sun*, declaring that "the right of freedom of contract" was the "most precious of all the possessions of a free people."[20] He also offered his view that great trusts should not be regulated by government commissions (which Roosevelt favored), even though businessmen who violated the law should be punished. As he said to the Princeton graduating class in 1909, labor unions existed primarily to keep production standards as low as possible.[21]

On the other hand, in his pronouncements during the Princeton controversies, Wilson had showed himself committed to social and educational democracy, and he had singled out the power of wealth as a corrupting influence on undergraduates. More and more he came to stress the need for ethical standards for businessmen and industrial leaders, which may well have derived from his experiences in dealing with the likes of Moses Taylor Pyne. What he sought were not political remedies, as Roosevelt did, but moral regeneration.[22]

If Wilson's ingrained conservatism was not enough to persuade Smith to back Wilson's gubernatorial nomination at this first lunch with Colonel Harvey, at a second lunch at Delmonico's a week later, Smith told Harvey that Wilson "came up to scratch in fine shape." He was sure that he could persuade the other party bosses to fall into line if Wilson himself was truly committed to run.[23]

After this meeting, Harvey sounded out Wilson. Would he accept the nomination if it were handed to him "on a silver platter?" Wilson slowly paced the room before responding to the colonel. Under those circumstances, he said, he would give it the most "serious consideration."[24] This was not the ringing commitment Harvey had hoped for, but it was enough for Harvey to swing Smith behind Wilson.

• • •

ALTHOUGH WILSON may have deluded himself into thinking that Harvey and Smith "recognized the fact that a new day had come in American politics, and that they would have to conduct them[selves] henceforth in a new fashion," this was not Smith's reasoning at all. He viewed Wilson as a man of high reputation who was likely to win the statehouse in November, cooperate with the party organization in the matter of appointments, and help him return to the Senate. United States senators at that time were chosen by the state legislature, and Wilson would probably carry with him into office a Democratic legislature.[25]

Throughout the summer and fall the progressive wing of the New Jersey Democratic Party saw Wilson as a tool of the bosses. As Bob Davis, the Democratic boss of Hudson County, put it: "How the hell do I know whether he'll make a good governor? He will make a good candidate, and that is the only thing that interests me."[26] Wilson's antilabor views were publicized by the reformers throughout the state, which caused Wilson to have to repudiate almost everything he had said previously about the ills of labor unions. At the Democratic state convention in September, progressives were preparing to vote for the strongest anti-Wilson candidate.

When the convention itself opened on September 15, Trenton's opera house was packed. Colonel Harvey occupied a prominent box, while some forty Princeton students were seated onstage and from time to time sounded out the college football yell. In the meantime, Smith and his fellow bosses worked tirelessly not only to quell the progressives but also to keep the regulars in line to vote for a man whom they hardly knew. In this effort they succeeded.

Wilson remained at Princeton during the convention, playing golf in the morning, and then readying himself to be picked up late that afternoon for the drive to Trenton. Dressed in a somber gray suit, Wilson entered the opera house a little after five o'clock to accept his party's choice for governor.

His rousing speech stunned the delegates. Here, all of Wilson's gift for public speaking came to the fore. He demanded "a renaissance of public spirit, a reawakening of sober public opinion, a revival of the power of the people." He called for a public service commission to regulate utilities, and urged stricter control of businesses. Above all, he declared that he would enter the governorship "with absolutely no pledges of any kind."

At this, the delegates rose to their feet and cheered. As Joe Tumulty, a progressive young assemblyman who later became Wilson's secretary, described it: "The personal magnetism of the man, his winning smile, so frank and so sincere, the light in his gray eyes, the fine poise of his well-shaped head, the beautiful rhythm of his vigorous sentences, held the men in the Convention breathless under their mystic spell. Men all about me cried in a frenzy: 'Thank God, at last, a leader has come!'"[27] After Wilson finished his address, they even tried to lift him to their shoulders and carry him into the street.[28]

Despite Wilson's declaration of personal independence and his clarion call for progressive reforms, Jim Smith and the other political bosses regarded his speech as mere campaign rhetoric. They had yet to learn what historian Richard Hofstadter has called "the ruthlessness of the pure in heart."[29]

The Heirs of Hamilton
and Jefferson

ROOSEVELT WAS DETERMINED to unite the Republican Party. For this reason he put aside his vow not to get involved in factional struggles during the summer and fall of 1910. But at a Harvard class reunion that June, New York's Governor Charles Evans Hughes persuaded TR to join him in championing the cause of reform. In the White House, Taft realized that to carry New York in the elections that fall, the state's Republican "Old Guard" must be defeated. Here was an opportunity for Roosevelt to support the reformers, vanquish the reactionaries, and even join forces with the Taft administration.

To accomplish this, TR agreed to run for temporary chairman of the New York state Republican convention. Taft seemed to approve this. But he also insisted that Roosevelt give an unequivocal endorsement of the administration, in return for which Taft would cast out Senator Aldrich and Speaker Cannon as counselors and ask Roosevelt to become one of the White House advisers. TR believed Taft's policies had become too conservative for him to be able to endorse the actions of the administration. He therefore dismissed the proposal scornfully.[1]

On August 1, the state Republican executive committee met to nominate a man to preside over the convention. Rather than choosing Roosevelt, they selected James S. Sherman, Taft's vice president and a leader of the reactionary element among New York Republicans. This was the rebuff admistered to TR for his refusal to support the president's policies. Taft, still vacationing in Beverly and playing golf as often as he could, may not have engineered the coup against Roosevelt, but he was certainly aware of what Sherman and his friends were planning. Archie Butt wrote in mid-August that Sherman was constantly on the telephone to the president, "giving the plans to defeat Mr. Roosevelt" at the convention that fall. Taft's only response was to ask Sherman not to drag him into a fight that would create an open rupture with his predecessor. When Taft learned of Roosevelt's defeat in the committee, he laughed contentedly. Butt commented: "If they want to force [Roosevelt] to run for the presidency again, they could not do it better than they have done since his visit here last month."[2]

Roosevelt, upon learning that Taft had switched his support to the conservative faction in New York, felt double-crossed. But he was relieved that he did not have to fight a losing battle for Republicans in the fall elections in New York state. "The truth is," he wrote Lodge on August 17, "that we have had no national leadership of any real kind since election day 1908. Taft is absolutely connected in the popular mind with Aldrich . . . Cannon . . . and company. The anti-Taft leadership, on the other hand, has tended to fall exclusively in the hands of narrow fanatics, wild visionaries and self-seeking demagogues, with the result that a great many sober and honest men are growing to hate the word 'Reform' and all reformers, including myself. . . . The split looks to me as wide and deep as it could be."[3]

DREADING THE EFFORT to explain his own beliefs while at the same time refraining from "anything looking like criticism of the Taft administration," on August 23, Roosevelt left for a three-week tour of sixteen western states in yet another vain attempt to unite the party. In the meantime he had not communicated with Taft, and his silence so unnerved the president that he even temporarily stopped playing golf. "If only I knew what [Roosevelt] wanted," Taft said plaintively to his military aide, "I would do it, but you know he has held himself so aloof that I am absolutely in the dark. I am deeply wounded, and he gives me no chance to explain my attitude or learn his."[4]

The western tour was one long ovation. Since his return to the United States, TR had been deluged with invitations to speak. Traveling by a private railroad car paid for by *The Outlook,* a small but influential journal of which he was a contributing editor, Roosevelt espoused a more radical position than ever before. He spoke in town squares and at picnics, in ballparks and at statehouses. In Colorado, he branded the Supreme Court a barrier to social justice and advocated checks on the power of the judiciary to overrule acts of the legislature. (President Taft grew so angry when he learned of TR's attacks on the judiciary that he flung a golf club across the fairway.[5])

As TR's train sped from Colorado into Kansas, crowds of applauding partisans stood in the rain to cheer him onward. But even this paled before the reception on August 31 at Osawatomie, Kansas, where in 1857 John Brown had launched his bloody crusade to save the nation from slavery. Roosevelt made one of the most radical speeches of his life, calling for a New Nationalism that would put national needs above sectional or personal advantage, and urging "a genuine and permanent moral awakening." He endorsed the graduated income and inheritance tax, a comprehensive workmen's compensation act, prohibition of child labor, downward revision of the tariffs, and increased power for the Interstate Commerce Commission to supervise all corporations engaged in interstate business.

"The New Nationalism," he asserted, "regards the executive power as the steward of public welfare." And in what seemed the ultimate betrayal to the conservative wing of the Republican Party, TR said: "Labor is the superior of capital and deserves much the higher consideration. . . . I wish to see labor organizations powerful." He also said that, like the big corporations, the unions must accept regulation by the government. Above all, "The man who wrongly holds that every human right is secondary to his profit must now give way to the advocate of human welfare, who rightly maintains that every man holds his property subject to the general right of the community to regulate its use to whatever degree the public welfare may require it."[6]

Roosevelt's radicalism had evolved after he had left the presidency. Although what he said in Osawatomie did not represent a dramatic departure from what he had expressed while in office, he was far more specific in spelling out what he believed government should do. He was also spurred on to articulate his thoughts by having read Herbert Croly's book *The Promise of American Life,* published to great acclaim the previous year, which attacked the Populist strain of progressivism with its Jeffersonian emphasis on free competition and its preference for a weak central government. Croly's work not only helped to refine Roosevelt's thinking, but it also portrayed him as a model for activist reform.

For Croly, who later became the editor of *The New Republic,* democracy meant the fullest and freest participation of all citizens in determining how Americans live and therefore America's future. The Land of Freedom had to become the Land of Equality. Freedom without equality leads to injustice, and the triumph of American democracy would show that freedom and equality need not be in opposition to each other, as long as "no individuals are allowed to have special privileges."

What America had seen after the Civil War, according to Croly, was a growing inequality. The tragedy was that the fulfillment of the American national promise was abandoned precisely because traditional American confidence in "individual freedom has resulted in a morally and socially undesirable distribution of wealth. . . . in the hands of a few men." Such a condition undermined democracy. "What individual competition has done in America has resulted not only in the triumph of the strongest, but in the attempt to perpetuate the victory." Thus, the economic problem had become a democratic problem.

Roosevelt welcomed Croly's insistence that greater democracy was America's promise. Both men deeply distrusted Jefferson's legacy of limited government and uncontrolled individualism. Both men praised Hamilton's legacy of strong government and elite leadership. Jefferson, Croly wrote, "understood his fellow-countrymen better and trusted them more than his rival," but was suspicious of any efficient political authority. The Hamiltonians (or Federalists) were flawed because they came "to identify both anti-Federalism and democracy with political disorder and social instability." With all their apprehensions about democracy, however, the Hamiltonians did believe in liberty. But they thought that the essential condition for "a fruitful liberty" was an efficient central government to promote the national welfare.

The Hamiltonian legacy, as Croly saw it, implied government "interference with the natural course of American economic and political business and its regulation and guidance in the national direction." Unfortunately, Hamilton did not seek a broad base to carry out his ideas; he thought he was fighting for stability and political order against the forces of anarchy and disintegration. He therefore insisted all the more on attaching to the government the support of "well-to-do people."

The result of this policy was that "the rising democracy came more than ever to distrust the national government." Croly lamented that instead of seeking to perpetuate the Union upon the special interests of a minority of well-to-do citizens, Hamilton would have been far wiser "to have frankly intrusted its welfare to the goodwill of the whole people."

Jefferson, even though he unjustly vilified Hamilton, was right in believing that any tendency to impair the integrity of the democratic idea would likely lead to disaster. Unfortunately, Jefferson had a narrow conception of democracy, for in his mind democracy was tantamount to extreme individualism. There should be as little government as possible, and the good things of life, which had been formerly held by the few, were now to be distributed among all the people.

The Jeffersonians' error was not their devotion to equality but their inability to see the degree to which they were sacrificing a desirable liberty to an undesirable equality. Hamiltonians, on the other hand, were more clear thinking. He knew that genuine liberty could be protected only by an energetic and clear-sighted central government.

Croly was sure that to fulfill the promise of American life, the country needed Hamiltonian means to achieve Jeffersonian ends. In this way, individual desires would be subordinated to the fulfillment of a national purpose and the excesses of inequality curbed to provide for the general welfare. The person who could best achieve this ideal, he believed, was Theodore Roosevelt, the first political leader to realize that "an American statesman could no longer represent the national interest without becoming a reformer."[7]

Roosevelt was certainly a moralist, but he was not a self-righteous one. His patrician values gave him a disdain for the newly rich of the Gilded Age. He wrote in his *Autobiography* that after the Civil War "our strongest and most capable men had thrown their whole energy into business, into moneymaking, into the development, and above all the exploitation and exhaustion at the most rapid rate possible, of our natural resources—mine, forest, soil, and rivers. These men were not weak men, but they permitted themselves to grow short-sighted and selfish."[8]

By the end of the former president's western swing, the Republican reformers were more fervent than ever in their desire that Theodore Roosevelt should once again occupy the White House and make good the promise of American life.

ON HIS RETURN to Oyster Bay, despite his increasingly radical positions, Roosevelt planned to support moderate Republicans. At the behest of the chairman of the New York County Republican Committee, he even agreed to meet Taft in New Haven in mid-September. It was a cordial meeting, but shortly afterward, Taft's secretary spread the story that TR had requested the meeting because he was in trouble in New York, and asked for Taft's aid. Outraged, Roosevelt gave out his own public statement that he had not sought Taft's help in New York state. Only a few days later, Taft told Archie Butt that Roosevelt and he had come to "the parting of the ways."[9]

Toward the end of September, TR, wearing a sombrero, set off an impromptu parade down the streets of Saratoga, where the Republican state convention was being held. In the convention hall a wild, cheering ovation greeted him. Far from picking Vice President Sherman as temporary chairman, as the executive committee expected, the delegates overwhelmingly voted for Theodore Roosevelt. Thanks to Roosevelt's support, Henry L. Stimson, a fellow patrician who had served as secretary of war in Taft's cabinet and would later serve in that same post again for Franklin Roosevelt, was nominated for governor.

TR had spent valuable capital in trying to reunite the party, but as he feared, the 1910 elections turned out to be a disaster for the Republicans. Taft's Ohio was lost to the Democrats. Stimson was defeated in New York state. Wherever the party was dominated by conservative interests, the progressive faction drifted to the Democrats, most notably in New Jersey, where Woodrow Wilson was running for governor. Theodore Roosevelt's star was suddenly in eclipse, and he retired, temporarily estranged from his party, to his beloved Sagamore Hill.

• • •

"A POLITICIAN, a man engaged in party contests, must be an opportunist," Wilson said in a speech in 1907. In an effort to explain his search
for a middle ground between principle and expediency, Wilson employed
a sailing analogy: "Because, although you steer by the North Star, when
you have lost the bearings of your compass, you nevertheless steer a path-
way to the sea—you are not bound by the North Star." Wilson's principles
were his North Star, which only pointed him in a general direction. To
reach the sea, to get elected, a helmsman had to take into account tides,
winds, and currents. In his quest for the New Jersey statehouse, Wilson
amply demonstrated his willingness to change course.[10]

In the weeks following his nomination, Wilson swiftly put aside his
previous sympathy for Jeffersonian limited government. The rapidity of
his conversion was doubtless affected by his calculation that progressive
reform, directed from the governor's office, was the wind that would carry
him to victory. There is also no doubt that his growing disenchantment
with the rich resulted from his Princeton experience.

As he soon concluded, if he had held to his creed as a conservative
Democrat, the man whom the New Jersey bosses believed they had chosen would probably not win the Statehouse. The choice he made after his
nomination to run as a liberal Democrat may or may not have reflected
his convictions; he certainly was aware that he had to choose, and that
the outcome of the election would very much depend on his decision. He
behaved expediently when he needed the bosses behind him to obtain
his nomination, and he was now behaving expediently when he needed
liberal support to win the election.

Wilson hated the traditional American style of campaigning—all the
hand shaking and baby kissing. Knowing full well the power of his oratory, he much preferred to give a speech each evening in each county. Jim
Smith and the other party leaders, Bob Davis and James R. Nugent, operated the party machinery with sure and certain hands and continued to
believe that Wilson was a conservative at heart. Nugent prepared an itin-
erary of speeches. But Wilson was disappointing in his debut, hesitant
and waffling, and unable to articulate what he stood for. Valuable weeks
passed, but on September 30, in Newark, the very heart of Smith's fief-

dom, he finally found a forceful voice. His critics had been saying he was not being specific and evading the real issues of the campaign. Very well, then, he would let loose: "I believe the people of this State are entitled to a Public Service Commission, which has full power to regulate rates. I believe it would be wise to . . . pass an act in favor of a constitutional amendment allowing the people to vote directly for their senators." He went on to say that he was convinced that the people of New Jersey were in the midst of a great political revolution, and that he would fight for their welfare against the corrupt corporations. Jim Smith, convinced that this was campaign rhetoric, thought it was a great speech and was surer than ever that his man was going to win.

Wilson knew he would win only if he committed himself wholeheartedly to the cause of reform. But Wilson's effort to explain away his previous criticism of labor unions was never wholly successful. In the meantime the Democratic machine ran as smoothly as ever. Moreover, Wilson refused to denounce the Democratic chieftains who were managing his campaign. It was not until George Record, a Republican candidate for Congress, posed a series of questions about Wilson's position that Wilson replied in a letter to Record that he would never submit to the dictates of any political boss or special interest. This letter may have been the turning point that would give the election to Wilson.

Smith was alarmed at Wilson's declaration of independence, yet he had no choice but to support him to the end and hope that after he was elected governor he would be manageable. Yet Wilson, making his last speech to the voters in Newark on the eve of the election, reiterated his pledge to "the regeneration" of the Democratic Party. He concluded his address in Rooseveltian tones by summoning the voters to a calling higher than mere local politics:

> We have begun a fight that, it may be, will take many a generation to complete, the fight against special privilege, but you know that men are not put into this world to go the path of ease; they are put into this world to go the path of pain and struggle. . . . And then trust your guides, imperfect as they are, and some day, when we are all dead, men will come and point at the distant upland with a great shout of joy and triumph and thank God that there were men who undertook to lead in the strugggle. What

difference does it make if we ourselves do not reach the uplands? We have given our lives to the enterprise. The world is made happier and humankind better because we have lived.

At the end of this speech, Jim Smith turned to Joseph Tumulty, a New Jersey legislator who later became Wilson's private secretary, who was sitting beside him, and with tears in his eyes said, "That is a great man, Mr. Tumulty. He is destined for great things."[11]

On election day, Wilson stayed at home in Princeton. By early evening returns showed that he had carried the state by a substantial majority. Two years before, the Republicans, with Taft on the national ticket, had carried New Jersey by 82,000 votes. Now Wilson won the state by a majority of 1,333,682 to his opponent's 684,126. Happy Democrats and about a thousand Princeton students joined in a parade in his honor. Fireworks were set off as the marchers headed through the streets to the Wilson home. He was now a figure of national importance.

As GOVERNOR, Wilson's first task was to establish his independence. Who would be the true leader of the Democratic Party in New Jersey—Woodrow Wilson or James Smith? Elected once before by the legislature for a term in the U.S. Senate from 1893 to 1899, Jim Smith had had an undistinguished career in Washington. He had been involved in questionable financial dealings when he used confidential knowledge for personal gain, and he was in poor health.

At the outset of the Wilson campaign, Smith had repeatedly assured his friends that his health would not permit him to seek legislative approval for another term in the Senate; but it seemed self-evident to New Jersey politicians that the reason he supported Wilson for the nomination was to gain Wilson's backing in the state legislature for another run for the Senate. After the Democrats achieved a majority in the legislature, Smith let it be known that he wanted the job.

But there was another candidate, James E. Martine. In 1907, the liberals had pushed through the legislature a law establishing preferential primaries for the U.S. Senate seat. The voters, however, did not finally control the election; results of the primaries were not legally binding on the legislature. Still, the 1907 law provided a mirror of the popular will.

In the 1910 election, a substantial majority of the Democratic electorate endorsed Martine. An affable but unimpressive Bryan Democrat, Martine claimed his right to the office. So did Smith. It was now up to the legislature, and Wilson's position would doubtless prove decisive. Smith had no reason not to assume that Wilson would pay him back for all the work he had done to elect him governor.

A few days after the election Smith went to Princeton to celebrate with the victor and to demand his reward. He informed Wilson that his health had greatly improved, and his friends were urging him to become a candidate for the Senate. Wilson promptly reminded him that Martine had won the senatorial primary. Smith responded by telling Wilson that the primary was a farce and Martine was a fool. Wilson agreed with him on both points but would not endorse a Smith candidacy at this time. Should he do so, it would only confirm in the voters' minds that a deal had been struck between the two men when Wilson first announced he was a candidate for the statehouse. The governor-elect suggested that Smith propose a compromise candidate who would be acceptable to all Democratic factions. Smith refused.

Wilson was determined not to back Smith. Not only was it morally the right thing to do, but it also meant that Wilson could break from Smith and assert himself as leader of the New Jersey Democrats. He would have almost surely preferred another candidate to the vacuous Martine, and the popular support for Martine in the primary made little impression on Wilson. One option was to remain neutral, but the liberals in his party would not let him off the hook quite so easily. For them, irrespective of Martine's qualifications, it was a simple matter of justice that Martine should be the next senator.[12]

Wilson, in a letter to George Harvey, wrote that he hoped Smith would withdraw. He knew he had no choice but to support Martine, no matter how little he thought of him. He knew that the liberals who had voted for him would turn away from the Democratic Party if he supported Smith. He knew that the liberals held the balance of power in the legislature and that it was essential that they support his legislative initiatives. Otherwise, he was very well aware that his political career would come to an untimely end.

Wilson visited the other state bosses to explain his position, and finally, on December 8, he issued a public statement declaring "it is clearly the duty of every Democratic legislator, who would keep faith with the law of the State and with the avowed principles of his party, to vote for Mr. Martine." The people of New Jersey had expressed their preference in the primary and "for me, that vote is conclusive."[13]

By Christmas, Wilson had made the case for Martine's election to almost every Democratic legislator-elect. He was confident that Smith would lose. On January 5, 1911, Wilson's speaking tour on behalf of Martine opened in Jersey City. St. Patrick's Hall was crowded to the rafters, countless flags floated aloft, and the sounds of cymbals and trumpets were heard as Wilson appeared. "Mr. James Smith Jr.," Wilson said, "represents not a party, but a system—a system of political control which does not belong to either party. . . . It is the system that we are fighting [and] any man who turns away from the right way will be marked, labeled, and remembered."[14]

Smith was astounded. That a man of Wilson's seeming integrity could renege on his pledge not to fight the Democratic machine contradicted everything Wilson had given him to understand. How could he betray the man who had helped him to win the governorship?

On January 24 to 25, the New Jersey legislators voted for the next Senator from their state. The final vote was Martine 47; Smith 3. "I pitied Smith at the last," Wilson wrote to a friend. "He left Trenton [where his headquarters had at first been crowded] attended, I am told, only by his sons, and looking old and broken. He wept, they say, as he admitted himself utterly beaten."[15]

WILSON HAD FIRST met Roosevelt in 1896 when TR was police commissioner of New York City and was in Baltimore to address the voters on the issue of civil service reform. Wilson, then a professor at Princeton and considered an authority on municipal government, also spoke. Apparently, the two men liked each other. When Roosevelt became assistant secretary of the Navy in 1897, Wilson appealed to him to allow some deserving Democrats to retain their posts in the Navy Department. As governor of New York the following year, Roosevelt urged Wilson to make a trip to Albany to talk things over. This visit never took place. Nor, because of a carriage accident, was Roosevelt able to attend Wilson's inauguration as president of Princeton.

They finally did meet again at the Army-Navy game of 1902, which was held at Princeton. TR was now president. Once again, they showed great cordiality toward each other, and Wilson offered the president a lunch at his home. At halftime the two men walked across the field, Roosevelt smiling, waving his hat to the cheers of the spectators and pulling a less-than-ebullient Wilson along.

The friendship waned once Wilson became active in Democratic politics. He was quoted in the *New York Times* in 1907, saying that Roosevelt "no sooner thinks than he talks, which is a miracle not wholly in accord with the educational theory of forming an opinion." Mutual admiration had come to an end.

Despite Wilson's public homage to "the spirit of Jefferson" in the days before he became governor and wanted to tell his listeners about the need to resist regulation and centralization, Wilson shared with Roosevelt an admiration for Hamilton's model of bold leadership. Like Roosevelt, Wilson appealed in his gubernatorial campaign for public service that transcended special interests and called for a new birth of idealism. In a speech in October, he declared that Americans were on the threshold "of the age in which politics is a great altruistic undertaking."[16]

Both men distrusted the excesses of the reformists. Yet the model of leadership they offered was starkly different. Wilson wanted to "save and moralize [political] parties—save them by a sense of responsibility and teach them that right conduct is service of the community and what is right."[17] Roosevelt projected the dynamic image of the leader who would exhort the people to rise above their selfish interests to promote the public good.

Neither man was an ideologue. Both stood against the radicalism of the extreme left, whether through espousing the paternalistic nationalism of Roosevelt, or the self-righteous moralism of Wilson. In the presidential election of 1912, however, they would have to face down not only the judicious conservatism of William Howard Taft but also the socialist absolutism of Eugene V. Debs.

FOUR

The Debs Rebellion

I N THE WINTER OF 1910, the weather was so bitter that a man would have been either a fool or a saint to brave the snow and ice of Ohio and Pennsylvania on a seemingly quixotic mission to defend the principles of free speech. But Eugene Debs was convinced that commitment to a just political and moral cause was worth the pain of tramping through snow up to his waist after leaving the train in the large cities and climbing up gullies to shake the hands of miners. At one point he had to walk to the next town and wire for funds because he had given all his expense money to the miners' wives. Yet at the end of his tour, he declared that it was "in all regards the most successful of my experience."[1]

Debs, the Socialist Party's presidential candidate in 1904 and 1908, was a compelling orator. Not so much in the timbre of his voice, for he was rarely bombastic, but rather in how he used his body and his gestures to convince the audience of the righteousness of his message. He dressed somewhat formally, with vest and bow tie, and his long, bony body quivered with commitment. He paced back and forth across the platform, sweating, veins bulging from his balding head, or often kneeling at the edge of the stage to reach out to his listeners and persuade them that he was no doctrinaire Marxist, but someone who had risen above factionalism. He persuaded them that he was a man who understood the problems of the working men and women in the new world of industrial capitalism, who cared for them, and led the audience to envision, as he himself did, the new Jerusalem of a transcendent and fairer social order.

As one of his toughest listeners, who thought that calling one another "comrade" was "a lot of bunk," reported to the journalist Heywood Broun, "When Debs says 'comrade' it is all right. He means it. That old man with the burning eyes actually believes that there can be such a thing as the brotherhood of man. And that's not the funniest part of it. As long as he's around I believe it myself."[2]

Unlike Roosevelt and Wilson, Debs was far more than a reformist. As a radical, he preached that the power held by capitalist America should be transferred to those who made the products that created the wealth. But he also called for an American citizenship that transcended class barriers, a brotherhood that he believed was incarnate with the founding of the nation. In his campaign in 1908, speaking to a group of farmers and small merchants in Girard, Kansas, Debs called for a new "partnership"—when "we have stopped clutching at each other's throats, when we have stopped enslaving each other, we will stand together, hands clasped, and be friends. We will be comrades, we will be brothers, and we will begin the march to the grandest civilization the human race has ever known."[3]

THE INDIANA TOWN of Terre Haute, where Eugene Debs was born in 1855, was for him a kind of Eden. This "enchanting little village," as he described it to a friend two years before his death in 1926, lay on the banks of the Wabash River, a preindustrial society made up chiefly of French-Canadian trappers and Welsh and Scotch-Irish farmers, a population of fewer than six thousand. You could cross the village in less than fifteen minutes, starting at the covered county bridge over the Wabash.

Gene's father, Jean Daniel Debs, was born in 1820 in Alsace to a prosperous family. His father owned textile mills and meat markets. Daniel was sent to school in Paris and Waldersbach, where he steeped himself in the literature of the German and French romantics and idealists— Goethe, Schiller, Eugène Sue, and especially Victor Hugo. His forebears were bankers and merchants; Daniel, spurning business, became a lover of the latest poetry and knowledgeable about the quality of fine prints.

Family tensions—his Protestant father had refused him permission to marry a Roman Catholic working woman in his factory—filled Daniel with the belief that he would make his own way best in the New World. But it was the sudden death of his father in 1848 that spurred Daniel to seek a new life in America. In 1849, he landed in New York, all but penniless after an American businessman had cheated him of his money on the seventy-one-day voyage across the Atlantic. Soon after his arrival, he begged his beloved to follow him, and in September of that year, Mary Marguerite Bettrich arrived and married Daniel.

Settling in Terre Haute, where there was a sizeable French-speaking community, Daniel and Daisy (as he called her) found themselves economically hard-pressed: Daniel was working long, grueling hours at one of the packing houses but quit before the unsanitary conditions there destroyed his health. He then went to work laying ties for the Vandalia railroad, but he was laid off and went from one badly paid job to another. Two daughters died, one during their stay in New York and another shortly after her birth. Two more daughters were born to the couple, who left briefly for Brooklyn when an epidemic struck Terre Haute. Returning to Indiana, Daisy took the last of their savings, some forty dollars, and opened a grocery store in the front room of their house. It was in this two-story frame building that their first son, Eugene Victor Debs, was born, six years before the Civil War. He was named after Daniel's heroes, Eugène Sue and Victor Hugo, and the family finally did well.

Daniel Debs was determined that Gene would have a good classical education. After the grocery business flourished during the war, his father was able to send the boy to a local private institute, the Old Seminary School. In addition to the formal lessons, Gene would spend Sunday evenings at home where his father would read him passages from the German and French romantics: Schiller, Goethe, Dumas, Rousseau, Racine, Corneille, Sue, and his favorite, Victor Hugo. In this way Debs learned two foreign languages, and in later life he frequently reread Hugo's *Les Miserables* in the original.

After his mother dropped her Catholic religion he received little religious training. On the flyleaf of a Bible that he was given in school as a reward in a spelling bee was written: "Read and obey." He later commented: "I never did either."[4] This may have been true of his religious studies, but he was a good student in the Seminary and did equally well when he transferred to the public grammar school in 1867 and again when he entered high school two years later.

Terre Haute was not without its social distinctions, but the emphasis in the schools was, reflecting the words of Clarence Darrow, to present a "democratic vision that stressed individual potential and community progress within the context of the political traditions of the American Revolutionary heritage."[5] Most citizens of Terre Haute expected to better themselves through hard work, and although the business elite held power over the poorer classes, the democratic ideology and the close personal relations between employers and employees muted, at least in the period before the Civil War, the use of absolute power that would threaten a sense of community. Debs very much believed in the idea of citizens working together for the betterment of all; later, even when he experienced the brutality of industrial capitalism, he always yearned for the remaking of such a community for the American people.

Despite his love of learning and diligence in school, Debs quit high school at the age of fourteen in order to help the family, whose business had seriously slackened after the Civil War. His parents deeply opposed his decision to discontinue his formal education. But Debs was determined. As his brother Theodore said later, the family was not poor, there was always enough food, though "life at times was hard and suffering great."[6] Most likely, Debs wanted to strike out on his own as his father had, and working on the railroad might well have seemed to him an opportunity to advance to a position of engineer. He had a youthful infatuation for the railroad, dating from when he was a small boy watching the trains sweep through town to a world elsewhere.

And so in May near the end of the school year, Gene Debs, six feet tall, lean and hard, began cleaning grease from the trucks of freight engines at fifty cents a day. A most likeable young man, he was soon promoted, first to painting switches and stripes on car bodies and later, the letters on locomotives. He was open-handed, pockets filled with candy from his father's store, which he handed out to younger children. His brother Theodore, later to be his collaborator, adored him. The family was close, his father devoted to his children and his wife.

In 1871, Debs became a railroad fireman, with a raise that allowed him to use the extra money to go to a business college every afternoon, even though this meant he could sleep only a few hours in the morning. He sometimes regretted his decision to leave school, and in the spring of 1873 when his high school class graduated, he cried because he was not among them.[7] At the same time he continued his reading at night, shading his candle from the engineer with whom he shared a room.

During this period he came to identify himself with his fellow workers, especially the railroad firemen. When bankruptcy forced the railroads to shut down almost completely, Debs left Terre Haute to seek work. He found it in St. Louis and immediately experienced a rougher side of life in the growing metropolis. Life as he saw it there reflected much of the misery and retribution found in Hugo's story of Jean Valjean.

In 1874, after one of his friends slipped under a locomotive and was killed, his mother pleaded with him to come home, and her worries overcame his reluctance to leave railroading. He returned to Terre Haute and became a billing clerk at Hulman & Cox, the biggest wholesale grocery company in the Midwest.

Debs's commitment to improving the plight of the workingman was rooted in his vision of a cooperative community in which the bosses and workers needed one another for the common good. He was also growing to share the habits of the workingmen, drinking hard and enjoying Negro dialect jokes. He did not see the plight of the black American as so different from that of the white workingman, whose life would improve only if his economic circumstances changed for the better.

In a sense, Gene Debs struck out on his own to get ahead. His courses at the business school were meant to let him rise to a managerial position. In this respect, his leaving high school and his service on the railroad were not so much the result of an adolescent crisis as they were a reflection of the values of his hometown. For him and his peers it was an expression of manhood. As his biographer Nick Salvatore has described it, "Manhood was in large part defined through one's actions as a citizen, a member of a specific community, and a producer of value for one's family and the community and in one's personal relations with others."[8]

• • •

DEBS HAD WORKED on the railroad for fewer than five years, but as he later wrote, "I learned of the hardships of the rail in snow, sleet and hail, of the ceaseless danger that lurks along the iron highway, the uncertainty of employment, scant wages and altogether trying lot of the working man, so that from my very boyhood I was made to feel the wrongs of labor."[9]

He was nonetheless content at this time to join Hulman's, and he soon became the model of a rising young man in town, the son of a relatively prosperous retail merchant. He went to the opera house for orations, theater, and music, and the Occasional Literary Society, which offered debates and educational addresses. In February 1877, Debs attended the organizational meeting of the Brotherhood of Locomotive Firemen, which was primarily concerned with insurance and death benefits for its members. Debs, who continued having a feeling of solidarity with the firemen he had worked with, was elected recording secretary. He soon began devoting his evenings to increasing the membership of the Terre Haute lodge of the Brotherhood.

In 1878, he ran as a Democrat for city clerk and was handily elected. This was a job that was surely preferable to being a billing clerk at Hulman's, and in 1881 he was reelected, even though most Democrats were defeated. He was now a labor leader and politician; he knew most people by name and always had a smile for them. When the Brotherhood moved its national offices to Terre Haute, Debs became the new secretary-treasurer and the editor of the Brotherhood's journal, *The Magazine*. His brother Theodore, in turn, gave up a partnership in a local haberdashery and took a job as the Brotherhood's bookkeeper. His sisters, Emma and Eugenie, became unpaid stenographers. Under Debs, the Brotherhood flourished; by 1881 its membership had doubled, and the next year it doubled again to total five thousand. In 1884, Debs was elected to the state legislature for a two-year term, but he found the work in Indianapolis boring and the legislative compromises emasculating.

During this time Debs remained friendly with his former employer, Herman Hulman, and with other prominent businessmen in town. He was quite properly seen not as a radical but as a decent Democratic politician and labor leader, in short, a "sensible" man. He could write in an editorial in 1884 that the mission of the Brotherhood "is not to antagonize capital. Strikes do that; hence we oppose strikes as a remedy for the ills of which labor complains."[10] Even after the strike in 1877 of the Vandalia railroad, owned by a Terre Haute businessman, Debs did not surrender his ideal of a harmonious community.[11]

THE MARRIAGE OF Eugene Debs and Kate Metzel in 1885 at St. Stephen's Episcopal Church was a fashionable social event in Terre Haute. She was the stepdaughter of John Jacob Baur, who owned the largest drugstore in town. He had sent all his sons to college or to Europe, but not the women of his family, who were expected to learn the routine of housekeeping in preparation for a good marriage. Although Gene Debs was considered an admirably ambitious young man, he was marrying into a far wealthier social class, and not surprisingly, there was strong opposition from Kate's family to such a union.

The marriage was not an easy one. Debs's salary as city clerk at the time of their wedding was a decent $3,000 a year; it was not sufficient to provide Kate with the style of life she desired. A proud woman who aspired to a prestigious social position, she was a person of great strength and determination. Debs's passionate commitment to the ideals he held for workingmen and workingwomen doubtless captivated her, but the reality of their life once they had returned from their somewhat extravagant two-week honeymoon in New York City troubled her. (Upon their arrival back in Terre Haute after the trip east, Debs asked her if she had had a good time. When she excitedly said yes, he smiled and told her, "That's good, because we're dead broke now."[12]) Moreover, Debs's work with the Brotherhood kept him often on the road; and they were unable to have children. Their life was a public life, Debs involved in his work while Kate sought status and position. With money from an inheritance in 1890, she had a large house built in a stylish Terre Haute neighborhood, which soon became a local showplace, each room with a fireplace of blue tile and mantels of San Domingo mahogany.

Although Kate publicly supported her husband in his commitment to the trade union movement, when Gene's views became more radical as the rapidity and force of industrial capitalism grew, Kate feared that she would lose the social standing she had achieved. As an old Socialist put it some twenty years after Eugene's death: "When he embraced the Socialist movement she was, at first, a little bit hesitant, afraid that he was burning his bridges, afraid of the danger of losing a home, to which she had contributed so much *more* than he, by the way."[13]

FOR DEBS the great Pullman strike of 1894 was decisive in lifting him from a full-time union man to a national labor leader, a man who did not merely support the workingman but was also someone of such moral force that he was prepared to go to prison for his beliefs.

In the years following his marriage, workers throughout the country were demanding an eight-hour day, and the members of the railway firemen were beginning to rebel against the no-strike policy of the Brotherhood; in 1885, the firemen went out on strike to support the shopmen on the Wabash line, after Jay Gould, the owner of the railroad, reduced their wages by 10 percent. Forced to rescind the wage reduction, Gould had to rehire the strikers. But he soon fired some of the strike leaders.

Debs himself was finding it harder and harder to believe that the bosses and the workers shared the same ideals of community. The workingmen were demanding a new militancy from their leaders, and now at the gatherings of the Brotherhood he stressed the need for justice. Debs declared that "the men of brain and brawn who produce" should be given "a just proportion of the proceeds." In calling for an eight-hour day, Debs attacked the monopolists who demanded the greatest number of hours for the least possible pay, and he envisaged that the good of the nation would be best achieved from an active laboring class, for then "the government will rest upon the intelligence and virtue of the people."[14]

When Debs observed the effectiveness of joint action by labor Brotherhoods in the 1885 Wabash strike, and later witnessed the brutality of Pinkerton detectives used as strike breakers in 1888–89 in a walkout against the Chicago, Burlington and Quincy Railroad, he came to understand that only unity among the various Brotherhoods could ensure success. What Debs wanted was an inclusive union, a federation comprising engineers and firemen, switchmen and brakemen. If a man worked for a railroad, he should be in a broader brotherhood of all the railway workingmen. But his dream was to remain only a dream: other craft unions connected to the railroad refused to embrace his vision, and Debs resigned at the end of 1892 as secretary-treasurer of the Brotherhood of Locomotive Firemen, though he did agree to continue as editor of *The Magazine*.

In 1893, in the wake of the strike at the Homestead, Pennsylvania, works of Carnegie Steel, when the governor allowed strike leaders to be indicted for murder, aggravated riot, conspiracy, and treason, Debs succeeded in founding the American Railway Union (ARU). It would include *all* railway employees except for African Americans. Even though he opposed the ban on blacks—all the railroad Brotherhoods had denied membership to black Americans—Debs finally backed away from his challenge to the culture of the railwaymen.

When he became president of the ARU, Debs discovered a new and equally determined opponent. That man was Samuel Gompers, a Jewish immigrant from the London ghetto who had first worked as a cigar maker in the early 1870s in New York City. He rose in the labor movement through his iron will, and in his job with the cigar makers saw the need for a federation of workers from the skilled crafts that became in 1886 the American Federation of Labor (AFL). He excluded unskilled workers from his union, because he feared spontaneous strikes, any violence, and did not seriously question the capitalist structure. He strongly opposed the Socialist principle that involved ownership of the means of production by the people, and at the 1890 convention of the AFL he fiercely resisted political action by labor.

Believing that no trade union could win a strike against a major corporation at the turn of the century, Gompers worked closely with the National Civic Federation, a group of business and professional leaders dedicated to industrial harmony, and served on its arbitration board. In 1901, the chairman of the Federation was Mark Hanna. Gompers did not allow people of color into the union, and this usually meant that African Americans could get factory jobs only when they came available during strikes. An implicit bargain was struck between the AFL and the big employers: as long as the AFL would not move to organize unskilled and African American workers, the corporations would make certain concessions to the unions. This policy of conciliation was supported by John D. Rockefeller, August Belmont, and J. Pierpont Morgan, among other financiers.[15] For Debs, on the other hand, labor's key to securing its rights from the industrialists required that a union include both skilled and unskilled workers.

THE AMERIAN RAILWAY UNION became a growing success after it was organized in 1893. Under Debs's direction, the ARU triumphed a year later in a strike for higher wages against the Great Northern Railroad, which Debs rightly called the "only clear cut victory of any consequence ever won by a railroad union in the United States."[16] The Pullman boycott that same year proved to be far more difficult and dangerous for Debs's union and challenged his view that it was possible to achieve social harmony in a rapidly industrializing America.

In the most severe economic crisis the country had ever experienced following the Panic of 1893, in the small Chicago suburb of Pullman, Illinois, a local dispute over wages was fast turning into a full-scale rebellion. George Pullman, who manufactured sleeping cars that bore his name, had constructed a paternalistic system as a model for industrial relations. The company owned the land, workers' houses, and ran the churches; the sewage was pumped into Pullman's farm to be used as fertilizer. When the depression hit the country, wages fell on the average of 33 to 50 percent. But dividends were still being paid.

From July 1893 to May 1894 the working force was reduced from 5,500 to 3,300. Pullman deducted from the workers' weekly wages the costs of rent and water, library fees, and grocery bills. Yet when the company reduced pay, it refused to lower the rents. The eight-hour day was banned, along with the saloons and trade unions. The strike at Pullman, Debs declared, was against "tyranny and degradation" as much as against low wages.[17]

The winter of 1894 was grim, the weather harsh. Children were without schoolbooks and often without shoes and warm clothes. They were kept in bed all day because there was no coal in the houses. By spring, a majority of employees had joined the American Railway Union; in May, when a committee of some forty employees presented their grievances to the vice president of the company, the men received only promises that the company would look into their problems. At noon on May 11, three thousand workers left their jobs. Debs, who now rushed to the scene, cautioned the strike leaders to consider carefully whether or not a strike would satisfy their demands. As he later told a meeting of Pullman employees, "The paternalism of Pullman is the same as the self-interest of a slave-holder in his human chattels."[18]

The Pullman strikers wanted the American Railway Union to support a nationwide boycott of all of Pullman's sleeping cars. If the management of any railroad line refused to detach these cars, the ARU men were to stop running the trains. When Pullman still refused arbitration—which Debs had suggested might settle the dispute peacefully—and would not confer with any member of the ARU, the Pullman shops were to be struck at Ludlow, Kentucky, and at St. Louis, and the ARU would no longer handle Pullman sleeping cars. Debs now ordered a national boycott of sleeping cars to begin at noon on June 26. This was the beginning of what newspapers came to call the Debs Rebellion.

The *New York Times* labeled it "a struggle between the greatest and most powerful railroad labor organization and the entire railroad capital."[19] This was no exaggeration, for the Pullman company was supported by the General Managers Association, which welcomed a confrontation with the ARU. Meanwhile, Gompers was reluctant to give the AFL's support for the strike, as were most of the railway Brotherhoods. Debs's broad-based union would stand virtually alone.

Nothing like the Pullman strike had been seen in the country. More than 100,000 men had quit work. As the strike got under way, there was no violence, and the railroads were losing vast sums of money, for they were all but unable to operate their trains between Chicago and San Francisco. It now appeared that Debs would win his greatest victory.

But he had not foreseen intervention by the federal government. The General Managers Association was determined to destroy the ARU and by so doing stamp out all militant unionism in the railroads. In these aims they found an invaluable ally in Democratic President Grover Cleveland's atttorney general, Richard Olney. Cleveland himself was unsympathetic to the travails of the working class, and he intensely disliked any hint of paternalism by the government.

In his first move to crush the strike, Olney used the 1890 Sherman Anti-Trust Act to have the courts issue an injunction on July 3, prohibiting strike leaders from any action to aid the boycott. As Cleveland himself admitted, this was an injunction aimed against Eugene V. Debs. At the same time federal troops were sent to Chicago should they be needed to enforce it. The excuse used was that no authority other than the U.S. Army could protect the mails. On Independence Day, 1894, Gene Debs and his brother Theodore woke up in their Chicago hotel room to see hundreds of federal troops camped along the lakefront.

In fact, no federal property had been destroyed in Chicago, and the mail trains were still moving. The main obstruction to interstate commerce was the boycott of the Pullman cars. In a telegram to Washington, John Peter Altgeld, the governor of Illinois who had pardoned the Haymarket rioters, said that Cleveland's action violated state law. The president's order effectively established military rule in Illinois.

Cleveland had no intention of withdrawing the troops. As he said to a friend: "If it takes every dollar in the Treasury and every soldier in the United States Army to deliver a postal card in Chicago, that postal card shall be delivered."[20]

Debs feared that the presence of the soldiers would lead to near civil war. On July 5 his foreboding seemed to come true. The railroad tracks were blocked, a signal house was burned, and the troops made a bayonet charge against a crowd, injuring several people. In addition to the soldiers, federal deputy marshals were sent in. These were men who had no regular employment and were made up of labor spies, strikebreakers, and small-time gangsters, what the governor of Colorado called "desperadoes."

Violence came in their wake. A freight car was set on fire, possibly by the railroads themselves in order to discredit the strike; deputy marshals, according to Debs, cut fire hoses when some cars were burning. Indeed, many of the deputies' salaries were paid by the railroads. Once again Debs spoke out against violence, arguing that it had been done by thugs, not by strikers.

On July 10, Debs and three union leaders were arrested on charges of conspiracy to interfere with interstate commerce; they were released on bail of $10,000 each. Debs then asked Sam Gompers to carry a request to the General Managers Association with an offer to call off the boycott if all ARU members were rehired. Gompers refused but did propose to accompany Debs to meet personally with the railroad. When the leaders of the railroad rejected this, Debs asked Gompers to have the AFL call a sympathy strike. Gompers said no. He was surely pleased at the likelihood that Debs's union would be destroyed, and that the Brotherhood might now be willing to join his organization. On July 13, the executive council of the AFL recommended that all those workers connected to the AFL who had joined in a sympathy strike return to work. Without the aid of the AFL, the Pullman boycott was doomed.

Mayor John Hopkins of Chicago finally did carry a message from Debs to the Managers with his offer to end the boycott if all ARU members were rehired. The offer was turned down. On July 17, Debs and the other strike leaders were again arrested on a contempt of court charge for violating the July 2 injunction. This time they refused bail and were imprisoned.[21]

THE COOK COUNTY JAIL was a filthy hole soiled with dirt and cobwebs. Bunks were three-deckers, their straw mattresses mildewed and crawling with vermin. Prisoners, stripped to the waist, scratched at the vermin bites until blood ran down their chests. For twenty hours a day they were locked in their cells with little or no light, and at night they listened to the giant rats that ran along the floor. Even a fox terrier that Debs obtained from the deputy sheriff to patrol his cell to kill the rats went into a panic when it first saw the huge and vicious rodents. Howling and whining, it had to be removed from the cell. Released on his own recognizance after eight days, an exhausted Debs returned to Terre Haute, where he spent the next two weeks in bed.[22]

During this period, the railroad had sent agents to each town where the workers lived to tell them that the men in neighboring towns had returned to work. When the locals wired Debs for confirmation, there was no reply, as he was behind bars. This dishonest maneuver persuaded the workers to return to their jobs. They were also forced to sign a contract promising not to join a union. A few days later, the United States Army left Chicago.

At the time of the November election, after a brief trial, Debs and the other directors of the union were jailed for contempt, Debs for six months, the other three for half that time. More serious was a second trial for conspiracy in January 1895, but Debs, with the aid of his defense lawyer, Clarence Darrow, and Darrow's associate S. S. Gregory, attacked the Managers for their deviousness, and the fact that not a single man had been indicted for obstructing the mail trains. Every day for nearly a month the defendants were brought fifty miles from their jail in Woodstock, Illinois, to a courtroom in Chicago. But unlike Cook County, the Woodstock jail was clean, and Debs now appeared in court in a well-tailored gray tweed suit, a handsome black and white tie, and a boutonniere; he looked like a natty businessman.[23] The prosecution seemed to be losing the case, and when the judge recessed the court after a juror became ill in early February, Darrow later claimed that the jury, when discharged, stood eleven to one for acquittal. The trial was never reopened.

In another effort to obtain justice, in January Debs's legal team argued against the contempt conviction before the United States Supreme Court. In its final ruling, however, the Court set down that an injunction, regardless of the validity of its provisions, must be obeyed. Debs and his fellow directors returned to the Woodstock jail in June 1895 to serve out their sentences.

Eugene Debs, a Democrat who had campaigned three times for Grover Cleveland, had lost all faith in the two great political parties. There had to be a different way to achieve justice for the American workingman.

DEBS CELEBRATED HIS fortieth birthday in Woodstock's McHenry County Jail. Sheriff George Eckert was exceptionally sympathetic toward his prisoners, whom he did not view as criminals. The strike leaders ate their meals with the sheriff's family, played football in the street behind the jail, and were rarely locked in their cells at night. They were allowed to wear business suits, and each morning Debs placed a fresh carnation in his buttonhole.

The prisoners followed a strict routine that they laid down for themselves. They rose at 6 A.M. and, after breakfast and exercise, devoted the morning to union and political affairs. From noon to 1 P.M. they exercised with dumbbells and chest weights. Then, after lunch, they studied until six o'clock and had a military drill before supper; from eight to ten in the evening they debated under the direction of L. W. Rogers, who had taught school before he became a brakeman.

There was also time for Debs to receive noted visitors, such as the British labor leader Keir Hardie and Victor Berger, the Milwaukee Socialist leader who published the *Milwaukee Vorwaerts* and who dropped off three volumes of Karl Marx's *Das Kapital*. Debs found Marx hard going and preferred to read Marx's German popularizer, Karl Kautsky. In later years the Woodstock imprisonment was seen as the turning point in Debs's conversion to socialism.

Discouraged by the use of traditional trade union tactics of striking for redress of the workers' plight, Debs saw how futile it was to expect victory as long as all the forces of government as well as corporations were against you. Debs, however, was often impatient or bored with Marxist theory and with the doctrinal battles among factions of the Socialist Party. As he told a reporter from his jail cell, "Socialism is a broad term. I believe in every man having the opportunity to advance to the fullest limits of his abilities. I do not believe in the kind of socialism that measures everyone in the same mould."

He was still a man who looked for the overthrow of the competitive capitalist system by the ballot box in what he saw as the American democratic tradition. His hero was Abraham Lincoln, who incarnated the classic virtues he believed in—"education, frugality, integrity, veracity, fidelity, diligence, sobriety and charity."[24]

Debs became a national celebrity while in Woodstock. At one point the Justice Department informed him that he was being considered for a pardon. But he refused this on the grounds that he was entitled to his freedom as a matter of justice and not as a matter of mercy.[25]

On November 22, 1895, Debs was released from prison. Eight inches of snow covered the streets of Woodstock, and Theodore Debs had to borrow a horse and cutter for Debs and his wife, Kate, who had arrived three months earlier to be with him after his comrades were discharged. Now the Debs family rode through the wintry streets to bid their farewells to the thousands of people who had come to see him off. At five o'clock that afternoon a special train of six cars arrived from Chicago, filled with bands and supporters, to accompany Debs to a great reception in Chicago that night. The crowd lifted Debs to their shoulders and bore him to the train.

At the Chicago depot, in a pouring rain, over 100,000 people gathered to welcome the famous prisoner of Woodstock. They shouted and screamed and beat upon their neighbors' shoulders. Here at last was Debs, who had led his followers into an epic struggle against the power of the railroads, and had defied the government and the U.S. Army rather than surrender his principles. Slowly, slowly, the Chicago worshippers, with Debs on their shoulders, moved through the crowd to the Battery D Armory on Michigan Avenue. At one point they tried to put Debs on a wagon, but he preferred to march with them through the slush. "If the rest walk," he said, "I shall walk, too."[26]

The Armory was filled to the walls with standing men, women, and children, and Debs summoned the principles of the American Revolution to make his case. "Manifestly the spirit of '76 survives. . . . The glorification and vindication of American principles of government, as proclaimed to the world in the Declaration of Independence, is the high purpose of this convocation." What is to be done? he asked. Against the betrayal of the traditions of the American republic, the working people were not defenseless. The very soul of the Republic could be restored by "the people," who possessed "the all-pervading power of the ballot." It could give "to our civilization its crowning glory—the cooperative commonwealth," but the people must use it wisely or it will bring them bondage instead of freedom.[27]

With that speech and with his own release from bondage, Debs, like an Old Testament prophet, became the living symbol of discontent with the oppressive order of unrestrained capitalism. He had entered Woodstock jail as a pragmatic labor leader. He left as a labor radical.

His HANDS WERE so swollen and his arm so badly wrenched from shaking hands that Debs had to stop off in Indianapolis to see a doctor before returning to Terre Haute.

More serious was the debt of $30,000 that the American Railway

Union owed for legal fees to its lawyers, as well as for its printing bills. The union itself was already moribund, but Debs was determined to try to save it. To do this, he embarked on a massive lecture tour to raise the money to pay back all that it owed.

On one level, his speeches were a great success. Debs drew overflowing audiences from Rhode Island to California, enhancing his newfound image as a national politician. But railroad detectives followed him, and any railroad employee who was caught attending his lectures was summarily fired. In a period of severe economic downturn, men needed their jobs, and many railroaders stayed away; nonetheless, this time his appeal to the broad masses of discontented people broadened. From every city he sent a check to his union's creditors, and his speeches became more radical.

With both the Brotherhoods as well as the railroads determined to destroy the union, and with the AFL only too ready to pick up the pieces, the ARU could not be brought back to life. Debs's future now lay in national politics, but at this time he was still reluctant to declare himself a Socialist. Disenchanted with mainstream political parties, it seemed that the only avenue open was the Populist or People's Party, with its roots in southern and western agrarian sentiment directed primarily at the great corporations. With a presidential election looming in 1896, there was even some talk among the Populists of running Debs for president, but by the time the Democratic convention met in Chicago in early July, it was clear that William Jennings Bryan would try to fuse populism with the Democratic Party and thus secure the Democratic nomination for president.

Since the founding of the Populist Party four years earlier, the issue of free silver had been at the heart of the party's beliefs. For thirty years the dollar had strengthened under the system of tying the dollar to the gold standard, a "sound money" position that was supported by the bankers and industrialists of the East. During this same period the cotton-growing farmers in the South and the wheat growers in the West saw a fall in the prices of their products. Moreover, the farmers were mostly debtors, and their long-term indebtedness was increasing. For example, a debt that could have been covered in 1865 with 1,000 bushels of wheat now cost 3,000 bushels.

To many farmers, the remedy for this situation was simple: if money was scarce, increase the money supply. Silver was cheap and plentiful, and by adopting a policy of bimetallism, linking the dollar to silver and gold at a sixteen-to-one ratio, the currency would inflate and the costs of paying long-debts would diminish. The free coinage of silver seemed the answer, as long as a silver dollar was worth intrinsically less than a gold dollar.[28]

At the Democratic convention Bryan's speech electrified the delegates, as he famously cried out: "You shall not press down upon the brow of labor this crown of thorns, you shall not crucify mankind upon a cross of gold."[29]

Currency reform alone could not end the miseries that afflicted the farmers. High tariffs, middlemen, speculators, monopolistic producers of farm equipment, and the railroad owners all contributed to putting the farmers in debt. Nor were these issues ignored by the agrarian rebels. But Bryan was a man whose heart invariably ruled his head. He believed that free silver was the cure for almost all the ills of the farmers and the workingmen. In his campaign for Congress four years earlier, he told an audience: "The people of Nebraska are for free silver and I am for free silver, I will look up the arguments later."[30]

Essentially, Bryan was an evangelist. Born in Illinois in 1860, at the age of twenty-seven he moved to Lincoln, Nebraska, which he represented in Congress from 1891 to 1895. His father, Silas Bryan, was a Baptist and a Democrat of southern origins, a man who became a judge in the state courts and who believed in the supremacy of the white—and particularly the Anglo-Saxon—race and in expanding the currency. Bryan saw no particular reason to question these beliefs. At college the Great Commoner read mostly fiction, especially enjoying the novels of Charles Dickens. He showed little intellectual curiosity either then or later. His oratory and his convictions stirred audiences, and he won the Democratic nomination not only in 1896, but also in 1900 and 1908. In 1896 the Populist convention endorsed Bryan. Its platform included proposals for unemployment relief, public works, and government ownership of all forms of communication and transportation; Bryan simply stated that there were some planks in the Populist platform that he didn't approve of.

The historian Richard Hofstadter has described Bryan as a man who was lacking "a sense of alienation. He never felt the excitement of intellectual discovery that comes with rejection of one's intimate environment." The liberal journalist Oswald Garrison Villard put it more bluntly: "Of all the men I have seen at close range in thirty-one years of newspaper service, Mr. Bryan seemed to me the most ignorant."[31]

THOUGH A POPULIST by affiliation, Debs, who rejected free silver as a key issue, nevertheless supported Bryan in 1896. He doubtless saw in Populism the only broad-based alternative to the values of industrial capitalism. And Bryan's appeal to rural townships seemed to lend more ballast to Debs's own appeal to the industrialized working class. The Populists, after all, had their strongest base among southern farmers, who saw urban life as morally destructive and lamented the flight to the cities of so much of the farming population as agriculture itself became more mechanized.

With the defeat of Bryan by William McKinley, who won the eight major industrialized states with their decisive electoral votes, Debs had observed how the businessmen threatened to fire workers who did not join McKinley organizations. Seeing both major parties as prisoners of capitalist corporations, Debs was now prepared to publicly endorse socialism, declaring: "The issue is Socialism versus Capitalism. I am for Socialism because I am for humanity."[32]

As Debs took his vision of socialism to the remnants of the American Railway Union, he even embraced a utopian scheme for a cooperative colony where men and women would work together in harmony with industry; in part, Debs saw this colony as a haven for the workers who had been blacklisted after the 1894 Pullman strike.

At his union's convention in June 1897, Debs named his new organization Social Democracy of America; this effectively marked the burial of the ARU. Nor did most Socialists endorse the new Jerusalem of a cooperative society. They stressed the necessity of grounding socialism in the class struggle, whereas Debs clung to his essential vision of a classless society. Asking rhetorically, "What is socialism?" Debs responded: "Merely Christianity in action. It recognizes the equality in men."[33] At the Socialist convention in 1898, Debs sharply attacked those who preferred

a rigorous class analysis. Yet Debs did not want to break with Milwaukee's
Victor Berger, the prominent socialist who had visited him in Woodstock.
He finally supported Berger's Socialist Democratic Party platform, which
called for the immediate overthrow of capitalism, as well as for national-
ization of resources, legislation to improve working conditions, and
equality for women.

Above all, Debs did not want to embroil himself in factional disputes
between Berger and New York's Morris Hillquit, who headed the right
wing of the Socialist movement. Nor did the ideologues of the party want
to alienate Debs, whose national prominence might allow the Socialists a
far greater share of the popular vote than they had ever known.

AT THE SOCIALIST CONVENTION in March 1900, which would choose
a candidate for the presidential election, Debs was by far the most important personality in the movement. He was nominated as a man who had
undergone a Christian-like conversion to Socialist ideals. At first, Debs
refused the nomination because of his health, but during the night he
received delegations that begged him to reconsider. Finally, Berger
wrested from him a reversal and so added to the legend that Debs had
sacrificed his personal desire for repose for the good of the cause.

Although Debs advocated political action as a means to power, he also
clung to the democratic tradition. Citizens must have control over their
lives, whether it be from the bosses of industrial capitalism, or from the
autocracy of the Socialist ideologues. Debs continued to find himself
squarely in the tradition of the founders of the republic.

Throughout 1900, Debs undertook an arduous speaking schedule. As
usual, these national tours both nurtured and exhausted him, especially
when he slept upright on long train trips, refusing to use a Pullman car.

Debs polled just under 100,000 votes, but that didn't discourage him
or his comrades. This was their first truly national campaign, and the disputes within the movement had certainly hurt the candidate. Nonetheless, Debs remained the only Socialist standard bearer with national
recognition. What Debs saw as his task was to make clear to the working
class the contradiction between the reality of industrial capitalism and
the promise of American life.

The following year at a convention in Indianapolis the effort to unify all factions produced a new name, the Socialist Party of America. Although factionalism was not eliminated, in the 1904 presidential campaign with Debs again the party's nominee, the total vote came to an astounding 402,000. Electoral victory seemed to many committed Socialists only a matter of time.

Debs did not preach a struggle of class against class. He urged both the working and the middle classes to support the Socialist revolution in the spirit of the Declaration of Independence. "I like the Fourth of July," he said. "It breathes the spirit of revolution. On this day we affirm the ultimate triumph of Socialism."[34] The vision of Eugene Debs was not unlike that of Governor John Winthrop of Massachusetts who, in 1630, declared that America should be as a city upon a hill, the eyes of all people upon it.

He never perceived that a centralized bureaucracy, necessary to direct a centralized economy, would be a danger to the very individualism that he believed in. The humanistic vision he presented of men and women striving together to restructure society, and his call for a broad-based Socialist movement that would oppose and ultimately destroy the elite control of the economy, was a message that appealed to both native-born and immigrant citizens.[35]

DAISY DEBS, at the age of seventy-eight, died in the spring of 1906. Largely blind, eighty-six years old, and alone now, Daniel Debs died the following fall. For Gene, these losses were very deep. He had returned again and again to Terre Haute to mark the holidays with his parents, and his love for them was probably more profound than his depth of feeling for Kate.

With his parents' passing, only his brother, Theodore, gave him the unstinting love that he required. After his mother's death, which Debs mourned as "the light [that] had gone out of the world," he spoke of his brother in terms he once reserved for their mother. Theodore was his secretary, his political adviser, his closest confidant, a man who devoted his life to fulfilling his brother's needs; Gene wrote to him in 1908 that "no mortal has ever had a dearer brother, a more loyal pard, a sweeter soul, a more perfect ministering angel than you have been for me and I love you with all the holy power that one soul can love another."

During the 1908 campaign, he once spoke for sixty-eight consecutive days, and after one exceptionally tiring speech, Theodore "stripped me naked, put me in a bath with just the right temperature and then rubbed me till my flesh was all aglow . . . and that's only one of a thousand things he did for me for which I love him as devotedly as a mother does her first born."[36]

His marriage to Kate did provide Debs with a haven from the internecine warfare among the Socialists as well as, on occasion, a respite from his exhausting schedule of travel and speechmaking. But he was at home less than ever once he had agreed to become a contributing editor of the Socialist paper the *Appeal to Reason,* in January 1907. In partnership with Fred Warren, known among the prairie Socialists as the Fighting Editor, Debs wrote a column that reached an audience of about 250,000 and was soon to rise to approximately half a million. Working so closely with Warren meant frequent and prolonged trips to Girard, Kansas, where the paper was published.

At home, Debs's bedroom began to resemble an infirmary. After the 1904 campaign, Debs stayed in bed for several weeks. He told his friend and admirer, the Hoosier poet James Whitcomb Riley that he was suffering from "nervous exhaustion," accompanied by "the most violent and incessant headaches that mortals ever suffered."

Even without a presidential campaign in 1907, Debs began the year by recuperating from a "rheumatic attack." Without his wife, he then went to Girard, where he lived through the spring. Returning sick and again exhausted to his home base in Terre Haute, he remained there for six weeks, Kate nursing him. Recovering by September, Debs again embarked on a western swing that brought him home only for a Christmas holiday, and then on to another eastern tour that lasted until February 1908. It is hard not to conclude that many of these illnesses were psychological rather than strictly medical. In most cases, Debs's doctors could find no illness to cure. Rest and occasionally a special diet were all that anyone could prescribe for him.[37]

There was no evident estrangement between husband and wife, but their attitude toward the worlds they inhabited emotionally could not have been more different, as was evident during the Pullman strike, when Kate had visited him in jail wearing diamonds. Even when he wrote Kate to express his love from time to time, it is symptomatic that on the twenty-fifth anniversary of their marriage, in June 1910, Debs was on the road.

Back in Terre Haute, Kate, as the wife of a charismatic Socialist, withdrew from the rich social life she had envisaged for herself. She once complained that she knew "what a let-down there is after he gets home and how he suffers and how I have to take care of him to get him in readiness for the next dose." The decorum of their marriage meant that it would remain intact; his emotions were reserved at this time for his brother and later for the *Appeal's* editor Fred Warren, the men who shared his life to the fullest.[38]

BY THE 1908 presidential election, Debs was once again the candidate of the Socialist Party. He reaffirmed the value of trade unionism and especially the industrial union that would be open to both skilled and unskilled workers. In so doing, Debs understood that a Socialist need not choose between an emphasis on democratic rights and class struggle. But he never gave up his ideal of the community that would embody the democratic promise on which the nation had been founded.[39]

Boarding his three-car railroad train, nicknamed the Red Special, between late August and election day, 1908, Debs and his traveling companions, which included a brass band and a baggage car filled with Socialist handouts, traveled to more than three hundred communities in thirty-three states. Cheering crowds greeted the candidate at every stop. Newspapers wrote worshipful articles about him: here was a man whose commitment to the workingman was unquestioned, and writers characterized him as a disciple of Jesus Christ. More apt in Debs's mind was a letter that was published in the *Appeal to Reason* that compared Debs to Lincoln.

Debs was always a preacher more than a political leader, and his ability to attract large crowds always exceeded his ability to gain further political support. Even in Cincinnati, Taft's hometown, the Republican candidate for president barely filled the Music Hall, while at Debs's meeting in that same hall people had to be turned away. And when Taft spoke, admission was free; it cost a dime to listen to Debs. Perhaps Debs saw most clearly his appeal when a man said to him that the audience all seemed to love him. Debs replied, "They love me because they know I love them."[40]

By the time Debs's train, the Red Special, arrived in Chicago toward the end of September, Debs had already spoken to 275,000 persons in less than a month. At the climax of the campaign in the East, when the train pulled into Grand Central Station, a hysterical crowd pushed and shoved along the platform to catch a glimpse of the candidate; people were knocked down and trampled under, and even Debs could not calm them and had to escape from the station by a rear exit. The next day when he spoke at the Hippodrome, the *New York Times* called it the largest political meeting ever held in the city.

Back in Chicago on November 3, Debs marched at the head of a parade of fourteen thousand longshoremen in a line that stretched for more than two miles. An estimated sixteen thousand people filled the Seventh Regiment Armory to hear the hero of Woodstock speak. Then he returned to Terre Haute to wait for the results with his wife and his brother. The vote was a disappointing 420,973, little more than in 1904. Perhaps it was the growing prosperity in Theodore Roosevelt's second term that most hurt him. Bryan, once again the candidate of the Democratic Party, had siphoned off much of the reform vote. The AFL leaders had urged their members not to vote for a Socialist. But Debs would not allow himself to be discouraged. The *Appeal to Reason* said it all. Its headline read: "Taft Is Elected; Bryan Defeated; Debs Victorious."[41]

PART TWO

Chicago and Baltimore

FIVE

"Stripped to the Buff"

I N EARLY 1911 Roosevelt was not prepared for a final break with Taft. "One loves him at first sight," TR had once said of him. Nor was Taft at all ready to split with Roosevelt. "When I love a chief," Taft had declared in Boston when he was secretary of war, "I admire him from top to toe."[1]

From the moment he had set foot onshore after his trip to Africa, Roosevelt had uttered not one word of public criticism of Taft. Almost a year had passed since they had met on Taft's front porch in Beverly, and almost nine months since their brief encounter in New Haven. Now they were to see each other in Baltimore on June 6, 1911, at the fiftieth anniversary of the priesthood of James Cardinal Gibbons. It would turn out to be their last encounter before the Republican presidential convention the following year.

Roosevelt was waiting for the president in the gymnasium adjoining the armory. As Taft entered, according to Archie Butt, "TR came forward and grasping him by the hand called him 'Mr. President' and expressed great pleasure at seeing him. The President called him 'Theodore.'" After this exchange the two men went to one side and talked, and then they were separated, as first Roosevelt and then Taft were escorted into the hall. Butt sat behind them and reported that the "eyes of thousands in the hall—who, by the way, were all standing, and packed in like fish in a kit— were riveted on the faces of Taft and Roosevelt, eager to catch any signs

93

which might be construed into friendship or hostility. Once, when they whispered together and got to laughing, it so pleased the people that they all broke into cheering and applause. All during the speeches they were cracking jokes."[2]

What Butt had not overheard was the private conversation between the two men. Roosevelt, against Taft's advice, said he would agree to testify before a congressional committee investigating Roosevelt's reluctance to take action against U.S. Steel during his presidency.[3]

In the immediate aftermath of the Republican debacle in the congressional elections of 1910, Roosevelt had been despondent. He felt that his influence had been gravely diminished after his campaign for Henry Stimson as governor of New York state. The hero's welcome he had received when he landed in New York City was simply further evidence of the fickleness of the public. Even though the balance of power in the Senate was in the hands of the progressive Republicans who admired TR, the House was now in the hands of the Democrats. Moreover, the defeats of Taft's candidates in the November election in Ohio caused the Republican progressives to believe that they could deny Taft the renomination. As Mr. Dooley warned his friend Hennessey, there was a time that "gin'rally speakin' a Demmycrat was an ondesirbale immygrant that had got past Ellis Island. But it's different this year, Hennessey. The Demmycrat party is no longer low an' vulgar. Its the hite iv fashion an' th' home iv wealth."[4]

As both Butt and the *New York Times* reported, most of the crowd may have welcomed what they saw as a renewal of affection between the two men, but any such hopes were in vain. The last correspondence between them for years to come was a short note from Taft thanking Roosevelt for his gift on the occasion of the president and Mrs. Taft's silver wedding anniversary later that June, a celebration to which Taft had invited Roosevelt in Baltimore but which neither TR nor Edith chose to attend.

Whatever Roosevelt thought, he continued to say nothing publicly that was derogatory of Taft. That June he wrote to Henry C. Wallace (the father of FDR's secretary of agriculture) that he felt "very strongly that what is needed for me is to follow the advice given by the New Bedford whaling captain to his mate when he told him that all he wanted from him was silence and damned little of that."[5]

It seems likely that Roosevelt still believed, as he wrote to Arthur Lee in November 1910 after the congressional elections, that "the best thing that could happen to us now would be to do what we can with Taft, face probable defeat in 1912, and then endeavor to reorganize under really capable and sanely progressive leadership."[6] And, of course, who but Theodore Roosevelt would be able to provide this? Under this scenario, TR had to be circumspect and alienate neither wing of the fractured party.

TAFT, MEANWHILE, was displaying his progressive credentials by crusading in the autumn of 1911 against big business by pursuing strict enforcement of the Sherman Anti-Trust Act. Indeed, by the end of his administration, Taft the jurist would honestly be able to say that he had done more to enforce the Sherman Act than the renowned trust buster, Theodore Roosevelt. The act declared illegal "every contract, combination in the form of trust, or conspiracy in restraint of trade or commerce among the several States," whether or not the intent was to suppress competition. As far as Taft was concerned, to allow the courts to distinguish between righteous and wicked trusts would give them power that would be dangerous, if not impossible for them to exercise.[7] The paramount question for Taft was not the size of the trust but whether or not the trust broke the law.

In a speech in Boise, Idaho, in early October, Taft warned big business that he would continue his efforts to force monopolies to enter into a competitive system, "no matter whether we be damned or not."[8] This threat was not wise politics, since Taft would have to depend on the conservative wing of the party to win renomination.

Then, on October 27, 1911, Taft made a disastrous political error. His administration initiated a suit against the United States Steel Corporation for violating the Sherman Anti-Trust Act. This action enraged not only Republican conservatives, but it also negatively affected Roosevelt's reputation. In particular, the attorney general charged that U.S. Steel had become a monopoly by buying the Tennessee Coal and Iron Company four years earlier under circumstances that had misled Theodore Roosevelt.

The deal that had given U.S. Steel its monopolistic position through the acquisition of Tennessee Coal and Iron had been engineered by J. P. Morgan, arguably the most powerful banker in the world. In doing so, he had quelled the Panic of 1907, the last time that private bankers rather than government regulators controlled a financial crisis. Although there had been waves of panic selling on Wall Street since March of that year, the crisis crested in late October. Too many trust companies, once seen as safe havens for investment, had become highly speculative. As historian Ron Chernow describes it, "To draw money for risky ventures, they paid exorbitant interest rates, and trust executives operated like stock market plungers. They loaned out so much against stocks and bonds that by October 1907 as much as half the bank loans in New York were backed by securities as collateral—an extremely shaky base for the system. The trusts also didn't keep the high cash reserves of commercial banks and were vulnerable to sudden runs."[9]

As the panic worsened, Morgan decided that Wall Street must be rescued from its own folly, and he was the man who could do so. At seventy years old, Pierpont Morgan had demonstrated such integrity of character that his word was enough to stabilize roiling financial markets. His word was usually backed by his ability to raise tens of millions of dollars to secure a failing bank or company. On Tuesday, October 22, Morgan and other bankers met at a Manhattan hotel with Roosevelt's Treasury Secretary George Cortelyou. The next day, Cortelyou put $25 million in government monies at Morgan's disposal, a testimony to Roosevelt's regard for Morgan.

Morgan summoned George F. Baker of First National Bank and James Stillman of National City Bank and together they provided $3 million to save the Trust Company of America, which Morgan had designated as worth saving. That did not stop the panic. On Thursday, October 24, stock trading all but stopped. Ransom H. Thomas, the president of the New York Stock Exchange, crossed Broad Street and told Morgan that unless $25 million were raised immediately, at least fifty brokerage houses were likely to go under. Thomas wanted to close the Exchange. Morgan asked how long it usually stayed open. Thomas answered that closing time was three o'clock. Morgan retorted: "It must not close one minute before that hour today."

At two o'clock Morgan summoned the chief executives of the leading New York banks and warned them that dozens of brokerage houses would fail unless they came up with $25 million within ten to twelve minutes. By 2:16, the money was pledged. Morgan then sent his men across the street to the exchange to announce that call money for loans would be available at as low as 10 percent. Chernow recounts that "as news of the rescue circulated through the Exchange, Pierpont heard a mighty roar across the street. Looking up, he asked the cause: he was being given an ovation by the jubilant floor traders."[10]

The panic eased, but a few days later, Mayor George B. McClellan came to Morgan's library to tell Pierpont that the city needed $30 million to meet its obligations. Once again, Morgan, Baker, and Stillman provided the money.

The final act took place on Saturday night, November 2. The speculative brokerage house of Moore and Schley was $25 million in debt and was threatening to go under. But it held an enormous minority stake in the Tennessee Coal and Iron Company as collateral against loans. If it had to liquidate that stake, it would most probably collapse and bring down other houses as well. Once again Morgan gathered together the city's leading bankers.

Now, Morgan wanted something back for all his efforts to save Wall Street. He fashioned an ingenious scheme to save Moore and Schley, and thus avert the need to sell Tennessee Coal and Iron in the open market. He knew that U.S. Steel, perhaps his favorite creation, could profit from the Tennessee company's large iron ore and coal holdings in Tennessee, Alabama, and Georgia. Here was the deal: U.S. Steel would buy Tennessee Coal stock from Moore and Schley if the bank presidents he had assembled in his library would provide a pool of $25 million to protect weaker trusts. While the bank presidents pondered the proposal, Morgan locked the enormous bronze doors of the library. At 4:45 A.M., Morgan shoved a gold pen into the hands of Edward King, leader of the group. "Here's the place, King. And here's the pen." Exhausted by the all-night bargaining, King and the others signed.

Elbert Gary, chairman of U.S. Steel, would agree to the plan only if Roosevelt approved the takeover of Tennessee Coal before the stock market opened the following Monday. Otherwise the purchase might be seen as an illegal act in restraint of trade. On Sunday night, Gary and Henry Clay Frick, a director of U.S. Steel, traveled to Washington in a special Pullman car hitched up to a locomotive. They interrupted Roosevelt in the middle of his breakfast the next morning.

Gary and Frick told TR that "as a mere business transaction they do not care to purchase" Tennessee Coal stock; that "little benefit will come to the Steel Corporation from the purchase"; and that they were "aware that the purchase will be used as a handle for attack on them on the grounds that they are striving to secure a monopoly of the business and prevent competition." But they "feel it is immensely to their interest, as to the interest of every responsible business man to try to prevent a panic, and general industrial smash-up at this time." To their delight, Roosevelt answered that "while of course I could not advise them to take the action proposed, I felt it no public duty of mine to interpose any objection."[11]

Five minutes before the stock market was to open, Gary called Morgan partner George Perkins and told him that Roosevelt had agreed to the plan. The stock market rallied. The panic soon came to an end.

In the congressional inquiry of 1911, Gary testified that the brokerage house of Moore and Schley would have been saved if U.S. Steel had simply made a loan of its bonds to the house. The purchase of Tennessee Coal and Iron by U.S. Steel at a bargain price was very much to U.S. Steel's advantage. Much of the steel in the United States would eventually be produced from the iron ores of the Alabama region. Either Roosevelt was aware of the Steel corporation's using the panic as an excuse to buy up a competitor at a very low price, in which case Steel had violated the Sherman Anti-Trust Act, or Roosevelt had been duped.

Nothing angered TR more than to seem a fool, and when he appeared before the congressional committee, he insisted that his behavior was both wise and necessary. "The results," he told the committee, "were beneficial from every standpoint. . . . I would have shown myself a timid and unworthy public officer if . . . I had not acted as I did. . . . I never had any doubt of the wisdom of my action—not for a moment."[12]

In a letter to his former Secretary of the Interior James R. Garfield, Roosevelt reminded him that Taft was a member of his cabinet when he decided to permit U.S. Steel to acquire Tennessee Coal. "We went over it in full and in detail, not only at one but at two or three meetings. He was enthusiastic in his praise of what was done. It ill becomes him either by himself or through another afterwards to act as he is now acting."[13]

In an article in *The Outlook* in mid-November 1911, Roosevelt once again maintained that he had acted in the public interest. He criticized the Taft administration for its policy of the "destruction" of the trusts, and urged a thoroughgoing and effective regulation of trusts by a government commission, which would be comparable in power to the Interstate Commerce Commission. He would even go so far as to give that body the power to set prices on commodities produced by monopolies.[14]

Once again Roosevelt had put forth his view of how the trusts should be handled. He was certain that big business was here to stay and that a distinction should be made between size and behavior. His commission would compel transparency of accounts, and if investigation disclosed the existence of a monopoly, the commission would have two choices: if unethical practices had created the monopoly, then the trust should be dissolved under the Sherman Act. If the monopoly had come about through natural growth, which Roosevelt believed U.S. Steel's had, the commission should control it by setting the maximum prices for its products, just as the Interstate Commerce Commission set maximum freight rates. But in addition, TR thought that the commission should also be concerned with the treatment of employees, and so should have authority over hours, wages, and other conditions of labor.

To Roosevelt's thinking, big business required big government. He proposed to govern. This had been the case when powerful men, such as J. P. Morgan, fought TR when he initiated a suit in 1902 to break up the Northern Securities holding company, which was created to include the leading railroads in the northwest. Morgan thought he could bargain with the president, man to man, but Roosevelt made it clear that government was to be a superior rather than a negotiating partner.[15]

"If we have done something wrong," Morgan said to Roosevelt, "send your man to my man and they can fix it up."

Roosevelt refused. "We don't want to fix it up; we want to stop it."

"Are you going to attack my other interests?" Morgan asked. "The steel trust and others."

"Certainly not," said Roosevelt, "unless we find out that in any case they have done something that we regard as wrong."[16]

Roosevelt's article in *The Outlook* arguing his case for helping Morgan halt the panic of 1907, while at the same time reiterating his belief that trusts must be supervised by government, revived talk among politicians of his possible candidacy in the 1912 presidential election. Moreover, Roosevelt himself, still deeply angry with Taft for initiating the suit against U.S. Steel, wrote in a letter on December 23, 1911, that he now saw *The Outlook* article "as bringing me forward for the Presidential nomination." At the same time he declared that he "most emphatically [did not] wish the nomination." But—and this was key to his thinking—"I do not feel it would be right and proper for me to say that under no circumstances would I accept it if it came; because while wildly improbable, it was yet possible that there might be a public demand which would present the matter to me in the light of a duty which I could not shirk."[17]

Roosevelt was also aware that there was only one man, outside of Taft, who stood in the way of his nomination, and that was Senator Robert LaFollette of Wisconsin.

A LEADER OF the insurgent Republican senators, organizer of the National Progressive Republican League, LaFollette had progressive credentials that encouraged him to believe that he would be the beneficiary of the party's discontent with Taft. Progressivism as an idea had arisen in the 1880s, when men and women were transforming America from a largely agricultural country into a burgeoning urban one. But many Americans who had emigrated before the Civil War retained a certain moral nostalgia for their American past. They were not about to reject the benefits of modernization. They wanted to share in the profits of industrial America and enjoyed many of the efficiencies of the great cities. But at the same time, they often hankered after the mythological decency of a rural America.

The Progressive movement at first was made up of consumers and taxpayers who were challenging the accumulated wealth and power of such men as John D. Rockefeller, Andrew Carnegie, Henry C. Frick, and J. P. Morgan. By 1912, however, progressivism was becoming more of a movement of farmers and industrial workers seeking relief from the onerous power of the great monopolies.

Robert Marion LaFollette understood these aspirations and became convinced that he was speaking for the discontented by defying the powerful corporations and political bosses, and as he repeated time and again, "The will of the people shall be the law of the land."[18]

Born in 1855 to a family that had been moving steadily westward in search of a better life, he grew up in or near Primrose Township, Wisconsin. The town's name was emblematic of a romanticized version of Jeffersonian America. Like his parents and his neighbors, LaFollette fully embraced the idea that education was the key to a prosperous and moral future. His widowed mother sought to realize her hopes for a more comfortable life than offered by the farm by moving the family to Madison so that Robert could attend the University of Wisconsin.

Naturally sociable, the young Bob LaFollette loved to act in plays, and his theatrical gifts later helped make him a great orator. At the University of Wisconsin, he was active in extracurricular activities, was publisher and editor of the student newspaper, and preferred social life to intellectual study. He barely qualified for a degree.

After taking courses at the law school, in the fall of 1879 he passed the bar and was admitted to practice the following year. Hoping to launch a political career, he cultivated Republican county politicians and finally was elected in 1880 as district attorney of Dane County. He was easily reelected two years later, and in 1884 ran for Congress and became the youngest member of the House when he and his wife, Belle, moved to Washington.

Even while he was uncomfortable having to cultivate the new breed of businessman-politician that was coming to dominate the Republican Party, he could not have moved across the aisle to join the Democrats, whose stronghold was the South, where they now engaged in depriving black citizens of the right to vote. LaFollette saw race relations through the lens of Horatio Alger—that the Democrats were denying black Americans the opportunity to fulfill the American dream of becoming self-sufficient farmers and small-scale businessmen. African Americans would have progressed beyond the new immigrants, LaFollete declared, if they "had been fairly treated, if they had received kindly recognition, if they had been given the opportunity to make homes for themselves, if their labor had been properly rewarded."[19]

After being defeated for reelection in the Democratic landslide of 1890, he moved his family back to Madison and ran for governor in 1898, embracing the ideology of the reformers—their hostility to the new combinations of big business, their contempt for materialism, and their nostalgic longing for a community of citizens who cooperated with one another, the kind of social fabric that the young Debs had also desired.

The depression that began in 1893 had caused more than one-fifth of Wisconsin's banks to fail, and by 1894 more than a third of Wisconsin's workers could find no jobs, a situation that would continue over the next three years. A deep social chasm opened between the poor and unemployed and the very rich; in six Wisconsin cities criminal prosecutors revealed that bankers had been thieves and embezzlers. As LaFollette's biographer David Thelen points out, to the new progressives the "best way to prevent corporations from dominating city councils and state legislatures and to prevent pressure-group leaders and religious spokesmen from controlling elections was to give real power to public opinion in the mass." This approach was called by the insurgents "direct democracy," which simply meant that the people would "initiate policy and rule directly."[20]

LaFollette in his run for governor responded to the new current running through Wisconsin's politics. He endorsed the direct primary, by which candidates would be chosen by people who had registered with their political party and selected candidates through the ballot box. This system would presumably take from the bosses the power to dictate who would get the nomination for public office.

After the machine politicians defeated LaFollette in his campaign for the governorship in 1898, he cooled his denunciations of the bosses. He was easily elected to the statehouse, and became increasingly convinced that an income tax was the only way to discipline the very rich.

LaFollette came very much to believe that he represented "the people." By reappointing incumbents to state boards, he thought he had enough legislative support to pass bills for a direct primary and for a railroad tax. In fact, he ran into fierce opposition. It took him two terms as governor to get what he wanted. The direct primary was finally approved by referendum—an example of the direct democracy that LaFollette championed. At one point he collapsed with acute stomach pains and several times came near death; a prominent Chicago doctor diagnosed his condition as "an unbalanced nervous apparatus, the result of overwork, and in consequence a neurosis of the stomach."[21]

Elected to the Senate in 1906, he continued his call for radical legislation but was also coming to distrust the Wisconsin voters' preference for voting issues through the referendum process. He began to see the virtues of representative rather than direct democracy. Yet whatever his reservations, he could not escape his appeal to voters, who saw themselves as representative of direct democracy.

By 1911, the loss of seven conservative Republican senators and the new Democratic House of Representatives gave LaFollette and his fellow progressive insurgents the balance of power in the Congress. LaFollette, with his compelling oratory and handsome bearing—his thick hair was brushed upward, which gave him an almost military look—was the epitome of the strong leader. When he launched the National Progressive Republican League, he saw it as a vehicle to wrest the Republican nomination from Taft in 1912 and secure it for himself. The muckraking journalist Lincoln Steffens once described him as a "boss," dictating democracy in his unchained assault on conventional politics.

WHAT DISTURBED LAFOLLETTE was Theodore Roosevelt's refusal to endorse the National Progressive Republican League. Where LaFollette wanted to smash monopolies into pieces, Roosevelt continued to believe that they were inevitable and wanted to regulate them more fully. In short, LaFollette often seemed to prefer arousing the public and publicizing issues rather than working, as TR did during his presidency, to put together legislative majorities to pass bills.

Once Roosevelt had decided not to rule himself out of seeking the Republican nomination, many of LaFollette's close supporters, such as Gifford Pinchot and James R. Garfield, were prepared to defect to TR. LaFollette soon became even more incensed over TR's refusal to get behind his candidacy. According to historian Mark Sullivan, in the midst of one of LaFollette's "abusive" harangues against Roosevelt, Gifford Pinchot cut him short: "What can you do? You must know he has this thing in his own hands and can do what he likes."[22]

Meanwhile, as Roosevelt lingered in Oyster Bay to evaluate the shape of the electoral year, he was becoming convinced that Taft would defeat LaFollette for the nomination. This would mean that the prospects for a Republican victory were poor. A victory for the Democrats, in his view, would be a national catastrophe.

Taft's suit against U.S. Steel only strengthened TR's conviction that he, not Fighting Bob, was the providential leader. In addition, Roosevelt was truly committed to implementing the reforms he had outlined in his "radical" speech in Osawatomie, not only because of the rightness of his proposals but also because he wanted to halt the rising tide of the extreme radicalism of Debs and his Socialist followers.

The debacle that finished LaFollette off as a serious candidate came on February 2, 1912. The senator, tired by a lengthy speaking tour of the West and sick at heart at the news that his daughter Mary would need an operation the following day to remove a gland near her jugular vein, knew that he should rest. But he was worried that any cancellation of a speech would imply his withdrawal as a candidate. So he went ahead with his scheduled appearance before the magazine publishers in Philadelphia, an audience important to anyone seeking the presidential nomination. Unfortunately for his candidacy as standard-bearer of the Progressives, his two-and-a-half-hour speech became a harangue, where he all but indicted the publishers themselves as tools of organized capital.

Novelist Owen Wister was present and described LaFollette's crack-up:

> The speaker's voice grew acid and raucous, his statements had ceased to be even caricatures of reality. . . . and people began to leave the room by the glass doors at the end opposite him. He shook his fist at them and said: "There go some of the fellows I'm hitting. They don't want to hear about themselves." The chairman called him to order, and told him that personal abuse would not be permitted.
>
> He continued his speech, and a new astonishment came over us; whole passages were being repeated. At first one was not sure, then it was obvious. And the repetitions made havoc with his coherence. . . . At half-past eleven I went home. He had been speaking since ten. The hall was half-empty. Next day, I learned

that he had spoken until half-past twelve, and then sank forward
on the table.

Eight days later, the Republican governors of seven states wrote Roosevelt, asking him to be their man.[23]

With this call to arms in mind, Roosevelt traveled to Columbus in late February to address the Ohio Constitutional Convention. He called his oration a "Charter for Democracy." In it, to assure the business world of his moderation, he qualified the assertions he had made at Osawatomie. But he included among his proposals something that would inflame conservatives—his plan for the democratization of the judiciary. "Justice between man and woman, between the State and its citizens, is a living thing whereas legalistic justice is a dead thing. Moreover, never forget that the judge is just as much the servant of the people as any other elected official." It was "nonsense," he added, to suppose that impeachment was a practical remedy for a bad judiciary. A "quicker . . . more summary" method was needed.

True, the recall of judges should be applied with caution. But "when a judge decides a constitutional question, when he decides what the people as a whole can or cannot do, the people should have the right to recall that decision if they think it wrong." (He was referring to state judges.) "Our aim," he concluded characteristically, "must be the moralization of the individual, of the government, of the people as a whole."[24]

It was an egregious political error. Judicial recall was anathema to many Republicans, including two of Roosevelt's closest confidants, Elihu Root and Henry Cabot Lodge. TR's proposal reflected his view that a comprehensive program of reform could not be passed unless the nation's courts were first curbed. Throughout his presidency he had witnessed how often the courts had been shaping the federal Constitution, and several state constitutions, into a formidable barrier against social legislation. Although the newspaper headlines implied he meant that the public could ask for recall of *any* judicial decision, even homicide or a civil case of trespass, he actually meant that only in cases involving a juridical interpretation of the Constitution should the people have a right to pass on the decision. He later admitted that it was a major error for a man in public life not to make himself clear.

. . .

ON THE WAY HOME from Columbus, responding to a question asked of him in the railroad station in Cleveland, he happily declared—"My hat is in the ring," adding "the fight is on and I am stripped to the buff."[25]

A few days later he gave out to the press the letter signed by the seven governors and his reply: "I will accept the nomination for President if it is tendered to me, and I will adhere to this decision until the convention has expressed its preference."[26]

SIX

"A Rope of Sand"

JUST BEFORE AN early dinner at the White House, the president was handed a note from the Associated Press, reporting Roosevelt's letter to the governors saying he would accept the nomination if offered. Taft read the news without comment and then passed the piece of paper to the others. No one spoke as they sat down to the table until Mrs. Taft broke the silence: "I told you so four years ago, and you would not believe me."

The president laughed. "I know you did, my dear, and I think you are perfectly happy now. You would have preferred the Colonel to come out against me than to have been wrong yourself."[1]

A few days earlier, Archie Butt had gone walking with the president just after Roosevelt had quipped that his hat was in the ring. Taft told Butt of his "strong presentiment that the Colonel is going to beat me in the Convention. It is almost a conviction with me. I shall continue to fight to the last moment but when you see me claiming victory, or my friends claiming victory for me, remember that I feel that I am losing a battle and that I cannot blind myself, no matter what my friends say."[2]

Taft was despondent and feeling the stress that accompanied the news that TR was planning to run. For a man who had not wanted to be in the White House in the first place, Taft now had to strengthen himself to run hard against his predecessor for the nomination that he expected would be denied him. As often happened in time of trouble Taft had put on more weight: at 332 pounds, he talked of going on a diet. After the historian Henry Adams, who lived across Pennsylvania Avenue from the White House, ran into the president and Archie Butt, he wrote to a friend that Taft resembled a hippopotamus. Invited to join Taft and Butt on the White House porch, Adams noted with characteristic maliciousness that the president "looks bigger and more tumble-to-pieces than ever, and his manner has become more slovenly than his figure; but what struck me most was the deterioration of his mind and expression. He too is ripe for a stroke. He shows mental enfeeblement all over, and I wanted to offer him a bet that he wouldn't get through his term."[3]

Taft's sadness at the prospect of a run against Roosevelt came through in a remark he made to Archie Butt on New Year's Eve, 1911: "It is hard, very hard, Archie, to see a devoted friendship going to pieces like a rope of sand."[4]

In early March, Henry White, who had been Roosevelt's ambassador to France, wrote TR that Taft had said that "nothing would induce him to say—or allow anyone whom he could control to say—anything against [Roosevelt] personally; and that he never can forget the old and happy relation of intimacy. . . . he could not help hoping that when all this turmoil of politics had passed, you and he would get together again and be of old."[5]

Roosevelt's bitterness toward Taft was such that he could not respond the way White might have hoped. As Elihu Root said of Roosevelt, "When he gets into a fight, he is completely dominated by the desire to destroy his adversary completely."[6]

Taft, moveover, had unwittingly strengthened Roosevelt's animosity. In a speech on February 12, Taft had described the Progressive movement and its leaders as extremists who "would hurry us into a condition which I would find no parallel except in the French Revolution. . . . Such extremists are not Progressives, they are politically emotionalists or neurotics." TR wrongly assumed that Taft was calling him neurotic, or "crazy," as many of Taft's supporters were labeling him. This did not matter so much when it came from TR's opponents in the political warfare of the time; it did matter when it came from Taft.[7]

· · ·

IT HAD LONG BEEN Roosevelt's plan to obtain the nomination as much as possible through direct primaries. This would allow him to say that the people had called on him to lead them, and give him the right to accuse Taft of being a creature of political bossism. Certainly a central credo of the reform movement was to persuade state legislatures to allow direct primaries in which the voters could express their preference. Soon Roosevelt was able to rightly charge that Taft supporters were trying to block direct primary legislation in states such as Massachusetts and Michigan where it was pending. Taft's strategy was to get the nomination through patronage officeholders who would be delegates to state nominating conventions.

In New York, for example, there was no doubt that corruption was marking the process. Roosevelt was outraged. "They are stealing the primary elections from us," he said. "Never has there been anything more scandalous than the conduct of the Republican New York County machine in this fight. . . . All I ask is a square deal. If the contest goes against us in a square fight . . . I have no complaint to make. But I cannot stand by quietly while the opinion of the people is being suppressed and their will thwarted. I am fighting for the people and not for myself."[8]

Meanwhile, Roosevelt had put a national campaign organization together. Senator Joseph M. Dixon, a decent, likeable man, headed the National Executive Committee. The headquarters were to be in New York City. The financial angels of the campaign were Frank Munsey, a rich newspaper publisher, and George Perkins, the elegant Morgan partner who approved of Roosevelt's views that regulation, not destruction, was the fairest way to handle big business. The campaign was well funded, and Roosevelt was very well aware that the larger the campaign's bank balance the more likely the final victory.

Unfortunately for TR, it was not a tightly run campaign. Poor coordination and constant bickering divided the New York, Chicago, and Washington offices. In Oklahoma, for instance, two Roosevelt leaders, backed by two rival organizations, were in a bitter struggle for a place on the National Committee. It took much time and energy for such tangles to be sorted out. What was happening was that TR, who had perfected presidential control of the Republican Party, had given it to Taft, who was now using it to thwart him.

The Taft forces were already busy securing the South, where there was no threat of direct primaries. Political realism ruled. Any federal employee who made it known that he was for Roosevelt lost his job. Local postmasters were told straightaway that they would not be reappointed if they did not put together a state delegation committed to Taft. Cecil Lyons, a Roosevelt man who was Republican state chairman of Texas, was eliminated from his position as patronage adviser. Each state chairman was ordered to hold conventions to select delegations for the national convention months before the usual time in order to prevent Roosevelt's forces from getting fully organized.

It was different in the North and West. At the beginning of the electoral year, only six states used the direct primary system to select delegates, but Roosevelt men intended to secure a selection of delegates by direct vote of the people in additional states. In the end, Illinois, Massachusetts, Pennsylvania, Maryland, Ohio, and South Dakota joined the six states of California, Nebraska, North Dakota, Oregon, Wisconsin, and New Jersey in holding direct primaries.

At first TR had planned to make few speeches, perhaps one in every state, and to leave it to his followers to gather the delegates. But when it became evident that the Taft forces were very well organized, Roosevelt embarked on one of the most grueling campaigns in American political history. He battled in every important state, speaking sometimes as often as ten times a day, and his voice almost gave out as the spring wore on. In addressing the Massachusetts legislature, he defended his call for judicial reform by claiming that it would give back to the people the right to direct their own destinies. "If that is revolution," he cried, "make the most of it."[9]

It was also in Massachusetts that Taft could no longer refrain from attacking what he called his opponent's "false accusations."[10] He kept saying to those who gathered at the rear of his train as it made its measured way from Springfield to Boston, "This wrenches my soul. I am here to reply to an old and true friend of mine, Theodore Roosevelt, who has made many charges against me. I deny those charges, I deny all of them. I do not want to fight Theodore Roosevelt, but sometimes a man in a corner fights. I am going to fight."[11]

At the Arena in Boston, Taft refuted at length all the criticisms that TR had leveled against his policies. He vehemently denied he was a reactionary, or that he had joined the bosses after having been elected president. He defended the actions his administration had taken: the amended railroad-legislation act and various laws for the protection of labor, all of this "progressive legislation." He criticized Roosevelt's proposal to differentiate between "good" and "bad" trusts and declared that this approach would alarm the business community and cause a depression. Then, before an overflow crowd in Boston's Symphony Hall, Taft, exhausted, pleaded with the audience to see that "Mr. Roosevelt does not understand the rule of fair dealing."[12]

His voice reduced to a whisper, Taft then made his way to the waiting train. Louis Seibold from the *New York World* went to the president's car to ask a question. Taft was slumped over in one of the lounges, his head between his hands. As the journalist entered Taft looked up and said: "Roosevelt was my closest friend." Then he could restrain himself no longer and began to weep.[13]

Twenty-four hours later, in Worcester, Massachusetts, Roosevelt struck back. It was the "grossest and most astounding hypocrisy" for Taft to claim that he had been loyal. Taft, he said, had been "disloyal to every canon of decency and fair play." Accusing Taft of base ingratitude, Roosevelt read from the old letter Taft had sent him, which declared, "I can never forget that the power I now exercise was voluntarily transferred from you to me."[14]

In early May, after narrowly winning the Massachusetts primary, Taft pleaded with an audience in Maryland to understand his dilemma. "I am a man of peace, and I don't want to fight. But when I do fight, I want to hit hard." He then uttered an unfortunate phrase: "Even a rat in a corner will fight."[15]

IN MANY STATES the conventions were splitting into two sets of delegates, each showing little concern for the niceties of parliamentary procedure. At the Michigan meeting, despite the presence of state troopers, a mass fight broke out on the platform when a Taft supporter threw a football block into a Roosevelt speaker. By the end, unable to agree on anything, the delegates elected two chairmen, and in a disorderly finale, the

Taft and Roosevelt delegates, from the same platform, each selected its own set of delegates for the national convention.[16]

By the end of March, Taft forces were dominant in the South and in the important states of New York, Indiana, Michigan, and Kentucky (none of them used the direct primary system). Taft had won in Massachusetts primarily through the efforts of Cabot Lodge, now convinced that TR was wrong to run. In the Midwest, Roosevelt had lost the primary in North Dakota to LaFollette by a margin of two to one.

Then in April the Taft tide receded. Roosevelt won the Pennsylvania primary, giving the former president sixty-five of the state's seventy-six delegates. Progressive forces hailed the victory, Idaho's Senator William E. Borah declaring, "There can be but one result, and that is the nomination of Mr. Roosevelt." Senator George Norris of Nebraska asserted that "Taft is out of the race." If Taft could not carry Pennsylvania when he had the machine fully mobilized behind him, his chances looked bad elsewhere.[17] At Louisville, Roosevelt declared: "The Republican Party is now facing a great crisis. It is to decide whether it will be as in the days of Lincoln, the party of the plain people. . . . or whether it will be the party of privilege and of special interest, the heir to those who were Lincoln's most bitter opponents."[18]

From that moment on, almost every week until the middle of May saw a Roosevelt victory. California, Minnesota, Nebraska, Maryland, and South Dakota fell into Roosevelt's hands. With the primary in Ohio— Taft country for generations—the climactic battle was joined. Roosevelt traveled in one week eighteen hundred miles within the state and delivered some ninety speeches. Taft, desperate to win at home, covered even more ground and, for someone who disliked public speaking, spoke more often.

Both men hurled vicious epithets at each other. Taft branded Roosevelt a "dangerous egotist," a "demagogue," and a "flatterer of the people." Roosevelt called the president a "puzzlewit" and a "fathead" whose intellect was little short of a guinea pig's. In Steubenville, the private railroad cars of Roosevelt and Taft stood side by side, and as historian George Mowry writes, "Hopeful onlookers expected a street fight. But both men refused to recognize the presence of the other, and by morning the cordial friends of but four years back had gone their separate ways."[19]

Ohio was a disaster for Taft. Roosevelt won the state by a sizeable majority over both Taft and LaFollette. Many politicians now believed Roosevelt would win the nomination. New Jersey's results mirrored Ohio's. The total vote cast in states that held direct primaries was: Roosevelt 1,157,397; Taft 761,716; LaFollette 351,043. Even though he could not win the presidential nomination on the first ballot, Roosevelt now believed he could control the national convention.

There would be a total of 1,078 delegates at the convention, with 540 needed to win the nomination. Roosevelt had won 278 delegates, Taft 48, and LaFollette 36. The rest of the delegates would be chosen by district conventions, caucuses, state conventions, or some combination that nonetheless did not permit voters to directly elect their delegates. At the end of the primary season, 254 delegate seats were contested, with the disputes to be adjudicated by the Republican National Committee, which would convene in Chicago on June 7 before the convention opened.[20]

Since the end of the Civil War, the Republican Party had been the traditional party of conservatism. But the primaries indicated that the great mass of Republican voters had clearly moved into the Progressive column—for every vote that Taft had received, Roosevelt and LaFollette together had obtained two. These were citizens who might well embrace the tenets of the New Nationalism, which TR had so forcefully expounded at Osawatomie when he called for "a genuine and permanent moral awakening."[21]

SEVEN

Standing at Armageddon

H AD ROOSEVELT CHOSEN not to oppose Taft's renomination and let him lose in 1912, he would surely have been the party's choice to run for president in 1916. Or he could have kept silent and waited for Taft, who had never enjoyed the presidency, to withdraw, and at that point anxious party leaders might well have drafted him to run. All he really had to do was to say nothing controversial and just wait.

But this was not possible for a restless, relatively young man of fifty-three. The habit-forming drug of public life was too strong to be put aside, even for someone whose ability to gauge the political winds was legendary. As Elihu Root, whom TR had once described as the "ablest statesman on either side of the Atlantic Ocean in my time,"[1] wrote to him on February 12, 1912, regarding his promise not to seek a third term: "No thirsty sinner ever took a pledge which was harder for him to keep than it will be for you to maintain this position."[2]

By the time of the Republican convention, it was clear that the outcome of the struggle between Roosevelt and Taft would shape the course of the Republican Party for years to come. Theirs was a breach that would never be fully healed.

• • •

ON JUNE 5 a coach of the Twentieth Century Limited filled with both Taft and Roosevelt supporters left Grand Central Station for Chicago. It was called the "Harmony Special," an ill-named traveling circus, for there was little if any harmony between the two factions. Ten days later, at Oyster Bay on June 14, Roosevelt breakfasted early, and after hasty good-byes to neighbors who came to wish him luck, he climbed into an open car and, with Mrs. Roosevelt beside him, started for New York.

After he reached the offices of *The Outlook,* where the corridors were packed with hundreds of people, a reporter asked him if he were going to Chicago. Roosevelt answered: "When am I going to Chicago? I do not know yet. I may return to Oyster Bay this afternoon. But sometimes things move quickly these days." Inside, Roosevelt talked on the telephone to his Chicago operatives. Soon he emerged and handed out copies of a statement saying that he was going to the convention city. Later that day Roosevelt, wearing a new, broad-brimmed hat that had the look of a sombrero—the hat of a Rough Rider—boarded a train for the Midwest.[3]

In Chicago thousands of handbills littered the streets, announcing that at three o'clock Thursday afternoon, Theodore Roosevelt "will walk on the waters of Lake Michigan."[4] Finley Peter Dunne's Mr. Dooley predicted that the Chicago convention would be "a combinaytion iv th' Chicago fire, Saint Bartholomew's massacree, the battle iv th' Boyne, th' life iv Jesse James, an' th' night iv th' big wind."[5]

Meanwhile the Republican National Committee, which had been meeting since June 7, had been stealing Roosevelt's delegates. Of the 254 contested seats, it awarded 235 to Taft and 19 to Roosevelt. There is no question that TR was entitled to more delegates. Roosevelt's own estimate was that he should get 80 or 90 more. Senator Borah, who represented Roosevelt at the committee sessions, estimated that his candidate should have received about 50 contested seats. If Roosevelt had won just 70 of the seats, he would have had enough to obtain the nomination. Fifty delegates would have given Roosevelt control of the convention and probably the nomination as well. He certainly could have blocked Taft's victory on the first ballot, and gone for the nomination on the second.[6]

The thievery was well under way when TR arrived in Chicago. At noon of June 15, a hot, muggy day with the threat of rain, people began to gather on Michigan Avenue to await his arrival. At the LaSalle station, where he was scheduled to arrive at 4 P.M., a merry mob that the police were unable to control overflowed the railroad yards. The sight of Theodore Roosevelt waving his romantic soldier's hat drove the crowd into a frenzy. They followed him down the street, three brass bands playing, shouted at him from office windows, stood on windowsills and the tops of automobiles, and ran beside his car until he reached the Congress Hotel. (Mrs. Roosevelt remained in the railroad station and later went to the hotel by a different route.)

After Roosevelt arrived at the hotel and went up to his room, people refused to disperse and flowed into Grant Park. Roosevelt had to speak to them, and after a wait, he did appear on the balcony. "Chicago is a bad place for men to try to steal in," he shouted. Every sentence that followed was greeted with cheers. He continued in this vein—"the receiver of stolen goods is no better than a thief. . . . It is a naked fight against theft and thieves, and the thieves shall not win."

Just before dinner in the hotel with his wife and Kermit, a newspaperman asked TR a simple question about how his health and spirits were holding up. "I'm feeling like a bull moose!" Roosevelt said. This image—of a huge antlered member of the biggest deer family—became the symbol of Roosevelt's campaign. Crude, hand-drawn pictures of the animal soon appeared in enormous posters on the walls of hotels and as placards at the head of parades. Roosevelt partisans henceforth called themselves "Bull Moosers."[7]

ON MONDAY, June 17, the day before the convention was to open, Roosevelt went to the Chicago Auditorium to address his followers. To a crowd of five thousand inside and thousands more outside, Roosevelt declared he would not be bound by the convention decisions if the credentials committee agreed with the National Committee on seating the 76 delegates whose seats were now being contested; this would allow them to take part in organizing the convention.[8] In fact, if 70 or more of Taft's 555 delegates were not allowed to vote, Roosevelt's 430 delegates plus some other scattered votes would allow TR to control the proceedings up to and including the nomination.

When TR arrived, the organ began playing "America," and the people in the audience joined in. As soon as they finished, they once again cried out for "Teddy—Teddy—Teddy!"

The contest for the nomination, Roosevelt insisted in his high-pitched voice, was more than an ordinary fight among contending factions: "We are warring against bossism, against privilege social and industrial; we are warring for the elemental virtues of honesty and decency, of fair dealing between man and man." The bosses would soon know whom they sought to destroy.

The audience listened with rapt attention to TR's words, interrupting only to echo their solidarity. All was quiet as he drove forward: "The parting of the ways has come." The Republican party must stand "for the rights of humanity, or else it must stand for special privilege."

As for his own fate, "What happens to me is not of the slightest consequence: I am to be used, as in a doubtful battle any man is to be used, to his hurt or not, so long as he is useful, and is then cast aside or left to die." Whatever happened to him, the fight must continue. The victory may not come at once. "But the victory shall be ours, and it shall be won as we have already won so many victories, by clean and honest fighting for the loftiest of causes. We fight in honorable fashion for the good of mankind; fearless of the future; unheeding of our individual fates; with unflinching hearts and undimmed eyes." His final words made the masses inside and outside the hall erupt in ecstasy: "We stand at Armageddon, and we battle for the Lord."[9]

To Theodore Roosevelt, as Supreme Court Justice Felix Frankfurter later recalled, Armageddon was not simply a rhetorical flourish: "That's the way he felt. And so did his followers, who would soon join him under the banner of the Progressive Party—Bull Moosers all—in his newfound freedom that came at an heroic but bitter price."

TAFT'S only really brilliant move of the campaign was to make sure the delegates would appoint Elihu Root as temporary and then permanent chairman of the convention. An excellent parliamentarian, he could be counted on to establish order and frustrate any shady maneuvers Roosevelt's followers might try.

There were few men in public life TR admired more than Root. A brilliant attorney, he had been one of a group of well-connected New Yorkers who had supported Roosevelt's early entry into state politics. Roosevelt had time and again looked to Root for sage advice—"the brutal friend to whom I pay the most attention."[10] He had already made it clear he did not want TR to run in 1912, and he would not let sentiment affect his political calculation of what was best for the Republican Party.

Throughout the week Root did not falter while he presided over the convention, albeit with a deep sadness within him. As he told a friend after the convention was over, "I care more for one button on Theodore Roosevelt's waistcoat than for Taft's whole body."[11] Nevertheless, he was determined to defeat Roosevelt and preserve the conservative heart of the Republican Party.

Root won the chairmanship by a vote of 588 to 502. When he rose to make his keynote address, Bill Flinn, the party boss of Pittsburgh who had led the pro-Roosevelt forces to victory over Philadelphia's Boies Penrose in Pennsylvania, shouted: "Receiver of stolen goods!"[12] This brought about laughter and catcalls while Root disdainfully contemplated the mob until several hundred delegates departed. Then, Root, his face impassive, delivered a pro-Taft oration.

The next day, June 19, the credentials committee moved to endorse the action of the Republican National Committee in barring Roosevelt's delegates. The issue centered on whether 72 Roosevelt delegates should be awarded seats held by Taft delegates. Roosevelt supporter Governor Herbert Hadley of Missouri took the floor to demand that it be done. Root, however, refused to do so by quoting the rules of the House of Representatives to sustain his argument: a delegate could not vote on the question of his own right to a seat. But he could vote on the validity of the other 71 seats.[13]

With this ruling, Root essentially handed Taft control of the convention.

WITH THE EVIDENCE piling up, hour after hour, that the Roosevelt forces were being beaten, the cry of "steamroller, steamroller" from TR's supporters echoed through the convention hall. Then one man squeaked out the refrain "toot, toot," and so it continued as Root ruled again and again in favor of Taft. Even so, the Roosevelt forces were not quelled. At one point, a Mrs. W. A. Davis, the wife of a lumber dealer, leaned out from the gallery and unfurled a large portrait of Roosevelt.

Mark Sullivan described the scene: "In pantomime she coaxed the Taft leaders to be fair to her hero, holding out her hand in mute appeal, and expressed in her mobile features a gamut of appropriate manifestations of feminine winsomeness." Her clear voice sounded throughout the convention hall: "A cheer for Teddy!" Fights broke out, men jumped on their seats, while others escorted the woman from her perch in the gallery and paraded her to the platform. She stood at the table where Root was sitting and called for cheers and songs. This lasted an hour, and then Root took up where he had left off in calling for votes on whether Taft or Roosevelt delegates should be seated.[14]

A few days after the convention ended, Root said that his activities as chairman had been "clouded by regret and sorrow but never for an instant by any doubt."[15]

At two o'clock in the morning of June 20, Roosevelt's men bolted from the room where the credentials committee was meeting, after that body refused to give a full hearing on all the contested cases. They convened at the Congress Hotel, and were soon joined by other sympathizers. Then Roosevelt spoke to them. "So far as I am concerned," he said. "I am through. If you are voted down, I hope you, the real and lawful majority of the convention, will organize as such. . . . I hope you will refuse any longer to recognize a majority thus composed as having any title in law or morals to be called a Republican Convention."[16]

Governor Hiram Johnson of California jumped on a table and declared that a new political party would be born later that day. Plans were made for a possible counter convention to be held in Orchestra Hall. Roosevelt, however, was not ready to go that far, at least not yet. In an interview with a reporter later that day, TR admitted that there "will probably be a new National Convention, but whether it will be held immediately after the convention adjourns or at some later date I cannot tell."[17]

Roosevelt was assured that he would have the financial backing he would need for a third-party run when his financial supporters, George Perkins and millionaire publisher Frank Munsey, met with him.

"Colonel," they said, "we will see you through."[18] At that moment the Progressive Party was born.

On Friday, the eve of the day that William Howard Taft was expected to be nominated for president, Munsey told the press: "Mr. Roosevelt will be nominated for president by a new party. He refuses to have anything more to do with the Republican Convention now in session in this city. He would not now take a nomination from that body if it were given to him.

"He regards it as a grossly illegal organization, formed by the force of men fraudulently seated. Taft will probably be nominated late tomorrow. It is now the earnest wish of Mr. Roosevelt and his friends that the nomination go to him. They regard him as the proper nominee of such a convention."[19]

Late on Saturday, June 22, Elihu Root began the task of calling on each state to sustain or reject what the credentials committee had awarded. The Taft men voted to uphold the committee, while the Roosevelt men mechanically and sullenly voted the other way. As the states reported, the refrain of the steamroller, "toot-toot, choo-choo," again echoed through the hall.

Some cheerfulness did break through when delegate Clark Grier of Georgia shouted to be recognized on a point of order: "I make the point that the steamroller is exceeding the speed limit!" Root's wintry face showed a sudden smile: "The Chair sustains the point of order." The house broke into laughter. Then Root continued: "But unless you let that steamroller run on for a while there isn't any chance of our getting home on Sunday."[20]

This was the only moment of levity. Things fell apart after Republican delegate Henry J. Allen of Kansas was allowed to have the floor. A fervent Roosevelt supporter, he not only castigated the convention, but he also ended his address by reading an angry statement released by TR earlier that day. This declaration not only repeated Roosevelt's accusation that the Taft forces had stolen "80 to 90 delegates," but also concluded by saying that any man accepting the nomination under these circumstances "would have forfeited the right to ask the support of any honest man of any party on moral grounds."[21]

With these final words—"on moral grounds"—fistfights broke out and policemen tried to eject delegates from the hall. But fighting continued to such an extent that the police were helpless to restore order. Nonetheless, after about twenty minutes the tumult faded, and the votes for the platform were held. Many pro-Roosevelt delegates simply refused to vote, and the platform was finally adopted by 666 in favor, 343 refusing to vote, and 53 against.

Nominations for president and vice president followed. TR had requested that his name not be put forward. At 6:15 P.M., therefore, Warren Gamaliel Harding, a small-town Ohio newspaper editor, rose to nominate Taft. Even as he spoke, brawls continued to break out; when partial quiet had been restored, Harding pressed on, but still his words brought forth hisses and cheers. Finally, he was able to conclude his nominating speech by declaring that Taft was "as wise and patient as Abraham Lincoln, as modest and dauntless as Ulysses S. Grant, as temperate and peace-loving as Rutherford B. Hayes, as patriotic and intellectual as James A. Garfield, as courtly and generous as Chester A. Arthur, as learned in the law as Benjamin Harrison, as sympathetic and brave as William McKinley, as progressive as"—and here Harding faltered, not daring to pronounce the next name—"as his predecessor, with a moral stamina, breadth of view and sturdy manhood all his own." And so, "for one hundred million of advancing Americans, I name for renomination our great President William Howard Taft."[22]

Taft received 561 votes, Roosevelt 107, LaFollette 41, with 344 delegates refusing to vote. "Sunny Jim" Sherman was renominated as vice president, and a conservative platform showed not the slightest hint of the impact of progressivism.

LESS THAN A MILE AWAY from the Coliseum in Orchestra Hall, with a huge portrait of Theodore Roosevelt on the stage, Governor Hiram Johnson of California presided over the rump convention. After his own jeremiad against the Republican National Committee, he introduced Senator Moses E. Clapp of Minnesota, who offered the resolution nominating Colonel Roosevelt. Then state comptroller William Pendergast of New York gave the nominating speech. That and the seconding speech over, TR appeared onstage, and the crowd went wild, men flinging their hats in the air, women tossing their gloves and fans about. When he said he would accept their nomination, there was pandemonium.

With narrowed eyes and bared teeth, Roosevelt embraced his fate. And when he spoke to his loyalists, his theme was theft. "I am in this fight for certain principles, and first and foremost of these goes back to Sinai, and is embodied in the commandment, 'Thou Shalt Not Steal.'" Above all, he promised, "If you wish me to make the fight, I will make it, even if only one State should support me."[23]

To have refused to run against Taft would have been an admission of weakness and, in Roosevelt's mind, an act of moral cowardice. Beyond these scruples, in Chicago in June of 1912, with the Democratic challenger yet to be chosen, Theodore Roosevelt may well have had a reasonable hope of victory.

EIGHT

The Fullness of Time

THE REPUBLICAN SPLIT augured well for a Democratic victory
in the fall. William Jennings Bryan happily declared: "When the
Republicans fall out, honest men come into their own."[1] The
Democrats, after all, had been absent from the White House for forty-
four out of the last fifty-two years. Bryan could even hope that he would
at last have the opportunity to run for president at an auspicious time. At
the very least, he would be the kingmaker at the convention.

Even though Woodrow Wilson had been a stunning success as governor of New Jersey, the Democratic Party was hardly ready to embrace
him as its candidate for president. The bosses were deeply suspicious of a
man who had turned on them when he ran, for Wilson's betrayal left a
shadow of suspicion on him that his rhetorical rectitude could never
quite remove.

The leading candidate for the nomination was James Beauchamp
(Champ) Clark, the powerful new Democratic Speaker of the House,
who could legitimately claim modest progressive credentials. An unin-
spiring speaker who certainly paled in comparison with TR, he was the
man the exuberant ex-president was betting on. Oscar Underwood, the
chairman of the House Ways and Means Committee, whose base of support lay in the solidly Democratic South, was also a threat. Judson Harmon, governor of Ohio, was a long shot. In a deadlocked convention,
exhausted delegates could turn to William Jennings Bryan.

And there was Woodrow Wilson, who had gained a national reputation with an astonishing record in passing progressive legislation in his first year as governor. Four major laws passed in 1911 had changed the face of New Jersey: an employers' liability and workmen's compensation act; the act creating a commission to regulate public utilities; another that revised primary and general election procedures; and a corrupt practices act that put stringent limits on those running for public office.

With understandable self-confidence, Wilson wrote to his amorous Mary Peck in April 1911 that he had succeeded because he had come to office "in the fullness of time, when opinion was ripe on all these matters, when both parties were committed to these reforms, and by merely standing fast, and by never losing sight of the business for an hour, but keeping up all sorts of (legitimate) pressure *all the time,* kept the mighty forces from being diverted or blocked at any point."[2]

Despite his success at curbing the power of the New Jersey Democratic political machine, he still had to deal with the bosses who remained in place, and in the spring of 1911, he overestimated his potential popularity as a son of the South. Wilson believed that what would eventually bring him the nomination for the presidency were his speeches spelling out what he stood for.

Unlike most politicians, who explained their views by going from the particular to the general, Wilson, in his thinking, went from the general to the specific. Unlike Roosevelt, who believed that people should rise above their sectarian interests to promote the general good, Wilson thought that the pursuit of such interests, free from any special privilege, would be the way to achieve a good society. In his next-to-last campaign speech for governor in November 1910, he had called for the restoration of economic freedom and—in an implied slam against Roosevelt—criticized paternalism. "Do you want big business beneficently to take care of you, or do you want to take care of yourselves? Are you wards or are you men? Do you want the court to appoint guardians for you or are you old enough to take care of yourselves?"[3]

The summer of 1911 Wilson vacationed in Lyme, Connecticut, and indulged in a fleeting desire to be a private citizen again. In a letter to Mrs. Peck, he wrote, "It is entertaining to see the whole world surge about you,—particularly the whole summer world,—but when a fellow is like me,—when, i.e., he *loves* his own privacy, loves the liberty to think of his friends . . . and to dream his own dreams . . . he flings about like a wild bird in a cage,—denied his sweet haunts and his freedom."[4]

Wilson returned to New Jersey to find that the task ahead of him was to be another test of his political skills—campaigning for the state legislative elections to ensure a Democratic majority in both the assembly and the senate.

Wilson, however, got rid of his main antagonist, James Nugent, chairman of the state Democratic committee. Enjoying himself at a party in late June, almost surely intoxicated, Nugent rose and with several New Jersey National Guard officers present, proposed a toast to the governor, "an ingrate and a liar. I mean Woodrow Wilson. I repeat, he's an ingrate and a liar. Do I drink alone?" Apparently he did.

A few days later, Wilson and a number of state committeemen were at Sea Girt, New Jersey, at the governor's official summer home, when they drafted a letter to the state chairman suggesting that he resign. At first Nugent refused to budge. Then in August, at the Hotel Coleman in Asbury Park, a majority of the committee met to consider the matter. To everyone's surprise, Nugent attended the meeting, accompanied by a mob of petty gangsters from New York. At one point Nugent's henchmen kidnapped one member of the committee in order to prevent a quorum. Nugent defiantly confronted the remaining members with a short speech defending himself, then left. Just when the meeting was about to break up, George C. Low from Ocean County arrived. The quorum was reestablished and Nugent was voted out of office.[5]

This action brought about a reorganization of the state Democratic Party along progressive lines. Nonetheless, there were plenty of old-line politicians who remained powerful, especially in populous Essex County, which was to be the battleground between the remnants of the Smith–Nugent machine and Wilson's newly organized forces. In the primaries on September 26, the machine won handily (even though only one-fourth of the registered Democrats voted). Elsewhere Wilson's supporters were victorious, and the governor was heartened.

For the rest of the fall campaign, Wilson denounced the bosses and the Republicans, but he said little about what his program would be. He essentially ran a negative campaign by asking only for a personal vote of confidence. The results were disastrous. The voters in Essex County rejected the Smith-Nugent slate, thus helping to elect Republicans. This outcome did not necessarily displease the bosses in their efforts to discredit Wilson and blunt his hopes for the presidential nomination. Had Essex County voted Democratic the party would have controlled both houses. As it was now, the Republicans had an overwhelming majority.

Wilson was sufficiently discouraged by the outcome to refrain from providing the dynamic leadership he had shown earlier that year. He did not try to woo the Republicans or energize the Democrats. The results were a barren session for his policies, and in the last days of the 1912 legislature, the Republicans passed bills easily over his veto. Wilson's response to adversity was characteristic. Just as in his Princeton debacle, Wilson, as his chief biographer Arthur Link wrote, "revealed his temperamental inability to cooperate with men who were not willing to follow his lead completely." Nor had he lost the habit "of making his political opponents also his personal enemies, whom he despised and loathed. He had to hold the reins and do the driving alone; it was the only kind of leadership he knew."[6]

ALTHOUGH WILSON had not finally made up his mind to run for president after the 1911 legislative elections, that possibility was never absent from his thinking. Colonel Harvey had always been convinced that Wilson would run for the White House, and win. It was Harvey who had first lined up the New Jersey bosses to support Wilson for the governorship, and no sooner was Wilson in the governor's chair than Harvey began planning for his run for the presidency.

Working with "Marse Henry" Watterson, the editor of the influential *Louisville Courier-Journal*, Harvey approached Thomas Fortune Ryan to help bankroll the forthcoming campaign. What bound these men together was anti-Bryanism; and to eradicate this strain from the Democratic Party, in 1910 Harvey had gathered around him almost every Democrat on Wall Street. The bosses in New York, Illinois, and Indiana were also receptive to a Wilson run for the White House.

In 1911, however, the Wall Street wing of the party had come to see Wilson as no better than Bryan. His reform legislation and his ruthless treatment of the Smith-Nugent machine won him the increasing support of the progressive Democrats but at the cost of alienating Harvey's backers. Toward Harvey himself, Wilson was becoming noticeably cool.

At the time, Wilson was growing more hospitable to an organized presidential movement, and he asked other supporters to confer with an old and trusted friend, Walter Hines Page, editor of *World's Week*. Soon, a small group of organizers came together. Page, a North Carolinian, had worked for decades to improve the educational system of the southern states and to help the small farmers in his native region. With him was Walter McCorkle; born in Virginia, he was the newly elected head of the Southern Society of New York and practiced corporate law in the city. The last member of the triumvirate was Arkansas-born William McCombs. A cripple since his youth, he had graduated from Princeton, where he had been one of Wilson's honor students before studying law at Harvard and later settling in New York.

By summer, a smart businessman had joined the group: William Gibbs McAdoo. His clear organizational abilities had led to his being put in charge of tunneling under the Hudson River. Though not as a student, he too had met Wilson at Princeton, and the governor valued him for his practical advice. Cool and ambitious, McAdoo was soon rivaling McCombs for the leadership of the undeclared campaign. (Though only seven years younger than Wilson, he later became his son-in-law by marrying Wilson's daughter Eleanor.[7])

While these men were trying to set up a formal "Wilson for president" organization, the would-be candidate was traveling to the South to establish his credentials as a native son and find political support from southern publishers and prominent political figures. In Georgia and Virginia, states that he could legitimately claim were part of his southern heritage, Wilson did not conceal his progressive leanings, but he tried to show himself as a respectable Democrat that was no creature of machine politics.

He also had to find some way of establishing a rapport with William Jennings Bryan, whose support would be invaluable if he hoped to receive the nomination. He had to somehow demonstrate to the Great Commoner that he was no longer contemptuous of his views. Bryan, not one disposed to hold grudges, was confused about where the governor stood. Wilson had declared himself a progressive; but then, Bryan asked, why were newspapers and journals that were generally friendly to big business, such as Colonel Harvey's *Harper's Weekly,* the *New York Sun,* the *New York World,* and the *New York Evening Post,* so enthusiastic about Wilson?

IT WAS ELLEN WILSON who finally brought her husband and Bryan together personally. Wilson was in Atlanta when she learned that Bryan was coming to speak at Princeton Theological Seminary on March 12, 1911. Without clearing it with her husband, Ellen asked Bryan to dinner. She then telegraphed Woodrow to get back to Princeton at once. Wilson, who had refused even to share a platform with Bryan in 1908, took a fast train and arrived in time to hear his speech.

The dinner at the Princeton Inn was apparently a great success, both men prepared to like each other. The next day Wilson wrote to Mrs. Peck, "I feel that I can now say that I know him, and have a very different impression of him from that I had before seeing him thus close at hand. He has extraordinary force of personality, and it seems the force of sincerity and conviction. . . . A truly captivating man, I must admit."[8]

Three weeks later, after meeting again at a Democratic rally at Burlington, New Jersey, Wilson and Bryan did not stint in declaring their admiration for each other. Wilson's tribute to Bryan reached new heights: "Mr. Bryan has shown that stout heart which, in spite of the long years of repeated disappointments, has always followed in the star of hope, and it is because he has cried America awake that some other men have been able to translate into action the doctrines that he has so diligently preached."

Bryan responded in like fashion: "I am glad to stand on this platform with [Wilson] and, of his constituents here, there is none more anxious to do him honor than I."[9]

AS 1911 DREW to a close, Wilson could feel himself satisfied that he had at least won Bryan's neutrality in the presidential sweepstakes, and maybe even his support. Although he no longer concealed his growing progressive convictions, he hoped to win adherents among the regular and even southern conservative Democrats who might keep in mind that he was a southerner by birth and upbringing.

In the *New York World* on Christmas Eve, 1911, a reporter tried to show how Wilson's features expressed his character: "The face is a pleasing one. Very refined but not exactly handsome, and yet it is hard to tell why. The eyebrows are beautifully arched and the mouth is uncommonly well shaped for a man. It is sensitive but firm. The eyes are blue gray, although generally very kindly, at times take on a hard, piercing expression."[10]

Then, on the night of January 8, 1912, before a festive Jackson Day dinner, held at the new Willard Hotel in Washington, D.C., things almost came unstuck. At the very moment Wilson believed that Bryan and he were now a political team, the *New York Sun,* a newspaper violently hostile to both Bryan and Wilson, published a letter Wilson had written in April 1907 to Adrian Joline, president of the Missouri, Kansas, and Texas Railroad and then a trustee of Princeton University. In response to an attack on Bryan by Joline earlier that month for his proposal to nationalize the railroads, Wilson replied that he had read Joline's address "with relish and entire agreement. Would that we could do something at once dignified and effective to knock Mr. Bryan once and for all into a cocked hat."

Joline, whose defeat for reelection to the Princeton board Wilson had later encouraged, released the damning letter at a time when it could inflict maximum damage to Wilson's candidacy. (As the *Sun*'s first version, published the day before the Jackson dinner, was somewhat garbled, the editor, with Joline's permission, printed the accurate copy the following day.)[11]

Luckily for Wilson, Bryan was visiting Josephus Daniels in Raleigh, North Carolina, when the letter was published. Daniels was the editor and publisher of the Raleigh *News and Observer.* By the time the two men arrived in Washington for the Jackson Day dinner, Daniels had calmed Bryan's anger with soothing words.

Wilson had drafted an awkward letter justifying his "cocked hat" remark. As Wilson's private secretary Joe Tumulty tells it, in a conference with Wilson and some of his backers at the Willard Hotel, he urged Wilson not to try to explain away his criticisms of Bryan, but rather "to make a virtue of necessity." Tumulty suggested he pay "a handsome tribute" to Bryan at the dinner.[12]

This is exactly what Wilson did in his speech, which came shortly before midnight. After a brief exposition of the Democratic progressive program, Wilson turned to Bryan. Admitting that they had differed in the past, he declared that "there has been one interesting fixed point in the history of the Democratic Party, and that fixed point has been the character and devotion and the preachings of William Jennings Bryan."

He went on to say that Bryan "has had the steadfast vision all along of what it was that was the matter and he has, not any more than Andrew Jackson did, based his career upon calculation, but has based it upon principle."

He then turned to Bryan again and said, "Let us apologize to each other that we ever suspected or antagonized one another; let us join hands once more . . . which will show us at last to have been indeed the friends of our country and the friends of mankind."

Bryan rose to his feet and put his hand on Wilson's shoulder and murmured, "That was splendid, splendid."[13]

On his return to Trenton Wilson told Tumulty that Bryan had urged him not to worry about the Joline letter, saying, "I, of course, knew that you were not with me in my position on the currency," and Wilson had replied, "All I can say, Mr. Bryan, is that you are a great, big man."[14]

THE BRYAN FRACAS may have been the most dramatic public affair Wilson had to deal with in the months leading up to the primary season. But a continuous campaign against him was being waged in the Hearst newspapers, which came about in no small part because of Wilson's break with Colonel Harvey and the Democratic conservatives.

A little over a week after the publication of the Joline letter came the revelation in the *New York Sun* that Wilson had betrayed Colonel Harvey, the original backer of his political career. Despite the banner above the masthead of the editorial page in Harvey's magazine, *Harper's Weekly*— "For President: Woodrow Wilson"—Harvey was quite unhappy with Wilson's attacks on the "Money Trust." It sounded like Bryanism, and Colonel Harvey was proud to boast that he had never voted for Bryan.

Harvey, along with "Marse Henry" Watterson, had met with Wilson in Watterson's apartment at the Manhattan Club on December 7, 1911.

They spoke of the financing that Princeton alumni were prepared to do for Wilson's candidacy, but when Harvey suggested that Wilson meet with Thomas Fortune Ryan, Wilson demurred. At one time, he had said some "uncivil things" about the utilities millionaire, Wilson reported, and if any knowledge of Ryan's contribution became known, it would hurt rather than help his candidacy.

As the three men were walking out, Harvey said to Wilson, "I wanted to ask you a frank question and I want a frank answer." He asked Wilson whether the support of *Harper's* magazine was "embarrassing your campaign." "I am sorry you asked me that!" Wilson answered. "Let's have the answer anyway," Harvey said. "Some of my friends tell me it is not doing me any good in the West," Wilson admitted. Harvey said he had feared that Wilson might "feel that way about it" and that he would "have to put on the soft pedal." They then discussed a way to counteract the impression that Colonel Harvey was controlled by J. P. Morgan and Wall Street. When they finally parted, Wilson thought their friendship was still intact.

Soon after the meeting, Harvey took Wilson's name off the masthead. But Wilson became alarmed only when his brother-in-law, Stockton Axson, as well as Joe Tumulty suggested that he may have offended Harvey. Wilson hastened to make amends. Writing Harvey on December 21, he protested that when Harvey asked him about the magazine's support, "I answered it simply as a matter of fact, and of business, and said never a word of my sincere gratitude to you for all your generous support, or of my hope that it might be continued. Forgive me, and forget my manners!"

Harvey replied in early January by reassuring Wilson that "no purely personal issue could arise between you and me," then essentially corroborated Wilson's version of what had transpired between them, and concluded his letter by writing, "Whatever little hurt I may have felt as a consequence of the unexpected peremptoriness of your attitude toward me is, of course, wholly eliminated by your gracious words."

Wilson was nevertheless alarmed by Harvey's admission that he had been hurt by Wilson's words. On January 11, 1912, Wilson once again tried to make amends, writing, "I am very much ashamed of myself, for there is nothing I am more ashamed of than hurting a true friend, however unintentional the hurt may have been."[15]

It seemed at first that good relations between the Colonel and the New Jersey governor might return. But Harvey was concealing his determination to do Wilson in. With Harvey's connivance, "Marse Henry" led the charge, and he was soon joined in his campaign of vilification by William Randolph Hearst, who was committed to supporting Champ Clark.

"He who abandons a friend will abandon a principle," one of Hearst's moralizing editors wrote, "and what a man does to an individual he will do to a people." In Washington, Taft believed that the Wilson-Harvey episode "shows Wilson in a perfectly bloodless chase for the White House and willing to sacrifice friendship."[16]

The effect of these attacks, which also included publication of correspondence between Harvey and Watterson, severely damaged the Wilson campaign. Contributions began falling away as the conservative forces arrayed against Wilson seized on the incident to unleash a torrent of criticism on a man who had behaved so ungratefully to his oldest supporter. In Tumulty's words, the " 'band-wagon' crowd began to leave us and jump aboard the Clark, Underwood, and Harmon booms."

But then a reaction set in. The progressive elements in the party began to see Wilson as unjustly condemned. One of Wilson's publicity men in Washington inspired a story that Wilson was being hanged because he had refused to accept the support of the Wall Street interests that Harvey and "Marse Henry" had offered him, and that "his refusal was the real cause of the break."[17]

In Nebraska, William Jennings Bryan was pondering how to help Wilson, who had so humbly asked his pardon for his earlier convictions. In a public letter, Bryan called the Harvey controversy an "Irrepressible Conflict" that demonstrated "the impossibility of co-operation between men who look at public questions from different points of view." Bryan pointed out that Wilson had begun his career as a conservative but had rapidly become a militant reformer. "As soon as it became apparent that he was a progressive Democrat the predatory interests were shocked. . . . The masses, on the other hand, were attracted and his political strength today is in exact proportion to the confidence that they have in the completeness of the change he has undergone."[18]

Bryan's words helped immeasurably. The Democratic Party had risked being seen as a loser's party, and Bryan's populism had seemed to many delegates, and indeed to many voters, the reason why. At the same time, a hard core of party regulars were devoted to Bryan. In 1912, with the tide of progressivism building against the Republican Party, the Democrats believed that they had a chance to recapture the White House. Bryan hoped that his support of Wilson at this juncture would help block the nomination of Champ Clark; then if Wilson could not gain a majority, he would back Bryan, who would once again receive the party's blessing.

Soon other important Democratic leaders rallied to Wilson's cause. When Watterson disclosed that Wilson had asked him to raise considerable sums of money for the campaign, even though Wilson vetoed any suggestion that Watterson solicit money from Ryan, Wilson denied doing any such thing. Few editors defended Watterson's attempt to place Wilson under some financial obligation to Ryan, who, one editor wrote, was associated by the public "with every rottenest and foulest transaction of rotten high finance, trust building and extortions."[19]

WILSON'S CANDIDACY not only survived but was even strengthened by the fracas. Nonetheless, the anti-Wilson forces were not giving up. George Williams, a former Populist leader in Massachusetts, wrote a public letter in February 1912 disclosing that in Wilson's 1902 *History of the American People,* "There is no note of sympathy for any suffering and protesting class." By quoting page after page from Wilson's own writings, Williams proved that Wilson "had a profound contempt for the Farmers' Alliance, the Populists, greenbackers, bi-metallists, trades unionists, small office seekers, Italians, Poles, Hungarians, pensioners, strikers, armies of unemployed." In fact, Wilson had praised Grover Cleveland's attack on Debs and the railway strikers of 1894, had harshly criticized the agrarian radicals, and had put forth the most unpleasant views of Poles, Hungarians, and Italians:

Now there came multitudes of men of the lowest class from the south of Italy and men of the meaner sort out of Hungary and Poland, men out of the ranks where there was neither skill nor energy nor any initiative of quick intelligence; and they came in numbers which increased from year to year, as if the countries of the south of Europe were disburdening themselves of the more sordid and hapless elements of their population, the men whose standards of life and of work were such as American workmen had never dreamed of hitherto.[20]

Hearst reveled in this exposure of Wilson as having been a bigot only a decade earlier, and the angry protests of various Polish-, Italian-, and Hungarian-American societies made front-page stories in the Hearst newspapers. Not that the men who read the anti-Wilson press were likely to vote for Wilson in those states that had direct primaries.

Wilson desperately tried to explain away his derogatory language by writing letters to Polish-, Italian-, and Hungarian-American leaders and declaring his great admiration and love for the "new immigrants." He claimed that the passages quoted were taken out of context. But even reading his words in the full context of the book does not change their meaning. Again and again he tried to excuse himself by saying that he was "only deploring the coming to this country of certain lawless elements which I had supposed all thoughtful Italians themselves deplored."[21] To Poles and Hungarians he wrote similar letters.

He was far from successful at his tortuous explanations. Finally, when one Polish-American group suggested he insert "erratum" slips in volume five of his history and then rewrite passages for the next edition, Wilson decided that a rewrite was indeed the best—indeed, the only—solution and asked his publishers if a new printing of that volume were in the works; if so, he wanted to rewrite one or two passages.

Beyond their justifiable anger at Wilson's slurs, the foreign-born voters feared that if he became president he would encourage legislation to restrict immigration. Fortunately for Wilson, the president of the National Immigration League of New York testified in his favor to groups of the new immigrants. To further counter Hearst's attacks on Wilson and support for Clark, the New Jersey Federation of Labor endorsed Wilson, and copies of the resolution were sent to labor organizations throughout the country.

Nonetheless, the anti-Wilson campaign grew in fury. German-Americans in Milwaukee were told he was in favor of Prohibition; nor was Wilson's statement that he believed liquor was an entirely social and moral question and should not be made a political issue a satisfactory response. Wilson's quest for the presidency was faltering badly.[22]

DURING THIS HARD WINTER for Wilson's ambitions, help came from an unexpected source—Edward Mandell House, an honorary Texas "Colonel" who had been helping to advance Wilson's cause in Texas.

In trying to realize the dream he had held for so long, Wilson had been largely alone. His family had certainly given him unqualified support. But the deluge of letters that Wilson sent Mrs. Peck testifies to his need to confide his hopes and share his problems with someone outside his family. He also required practical advice, and for this he had had to lean on the men who were his close advisers—McCombs, McAdoo, Tumulty—but with none of them did he speak without reserve. Once he had had a deep personal friendship with John Grier Hibben at Princeton, but he had cast that aside in the bitter struggles he had undergone there. When he met Colonel House at the Hotel Gotham in New York City on November 24, 1911, Wilson finally found the man who, he believed, would become his other self.

In the years of his presidency and, more important, in Wilson's relations with America's allies during the First World War, House would present himself as Wilson's absolute confidant—only to find at the Versailles conference in 1919 that Wilson would turn on him with all the bitterness of a betrayed lover.

House was born in Texas in 1858, the seventh son of one of the richest men in Texas. During the Civil War his father ran the Union blockade off Galveston, taking to nearby West Indian and Central American ports his usual cargo of cotton. On the return voyage the shipment was munitions, clothing, and medicine, which he then sold to the Confederate Army.

Edward House's earliest memories were of great turmoil in the years following the Civil War. Newly enfranchised black Americans and

Northern carpetbaggers seized the government of Houston, and these were, as House described them, "lawless and turbulent days. Personal encounters were frequent and nearly always resulted in fatalities. The courage manifested, the accuracy with which the participants shot, were told in detail by every fireside, and the most reckless dare-devil became the greatest hero. . . . They were bent on the gradual extermination of the parasites who had fastened themselves on a discouraged and defeated people, and were willing to give life for life in the accomplishment of this purpose."[23]

While young Tommy Wilson spent hours before the mirror practicing his oratory, House spent similar hours practicing the Texas fast draw of a six-gun. But when he was twelve, he was playing recklessly on a swing, making it go higher and higher. A rope snapped, and he fell, striking his head on a carriage wheel. His long recovery was interrupted by an attack of malaria, and when he finally recovered he no longer had his former strength. Nor could he get it back. From then on, his health was frail. He could no longer impose his will on friends by brute force, but he soon learned how to influence and manipulate his playmates psychologically. "I used to like to set boys at each other," he once said, "to see what they would do, and then try to bring them around again."

Applying to Yale, House had to spend up to two years at the Hopkins Grammar School in New Haven before he could be admitted to the college. He finally decided instead to seek entrance to Cornell. It was at Cornell and then Johns Hopkins that House became avidly interested in politics, and especially later in the daily workings of the Texas Democratic machine.[24]

With the death of his father, House was left with a substantial inheritance and returned to Texas to manage the estate. Business, like politics, was a game to House. He worked behind the scenes in the election of no fewer than four governors of Texas, an accomplishment that eventually made this now slight, soft-spoken man with a piercing gaze and a deceptively easy manner one of the powerful Democratic Party officials in Texas.

House, however, always preferred to remain anonymous. He refused to accept any office in return for his services. One governor did confer on him the honorary title of Colonel, and the nickname—which House disliked—stuck. By 1911, he had finished with governors and ready to take on the great challenge of the presidency.

When he was a young man, House had written a novel called *Philip Dru, Administrator*, in which an idealistic but tough young politician revamped the American Constitution, pursued a radical policy of political and economic cooperation with Britain, Germany, and Japan, and ushered in a period of peace and commercial prosperity that reached its apogee with the creation of a world political organization. The novel itself wasn't much good, but Woodrow Wilson would find the ideas behind it compelling.[25]

In the fall of 1910, House was considering whom he should support for the nomination. At that time, Clark, Underwood, and Governor Harmon were being mentioned as the most promising candidates. House was not satisfied with any of them. He believed an easterner would have the best chance of success if Taft—or even Roosevelt—should run. In the winter of 1911, he lined up the candidates in his own mind. Although he was leaning to Wilson, he was doubtful Wilson could get the nomination, but by the end of the year he could see that Wilson was the only viable candidate with a growing reputation nationwide.

As for Champ Clark: he had been a supporter of Bryan—even endorsing his free silver platform—and Bryan still seemed to look favorably on him. Clark had served in the House for twenty years and had consistently supported the progressive cause. Although he was not an exciting candidate, he had the support of William Randolph Hearst. In December 1911, Clark's strength was not as great as it would prove to be six months later. When House committed himself to Wilson, it was at a moment when the governor seemed to be leading the pack. (This was before the Jackson Day flap with Bryan and the subsequent campaign orchestrated by Hearst.)

House waited until Wilson was free of campaigning for the New Jersey legislature. When the propitious moment came, he sent a letter to Wilson that hinted at House's great influence within the party. "I have been with Mr. Bryan a good part of the morning, and I am pleased to tell you that I think you will have his support," House wrote on November 18, 1911. "The fact that you did not vote for him in '96 was on his mind but I offered an explanation which seemed to be satisfactory. My main effort was in alienating him from Champ Clark, and I believe I was successful there. He sent you several messages which he asked me to deliver to you in person, which I shall be glad to do sometime when you are in New York provided you return before I go South around December first."[26]

How could Wilson resist meeting the mysterious Mr. House after such a letter?

WHEN THEY FINALLY got together a few days later at the Hotel Gotham, the meeting released in Wilson the passionate desire for an intimate mentor that had been so painfully missing since the death of his father. "We talked and talked. We knew each other for congenial souls at the very beginning," House later wrote. It was a wide-ranging conversation, and "we agreed about everything." They also agreed to have a second meeting in a few days. That encounter was even more productive. Again, according to House—"I never met a man whose thought ran so identically to mine."[27]

"Mr. House," Wilson would later say, "is my second personality. He is my independent self. His thoughts and mine are one." It may be apocryphal that House told a friend after the Gotham meeting that Wilson would one day turn against him; but certainly House was a shrewd enough judge of human nature to have made such a remark.[28]

They met again several times that winter and soon found they knew what each other was thinking without anything having been said. House later wrote: "I asked him if he realized that we had known one another for so short a time. He replied, 'My dear friend, we have known one another always.'"[29]

What House was able to do during the primary campaign was to massage his good friend Bryan, writing him several letters reporting Wilson's views on issues that House knew would please Bryan. Throughout the turmoil of that winter—the Joline letter, the break with Colonel Harvey—House let Wilson know he had Bryan's ear at all times. Bryan was to be his guest in Austin, so House wrote Wilson in early February 1912, "Please let me know if there is anything you would like to have suggested to him, for there can be no better place to do this than by a quiet fireside."[30] The picture House conjured up was a seductive one—of House and Bryan speaking confidentially to one another on personalities and issues.

In Texas, House took the lead in building a strong base of Wilson supporters. But never did he put himself too forward, and he always understated his role while hinting to Wilson of his actual power. Nonetheless, despite his identification with Wilson, when Wilson's support was ebbing in the weeks preceding the June convention, House, too, thought Wilson would not secure the nomination. Three days before the convention opened, he wrote to Mrs. Bryan that he would support her husband if, in fact, he were nominated once again.[31]

House's strenuous work in Texas would keep the Texas delegation voting for Wilson at the Baltimore convention, but House himself did not play a major role there. Instead, he rested aboard the S.S. *Laconia* en route to England, sailing the day the convention opened and explaining to Wilson that he was too physically worn down to attend. He had done everything he could to anticipate any problems that might arise and had informed Wilson's campaign manager which delegates could be most relied upon. Wilson replied warmly, expressing his sorrow that House would be away from him and wishing him a good voyage. Were Wilson to receive the nomination, House assured him, he would be back in mid-August and planned to devote himself wholly to the election.[32]

As the spring wore on, Wilson's fortunes continued to fall. In Georgia and Virginia, which Wilson had once expected would be secure, the conservatives in the primaries were able to deliver the delegates to Oscar Underwood. In Kansas, the delegates were instructed to vote for Champ Clark.

Illinois was key, the third most populous state in the union, and here Wilson was prepared to expend all his energies. He began his tour at Springfield, paying tribute to Abraham Lincoln at his tomb. In Peoria, he sounded the call for direct democracy, endorsing the use of referendum and the recall of elected officials. From there he embarked on a tour throughout the state giving fifteen rear-platform speeches, followed by three mass meetings in Chicago. To a crowd largely made up of Polish-Americans, Wilson repeated his litany on immigration: that America was the home of the free and the eager.

Champ Clark did not appear in the state for the primary, leaving matters to his campaign manager. Nevertheless, on election day, the voters of Illinois gave Clark 218,483 votes, Wilson only 75,527. Only in Peoria did Wilson come out on top. These numbers had a devastating effect on politicians across the country; until then Wilson had been seen to be the front runner.[33]

Wilson did win the primaries in Oregon and Delaware in late April, but by the latter part of May Wilson's forces were still apprehensive. At the very end of that month, however, Wilson won—as he had to—New Jersey (though he lost Essex County), and on the same day carried North Carolina, South Carolina, and Wisconsin. And Colonel House made good on his promise to deliver Texas.

At the end of May, it was evident to Wilson's managers that the party professionals were still irredeemably hostile to Wilson. All his speeches seemed to go for nought. On the eve of the convention, 436 delegates were pledged to Clark. Wilson could count on between 245 and 248. Moreover, Clark was likely to attract most of the 224 votes controlled by the party bosses. With 729 votes—or two-thirds of the total—needed for nomination, Champ Clark, a Kentuckian by birth, a longtime Bryan supporter, and a spokesman for western agrarianism, was the favorite to win.

On June 9, three weeks before the convention was to meet in Baltimore, Wilson wrote to Mrs. Peck: "Just between you and me, I have not the least idea of being nominated, because the make of the convention is such, the balance and confusion of forces, that the outcome is in the hands of the professional, case-hardened politicians who serve only their own interests and who know that I will not serve them except as I might serve the party in general. I am well and in the best of spirits. I have no deep stakes involved in this game."[34]

But, of course, he did—and they were not to serve the party. The presidency had always been his highest ambition.

NINE

Baltimore

H OW COULD HE ever be nominated for president? Woodrow Wilson almost certainly asked himself this question when the news from Chicago revealed that Theodore Roosevelt would probably organize a new third party. This did not help Wilson's cause. His supporters had argued that Wilson alone could win the presidency because he was the only Democrat who could split off the insurgent Republicans from the regulars. That argument was now moot after Roosevelt had jumped in. Champ Clark or even William Jennings Bryan could win as easily as Woodrow Wilson.

Moving in mid-June to the Governor's Cottage at Sea Girt, New Jersey, Wilson had pretended (writing to Mary Peck) that "I am well . . . and underneath, deep down, my soul is quiet;"[1] but with Charles Murphy, the boss of New York's Tammany Hall, remaining silent and Bryan not to be trusted, he tried very hard to suppress his anxieties by embracing domestic life at the seaside resort. After church on their first Sunday there, the Wilson family sat by the fire that was lit in the upstairs sitting room, while the cold weather kept unwelcome visitors away. As Wilson's daughter Eleanor ("Nellie") later reported, the family "talked about everything except politics," until Wilson, thinking of the moment when the convention was expected to end, said with a sigh, "Two weeks from today we will either have our sweet Sunday calm again or an all-day reception and an army of reporters camped on the lawn."[2]

Throughout the week the reports of what was happening at the Republican convention overwhelmed the peace and solitude that Ellen and Woodrow sought. By telephone from Chicago William McAdoo kept Wilson directly informed; under the stairs at the cottage Joe Tumulty was on another phone. Bryan, too, was in Chicago, covering the convention for the newspapers. His interpretation of what Taft's steamroller tactics meant for the Democrats was far more favorable to the progressive wing of the party. "If the Democrats are guilty of the criminal folly of nominating a reactionary," Bryan wrote for the afternoon newspapers, "they will supply Mr. Roosevelt with the one thing needful in case he becomes an independent candidate, namely, an issue, and with two reactionaries running for President he might win and thus entrench himself in power."[3]

Bryan, who had attended national conventions since he was sixteen years old and had been the Democratic nominee for president in 1896, 1900, and 1908, now brought to bear on the gathering Democrats all of his political shrewdness. Even if he could not secure the nomination for himself, he could become the convention's kingmaker. To prevent Murphy and the conservative bosses in the East from dominating the convention, Bryan had decided to oppose their plans for choosing Alton B. Parker as temporary chairman. Parker had been the lackluster Democratic nominee for president crushed by TR in 1904. Bryan, sweating away at the press desk in Chicago, wired Norman Mack, chairman of the Democratic National Committee: "I have no choice among progressives for temporary chairman, but it would be suicidal to have a reactionary chairman when four-fifths of the whole country is radically progressive. I cannot believe such criminal folly is possible."[4]

Nonetheless, the National Committee voted to nominate Parker. Bryan, however, was relentless, determined to carry the fight to the convention floor. To prepare the ground, he demanded that all of the presidential contenders put themselves on the record. Would they stand with him or against him? He sent identical telegrams to Wilson, Clark, Underwood, and others, asking them to aid him in opposing Parker. And he gave them no way out by adding: "Kindly wire reply."

In Baltimore, Wilson's campaign manager was fearful. William McCombs was doing his very best not to anger Boss Murphy. Before Wilson had received Bryan's telegram he had been asked by the *Baltimore*

Sun, a paper that was supporting him, how he felt about the selection of Parker. Wilson responded immediately, writing that he had "neither the right nor the desire to direct the organization of a convention of which I am not even a member."[5]

McCombs was elated. But later that same day, Wilson received Bryan's message, which had by then been widely published. Joe Tumulty, arriving at Sea Girt, was surprised to learn that Wilson had nonetheless not even read Bryan's telegram. According to Tumulty, even when Wilson did read the message, he failed to grasp its importance. "In vain," Tumulty later wrote, "I tried to impress on him what I believed to be the purpose which lay behind the whole business; that his reply would determine the question as to whether he was going to line up with the progressive element which was strong in the West, or whether he would take sides with those of the conservative East, many of whom were bitterly opposed to him."[6]

Wilson admitted to Tumulty that he had been in touch with McCombs and would not answer Bryan's telegram until he had received McCombs's opinion. When McCombs finally telephoned Wilson, he begged him to be cautious and drafted a reply that echoed Wilson's position as put forth in the *Sun.* Wilson was at first inclined to accept this "hands-off" policy. Tumulty, on the other hand, urged Wilson not to do so.

It may well have been Wilson's wife who at last persuaded him to reject McCombs's advice. Seeking Ellen's counsel, Wilson found her in the bedroom and handed her the telegram without comment. According to Nellie, who was present, her mother did not hesitate. "There must be no hedging," she said.[7]

Sitting down beside her on the bed he wrote out his answer to Bryan. "You are quite right," he began and went on to point out that the convention was to be "a convention of progressives—of men who are progressive on principle and by conviction. It must, if it is not to be put in a wrong light before the country, express its convictions in its organization and in its choice of the men who are to speak for it. You are to be a member of the convention and are entirely within your rights in doing everything within your power to bring that result about."[8]

Champ Clark sent Bryan an evasive reply, calling for harmony, while Underwood and Harmon supported Parker. McCombs, moody and hypersensitive, reacted to Wilson's response to Bryan by escaping to a friend's house in Baltimore, Tumulty learned afterward, where "he was found in a room, lying across a bed, crying miserably." To his friends who asked what was the matter, "McCombs replied, weeping, that the Governor had spoiled everything by his telegram to Bryan; that had the Governor followed his [McCombs's] advice, he could have been nominated."[9]

ON TUESDAY, JUNE 25, the Democrats swarmed into Baltimore. The New Jersey delegation, with the exception of the delegates from Essex County, were rapturous in their support of Wilson. Arriving with a vast panoply of banners, posters, and several brass bands, they took up the entire fifth floor of the Stafford Hotel. Tammany Hall, led by Charlie Murphy, as well as Wall Street financier August Belmont, came in a special train. Thomas Fortune Ryan arrived as a delegate from Virginia to represent the southern reactionaries.

Murphy was in a quandary. His preferred candidate was Governor Harmon of Ohio, but Harmon had won only four delegates outside of Ohio before Baltimore and was barely holding on to his position as a favorite son. Murphy realized full well that this was the year of the reformers, and he had to find a candidate who could win.

Charlie Murphy was in the classic mold of a Tammany politico. He was born in New York City in 1858 to poor Irish immigrants and left school at fourteen to work in a wire factory. Later he worked in a boatyard and then became a driver of a horse-drawn bus for the crosstown Blue Line. Living frugally, he saved up enough money to open a saloon called Charlie's Place. But it was a respectable barroom; Murphy wouldn't put up with gambling or prostitution, rough language or fighting. As a young Democrat, Murphy prospered in the Gas House District. He eventually owned four bars and as he was widely known, he soon became district leader for Tammany Hall.

In the Democratic Party he was seen as a careful, smart, and cunning leader, and after he became the boss of the Democratic machine, he realized that Tammany Hall had to cleanse itself of excessive corrruption. Payoffs to the cops, and even so-called honest graft, which meant using inside information and government contracts to enrich the bosses, were under increasing attack by the reformers. In addition, the new immigrants—Eastern European Jews and Italians—were suspicious of the Irish politicos. If Tammany did not adopt some of the reformers' policies, it would soon lose its influence. It could not survive on patronage alone, and the question Murphy pondered was how much change was needed, and what kind of man could he trust to carry it out while still leaving patronage in the hands of Tammany.[10]

Murphy's absolute goal was to keep Bryan from ever receiving the nomination. Wilson he distrusted after the New Jersey governor had turned on the bosses who had picked him. Moreover, with Wilson now running against bossism and Wall Street, he threatened Murphy's power. The logical choice for him would have been Champ Clark. Clark, however, was vociferously backed by Hearst, and the newspaper magnate was no friend to Tammany. But as the convention got under way, Hearst and Murphy agreed to work together. The greatest problem for both of them was Clark's gray and docile personality. On the speaking platform, TR would devour him.[11]

Clark was at best an old-fashioned Democrat, ready to support moderate reforms. He has been described by Wilson biographer Arthur Link as "a distinguished-looking figure." As he stood at the speaker's desk "in his long coat" or appeared "on the street in his broad-brimmed black slouch hat, with a touch of color in his neck-scarf, he made one think—well, of Henry Clay."[12]

An attractive candidate would have been Oscar Underwood of Alabama. Moderately conservative but modern in his approach to issues, Underwood was a hardworking, able congressman who was the majority leader in the House. His easy southern manners and his undoubted integrity made him respected as a fair-minded and even courageous leader. He could stand up to Roosevelt, and he came into the convention with southern support. Wilson admired him far more than Clark and even thought of him as a possible vice presidential running mate.[13]

As the convention opened, Clark was pacing his office at the Capitol, Underwood was also in Washington, Wilson in Sea Girt, and Harmon in Ohio. The immediate question of who would chair the convention would test the relative strength of the potential candidates, and especially Bryan's power and prestige. Bryan had come directly from Chicago to Baltimore's Belvedere Hotel, in part in his role as a newspaper columnist. On the afternoon of June 25, he appeared at the armory for the opening ceremonies.

On the walls were portraits of Washington, Jefferson, and Jackson backed up by red, white, and blue bunting. In Catholic Maryland the venerable Cardinal Gibbons stood with raised hand: "Let the light of Thy divine wisdom direct the deliberation of this convention." Behind His Eminence sat Bryan. No sooner had the presiding officer, Norman E. Mack, declared that he had been instructed to put the name of Alton B. Parker forward as temporary chairman than Bryan moved in for the kill.

As the *New York World* described him:

> He looked older than a few days ago in Chicago, pale and very grim. His heavy black brows were contrasting over his piercing eyes. His hawk nose had an extra downward twist. His lipless mouth was like a thin dagger-slit across his broad face. He held his head erect, the magnificent dome of his brow contrasting with the curious lack of back to his head. The grizzled fringe of his dark hair was ruffled and moist with perspiration. He made a fine figure, standing up there, in an old dark sack suit, with a low collar and white string tie, holding his right hand up to quell the applause.[14]

Still the cheers would not stop. As soon as the band began to play, Bryan sat down and fanned himself with a big palm leaf. When at last the cheering died away, he stood and nominated Senator John W. Kern of Indiana as temporary chairman—the man who had been Bryan's running mate in the 1908 presidential campaign.

Bryan's speech, however, went on far too long. He recounted how he had been offered the temporary chairmanship but had refused the offer. He recalled his struggles for progressive democracy. And in the name of this democracy, he cried, "You cannot frighten it with your Ryans nor buy it with your Belmonts." Delegates leapt to their feet, waving their hats and shouting for Bryan. He should have stopped at this point, but unfortunately he went on to a lengthy condemnation of Parker. Before long, cries of "Parker, Parker" were growing louder and Bryan was being constantly interrupted. "And so," as the *New York World* put it, "with a last metaphor about a cloud of smoke by day, poor Bryan, who had begun as a prophet, concluded as a bore and sat down amid a roar one-quarter of enthusiasm, three-quarters of relief."[15]

Senator Kern, a small man in a sack suit, then mounted the platform. He called for Parker to withdraw from the contest. In the New York delegation the elegantly dressed Parker did not stir. Kern paused to survey the New Yorkers, then startled the convention by withdrawing his name from the contest and nominating Bryan himself. At first the convention was convulsed with noise, then there were demands for a roll call. Bryan asked for five minutes more of additional debate, as Cone Johnson of Texas elbowed his way to the platform and quieted the crowd with a voice as loud as a "human foghorn." He didn't care who had started the quarrel, he said, but "this one thing I know—the fight is on and Bryan is one side and Wall Street is on the other."[16] Nevertheless, the convention went on to endorse the selection of the national committee, electing Parker as temporary chairman by a vote of 579 to 508.

The victory of the Clark-Murphy coalition, however, was illusory. When the Tammany organization tried to force through a motion to retain Parker as permanent chairman, it was blocked by Edward House's Texans. Congressman Ollie M. James, now senator-elect from Kentucky, whom Wilson supported even though he was a Clark man, was elected permanent chairman. Wilson was convinced that James, a friend of Bryan's and a progressive, was a fair man. When Bryan had telephoned Sea Girt to discuss with Wilson the issue of the permanent chairmanship, he was surprised to hear the governor say that James would be an admirable choice: "He is our kind of fellow, and I am sure my friends can rely upon him to treat our cause well."[17] It was shrewd of Wilson to take this position: he not only once again displayed his progressive credentials, but he also found in James a man who would recognize Bryan when he wanted to speak up, which would demonstrate to Bryan Wilson's generosity.[18]

The next move by the progressives was to overturn the "unit rule." For example, the convention rules committee insisted that 19 Wilson delegates from Ohio had to vote for Harmon because the state Democratic convention had thus instructed. The principal champion for the abrogation of the unit rule was the young mayor of Cleveland, Newton D. Baker (later to be Wilson's secretary of war). In a passionate appeal to the convention, he insisted that the unit rule in Ohio would violate his sacred pledge to his constituents to vote for Wilson by forcing him to vote for Harmon. When another member of the Ohio delegation tried to defend the unit rule, by chance he mentioned Wilson's name, setting off a spontaneous demonstration that lasted more than half an hour. Banners were unfurled by delegates from Texas and Pennsylvania, and from the state of Wilson's birth, Virginia. When order was finally restored, the unit rule was overturned by a substantial majority.

It was now clear to Wilson that an avowed conservative like Harmon or Underwood could probably not garner enough votes for the nomination. But who would be the progressive chosen by the convention? Wilson himself, Champ Clark, or Bryan, playing for a deadlock between the two front runners?[19]

ABOVE ALL, Bryan wanted to crush the Tammany machine. Early Thursday morning, June 27, his brother told him that Clark's managers had come to an agreement with Tammany Hall: New York's 90 votes were to go to Clark sometime early in the bidding. Such an agreement would make the Democratic Party beholden to Wall Street and prevent Clark from carrying out a true program of progressive reform. The Great Commoner therefore made an astonishing proposal. The resolution he put before the convention later that evening demanded that "we hereby declare ourselves opposed to the nomination of any candidate for president who is the representative of or under obligation to J. Pierpont Morgan, Thomas F. Ryan, August Belmont, or any other member of the privilege-hunting and favor-seeking class." In addition, Bryan called for the withdrawal from the convention of "any delegate or delegates constituting or representing the above-named interests."[20]

In practically calling for the expulsion of Ryan and Belmont, Bryan set the convention in an uproar. The New York delegates were not in the hall to defend Belmont, but the Virginians fiercely attacked Bryan, who said he would withdraw that part of his resolution insofar as it related to Ryan,

President William Howard Taft at his desk in the White House, 1912.
Library of Congress

The Taft family, June 18, 1911. The president with his wife, Nellie, and (standing from left to right) their children, Charles, Helen, and Robert, who later became a U.S. senator and the leader of the conservative wing of the Republican Party. *Library of Congress*

Taft was an avid golfer, which allowed him to escape the cares of a presidency that he seldom enjoyed. Here he is teeing off on the golf links at Hot Springs, Virginia, c. 1908. *Library of Congress*

Taft campaigning in 1912. *Library of Congress*

Taft speaking from the back of a train in the 1912 campaign.
Library of Congress

Theodore Roosevelt saluting from the bridge of the steamship *Kaiserin Augusta Victoria*, arriving in New York Harbor, June 20, 1910, after his safari in Africa and a tour of European capitals. *Library of Congress*

Roosevelt in his library at
Oyster Bay, 1912.
Library of Congress

The Roosevelt family in 1907: Quentin, T.R., Ethel, Kermit, Ted, Edith,
and Archie. *Library of Congress*

Delegates arriving at the Progressive Party Convention in Chicago, August 1912, with a sign displaying their chosen slogan, the Bull Moose.
Library of Congress

The Progressive Party Convention in session at the Chicago Coliseum, August 6, 1912. *Library of Congress*

Whistle-stopping with
Roosevelt in Eugene,
Oregon, 1911.
Library of Congress

Roosevelt campaigning for president, October 1912.
Library of Congress

Cartoon of the 1912 campaign, with Taft mounted on the GOP elephant, Wilson riding beside him on the Democratic donkey, and Roosevelt on a bull moose that is nipping at the elephant's hide. Debs is nowhere to be seen. *Library of Congress*

Eugene V. Debs reaching out to his audience in gestures typical of his intense oratorical style. *Tamiment Library, New York University, Eugene Debs Photograph Collection*

Debs usually wore a suit with a vest and bow tie in public, as he does here in this photographic portrait created in 1912. *Library of Congress*

Debs's wife, Katherine Metzel Debs. They were a childless couple, and their marriage was not a close one.
Tamiment Library, New York University, Eugene Debs Photograph Collection

In the 1912 campaign, Debs rises above the battle, as T.R. and Taft trade insults, and Woodrow Wilson gives professorial speeches.
Tamiment Library, New York University, Eugene Debs Photograph Collection

A Socialist Party poster endorsing Debs for president in 1920. He was still in prison for having opposed American participation in World War I.
Tamiment Library, New York University, Eugene Debs Photograph Collection

Woodrow Wilson campaigning in the Middle West, 1912.
Library of Congress

Wilson and his first wife, Ellen Axson, at Princeton, c.1910.
Library of Congress

The Wilson campaign headquarters in New York in 1911.
Library of Congress

Wilson, the president-elect, and a jolly President Taft glad to be leaving office, at the White House prior to Wilson's inauguration ceremonies, March 4, 1913. *Library of Congress*

President Wilson barnstorming from the rear of his special train in the 1916 election. *Library of Congress*

The Big Four at the Paris Peace Conference, 1919. From left: Italian Premier Vittorio Orlando, British Prime Minister David Lloyd George, French Premier Georges Clemenceau, and President Wilson.
Courtesy of Photo History

OPERATING ROOM
SENATE COMMITTEE ON FOREIGN RELATIONS

PEACE TREATY

THE LAMB FROM THE SLAUGHTER

Republican Senator Henry Cabot Lodge, who opposed the Versailles Treaty that Wilson had signed, escorting the battered peace treaty from his Senate committee room. *Library of Congress*

President Wilson and his second wife, Edith Bolling Galt, 1920. The president bears the grim aspect of a man who has recently been felled by a stroke.
Library of Congress

as a delegate from Virginia. He would only withdraw it as it related to Belmont if the New Yorkers asked him to do so. The New Yorkers, according to the *New York Times*, "howled back a defiant 'No' in Mr. Bryan's teeth."

"What is the matter with Bryan?" Chairman Ollie James asked. "Does he want to destroy the Democratic Party?"[21]

Hal Flood of the Virginia delegation, his eyes blazing with anger, forced his way up the steps to the speakers' platform. Bryan held out his hand. Flood refused to take it and shouted that Bryan wanted "to destroy the prospect of a Democratic success." Confronted by a mob that cried for him to "sit down! down! down! sit down!" Bryan withdrew the second part of his resolution calling for the expulsion of Ryan and Belmont. In the New York delegation, Charlie Murphy tried to make Bryan look foolish by casting New York's vote for the amended resolution. The emasculated resolution passed by a vote of 883 to 201½.[22]

IT WAS NOW almost midnight, and the heat in the auditorium was all but unbearable. More than 20,000 people had somehow gotten into the armory. Delegates and spectators shed their coats, and almost everyone was equipped with a fan. The women, and there were thousands of them, had on shirtwaists.[23]

Chairman James called for the presidential nominations. Alabama went first. Senator John Bankhead yielded to his son William (father of the actress Tallulah Bankhead and later speaker of the House of Representatives) to nominate Alabama's Oscar Underwood. Bankhead tried to persuade the delegates that there was no North, no South, and that Underwood would represent all Americans. As the southern delegations cheered for their candidate, the song "Dixie" blared above the tumult. Despite the late hour, the demonstration lasted at least thirty minutes. At Bankhead's conclusion a dove flew into the hall, swooping about until it found a little boy in a white suit on the platform and perched on his shoulder. At the sight of this, the Underwood delegates cheered madly, though no one could explain the political significance of the dove.

After Alabama came Arkansas, which yielded to Missouri. Senator James A. Reed rose to nominate his fellow Missourian Champ Clark.

Along with his indictment of the Republican Party, Reed also took a swipe at Wilson—"Give me no political dilettante who comes into camp when honors are most ripe to pluck." After recounting Clark's legislative achievements over a quarter of a century, Reed nominated "the Lion of Democracy, Champ Clark, of Missouri."

At exactly twenty-five minutes after midnight, Reed finished and the demonstration for Clark began. His supporters were even more enthusiastic than Underwood's, with hundreds of horns blaring incessantly as dozens of delegates marched through the crowded aisles. It was not until one-thirty that the cheering stopped.

After the nomination of Governor Simeon E. Baldwin of Connecticut, the roll call of the states resumed. A little after two o'clock Delaware yielded to New Jersey and Judge John W. Wescott came forward to nominate Woodrow Wilson. Not to be outdone by the Clark supporters, the Wilsonians began their own demonstration, and it was not until 3:25 on that Friday morning that Wescott was permitted to speak. His was an eloquent oration in which he cited "the National Instinct" that centered on Wilson. The governor had been free of any political organization but had nevertheless accomplished great things for New Jersey because he was "the very incarnation of progress." Of course, he would do the same for the United States.

Day was breaking when Governor Thomas Marshall of Indiana and Governor Harmon of Ohio were nominated. It was about seven o'clock when the first ballot was taken: Clark—440½; Wilson—324; Harmon—148; Underwood—117½; and the rest—56. Bryan received just one vote. Under the two-thirds rule, 728 were needed for nomination.[24]

The convention adjourned.

AT SEA GIRT Wilson was determined to display no tension over the outcome in Baltimore. He frolicked with his children on the lawn and strolled about for ninety minutes while the second, third, and fourth votes were taken with little change in the numbers. Every afternoon he played golf, and most evenings he joined his wife in the sitting room, reading to her from John Morley's *Life of Gladstone*. His daughters Margaret, Jessie, and Nellie, along with Joe Tumulty, hardly slept at all. When one of the reporters who had staked out Wilson's cottage asked the governor what he had heard from the front, Wilson responded with an anecdote. From what he knew at present, it reminded him of a "friend who was riding in a buggy one day and asked a man by the roadside how far down it was to the next town. The man replied that it was twenty miles. He drove on a long way and asked a second man. This man also replied that it was twenty miles. In another half hour's driving a third passerby was encountered, and he also said the distance was twenty miles. Whereupon my friend remarked to a companion in the buggy, 'Well, John, I'm mighty glad we're holding our own.'"

As far as Wilson was concerned, it was probably going to be "a ten-inning game, and he wished some candidate would come forward and make a sacrifice hit."[25]

Wilson was not far wrong. When the convention assembled in the late afternoon of Friday, June 28, Murphy on the tenth ballot shifted New York's votes from Harmon to Clark. At least Clark, though a progressive, was not one to upset the party machinery. With New York's balloting, Clark was now far in the majority with 556 votes. This was also Tammany's signal for others to get on the bandwagon for Clark. Not since 1844 had a candidate who received a majority failed to get the nomination by the required two-thirds vote. The Missouri delegation rose and began a parade around the hall. More and more delegates waving their banners joined the marchers, and the demonstration lasted for over an hour. Bryan entered the hall at the peak of the demonstration and cried out, "A progressive candidate must not be besmirched by New York's vote!"[26]

But the stampede did not materialize. North Dakota held the line with its ten votes for Wilson. In the Oklahoma delegation, "Alfalfa Bill" Murray, collarless and wearing a red bandanna, declared that "we shall not join Tammany in making the nomination." Oklahoma stood firm for Wilson, and his supporters let loose a wild counterdemonstration that lasted forty-five minutes. The landslide was halted, and finally, after the eleventh ballot, at four o'clock in the morning, the convention adjourned.[27]

• • •

IT WAS AT ONE O' CLOCK in the morning when Wilson received the news of the fateful tenth ballot. He had already retired for the night, while Tumulty was in the newspapermen's tent to wait for word from Baltimore. No one else was in the tent but the telegrapher. Suddenly the instrument began to pound. The operator looked up and informed Tumulty that the New York delegation had now swung its votes to Clark. Tumulty later admitted that he almost "collapsed" at the news. In despair he walked back to the Sea Girt cottage before going home to Avon. As he was leaving the cottage, Wilson appeared at one of the upper windows in his pajamas and asked, "Tumulty, is there any news from Baltimore?" "Nothing new, Governor."

The next morning when they breakfasted together, Wilson confronted him: "You thought you could fool me last night; but I could tell from the serious expression on your face that something had gone wrong."[28]

In fact, Wilson was in despair. Writing out a message for McCombs, he told his campaign manager that his delegates had done all they could for him and should feel no compunction to change their votes. The same idea had occurred to McCombs, frail, sleepless, and discouraged. Early that Saturday morning, before hearing from Wilson himself, McCombs had requested that Wilson give his permission to release the delegates. "So you think it is hopeless?" Wilson asked McCombs on the telephone. Tears came to the eyes of Mrs. Wilson as the governor instructed his manager to tell the delegates that "they are now free to support any candidate they choose." After Wilson hung up the receiver, Ellen came over to him and put her arms around his neck and told him how sorry she was that he had failed.

When McAdoo went to see McCombs, he was told that Wilson had given up and had authorized McCombs to release his delegates, and that he also had a telegram from the governor to that effect. "You have betrayed the governor," the appalled McAdoo remembered saying. "You have sold him out." He then reached for the nearest telephone, called Sea Girt, and told Wilson that although Clark now had a majority of the votes, he did not have the nomination. Wilson seized the moment and countermanded his instructions to McCombs, insisting that the work continue. The telegram of congratulations to Clark that Wilson had prepared and was ready to put on the wire was now set aside. Once again, Wilson had had to overrule McCombs, who was obsessed with the notion that Wilson's only chance to win the nomination was with New York's votes.[29]

THE QUESTION OF BRYAN REMAINED. His Nebraska delegation was officially pledged to Clark. Then, on the fourteenth ballot that Saturday, Bryan for the third time dominated the convention. Convinced that a deal between Clark supporters and Tammany Hall had indeed been struck, Bryan demanded the floor to explain why he was casting his vote for Wilson. Nebraska was unwilling, he declared, to nominate any man who was prepared to violate the resolution that Bryan had earlier sponsored in which delegates had pledged themselves not to nominate any man connected with the "privilege-seeking, favor-hunting class." For that reason, he would withhold his vote from Clark "as long as New York's vote is recorded for him." When the applause and hisses finally died down, however, Bryan made it perfectly clear that he was ready to withdraw his support for Woodrow Wilson should New York vote for Wilson.[30]

Although the Wilson supporters cheered the gesture, they soon realized that Bryan had acted not out of conviction for Wilson, but only because Charlie Murphy's minions had voted for Clark. Surely this could only mean that Bryan was still angling for a deadlocked convention that would turn to him. Years later, Virginia's Senator Carter Glass said that "Mr. Bryan had not the slightest idea, when he changed the vote of Nebraska, of contributing to the nomination of Wilson. He merely desired to defeat Champ Clark, with the concealed hope and expectation of prolonging the contest and receiving the nomination himself."[31] When the twenty-sixth ballot was recorded Saturday night, Wilson did gain 83½ votes over his first tally, but he still was behind Clark by 56 votes. Victory for Wilson remained very much in doubt.

IN WASHINGTON, Champ Clark was outraged when he heard of Bryan's maneuver. He put out a statement declaring that he was under no obligation to Wall Street and demanded "proof or a retraction" of Bryan's charges.[32] He then sped to Baltimore to answer Bryan's challenge in person. He might have swung more delegates behind him had he arrived in time. But he was too late. He appeared on the scene just as the convention was adjourning. Now he was determined to stop Wilson.

Happily for the delegates, Sunday, June 30, was a day of rest. McCombs was not distressed at Bryan's action, for that meant that there was no bargain Bryan could strike to get New York's votes. McCombs tried to persuade Wilson by phone that the only way he could secure the support of the New York Democrats was for the governor to make a commitment not to appoint Bryan secretary of state. Wilson, however, refused to do so, citing Bryan's "fine service to the party in all seasons." In this, Wilson showed sound judgment. Had he agreed to do what McCombs suggested, Bryan would almost certainly have found out about Wilson's commitment and tried to dispose of him and Clark together.[33]

Wilson even issued a statement that "there cannot be any possibility of any trading done in my name; not a single vote can or will be obtained by means of any promise."[34] McCombs was nevertheless making deals wherever he could. He spoke to Thomas Taggart, boss of the Indiana delegation, suggesting that Indiana's governor Thomas Marshall, would be given the vice president's spot in return for Indiana's votes. Other agreements had been concluded with Roger Sullivan, boss of the Illinois delegation, and with the Underwood delegates.

On Monday, July 1, on the twenty-eighth ballot, Indiana's twenty-nine votes, formerly reserved for Marshall, went to Wilson. Iowa then took fourteen of twenty-six votes from Clark and gave them to Wilson. Now the New Jersey governor was the forerunner but still without a majority. Delegations from Vermont, Wyoming, and Michigan joined the Wilson forces. But unless Illinois's Sullivan or Alabama's Bankhead committed his delegation to Wilson, the governor would fail—and then Bryan's game could still play out.

Roger Sullivan was a secretive man who was opposed to Clark and probably preferred Underwood to Wilson. His wife and son were strong Wilson supporters, however, and argued Wilson's cause. There had also been a struggle within the Illinois delegation between Sullivan and the mayor of Chicago, who was supported by Hearst. There was no way that Sullivan could expect anything from Hearst.

Knowing Sullivan's political disposition, Wilson's managers in the opening days of the convention had struck a bargain. The Wilson members of the credentials committee had agreed to support Sullivan when two delegations from Cook County, Illinois—one controlled by Sullivan, the other by the mayor and Hearst—claimed to be the rightful representatives from Chicago. Sullivan did not promise to vote for Wilson for president, but he was not a man who forgot his "friends."[35]

When the convention adjourned after the forty-second ballot on the morning of July 2, the Illinois delegation held a caucus and voted, 45–13, for Wilson. On the first ballot after the convention met later that day, Sullivan then cast the fifty-eight Illinois votes for Wilson, giving the New Jersey governor at last a majority of the convention delegates.[36]

Virginia, under the unit rule, gave Wilson its twenty-four votes—including the vote of Thomas Fortune Ryan. West Virginia followed, and Wilson now had 602 votes. But New York's votes, because of Bryan, could not be used to put Wilson over the top. Clark's other delegates, along with Underwood's, could force a deadlock indefinitely.

Although Sullivan had earlier promised Bankhead that he would give the Illinois votes to Underwood sometime on July 2, he had not done so and continued to hold for Wilson through the forty-fifth ballot. At that point Bankhead approached Sullivan directly and asked him what he was going to do. The Illinois boss said he was going to throw Wilson overboard on the forty-sixth ballot and go back to Clark.

Why was Sullivan willing to double-cross both Wilson and Underwood? According to one story, when Clark learned that Sullivan had deserted him, he met with Sullivan in Baltimore and begged him to return to the fold. Sullivan replied that he had promised the Wilson people that he would vote for the governor for a certain number of ballots, but he would swing Illinois back to Clark on the forty-sixth or forty-seventh ballot. To gain such crucial support, Clark may well have agreed to recognize Sullivan as the leader of the state in the distribution of federal patronage.[37]

When Bankhead learned what Sullivan intended, he could see that Underwood would never be nominated. On the forty-sixth ballot, Bankhead therefore went to the platform to withdraw Underwood's name. Then the chairman of the Missouri delegation released the Clark delegates but announced that Missouri would cast its last votes for "old Champ Clark." Boston's John F. Fitzgerald (John F. Kennedy's grandfather) followed and gave Massachusetts's vote to Wilson. At that point New York's John J. Fitzgerald moved that Wilson be nominated by acclamation. Missouri objected, but it was over. The Harmon delegates were released; Wilson received 990 votes to become the nominee. Ironically, it was the machine politicians who finally made Woodrow Wilson the Democratic candidate for president.[38]

THERE WERE STILL two issues before the exhausted delegates—the vice presidential nomination and the platform. Wilson badly wanted Underwood, but the Alabaman refused to let his name be put forward. Wilson's managers were then able to suggest that the convention was leaning to Thomas Marshall of Indiana. Earlier, Wilson had protested to McCombs that Marshall "was a very small man." He could not have known that his campaign manager had promised the vice presidency to Marshall in return for Indiana's vote. Wilson was persuaded to go along only when he was told that Marshall was well located geographically and was a very good politician.[39]

The platform turned out to be a progressive one in the Bryan tradition. It criticized the Republican protective tariff and promised to destroy the great trusts and regulate business activities. It proposed constitutional amendments for the adoption of the income tax and the direct election of senators. It opposed establishing a centralized banking system. And it pledged that the Democratic candidate for president would serve only one term—a provision that Wilson opposed.

At Sea Girt, the leader of a western delegation wired Wilson: "The switch of the progressive leadership from Bryan to Wilson means that the progressive movement is passing from emotionalism to rationalism. Bryanism is dead, a new Democracy is being born." For reporters gathered at the governor's house, Wilson responded: "I think my western friend phrases it about right, and he does it quite aptly."[40]

. . .

As was the custom, Woodrow Wilson did not appear at the convention to accept the presidential nomination. He remained in Sea Girt, meeting with various Democratic and other national leaders. On the Fourth of July, thirty-five members of the Democratic National Committee, including the old bosses, came to the cottage to pay him homage.[41]

Happy to accept the peace offerings of the bosses, Wilson was prepared to tell them that he would launch no new assault on bossism. Many of them, after all, had been central to his nomination. "I can never forget Illinois," Wilson said to Roger Sullivan.[42]

He also met with Samuel Gompers and other officials of the American Federation of Labor. Gompers had been distrustful of Wilson because of his conservative reputation, but after their brief meeting, he later wrote: "I felt my prejudices disapearing before the sincerity and obvious humanitarianism of the man." The AFL heartily endorsed the Democratic nominee.[43]

The most awkward meeting was with Champ Clark, who dutifully if reluctantly made his way to Sea Girt; as he was an hour and a half ahead of schedule there was no one to meet him at the railroad station, so that Clark, carrying a large black umbrella, had to walk up the gravel path to Wilson's cottage. The meeting was polite but hardly cordial, and it was clear to reporters who spoke with Clark afterward that he had found the whole experience trying and unpleasant. (Clark later returned to Sea Girt with the Democratic members of the House of Representatives.)[44]

The incessant stream of visitors wearied Wilson. Writing to Mary Peck on July 14, he complained, "Not a moment am I left free to do what I would. I thought last night that I should go crazy with the strain and confusion of it."[45] Wilson finally did escape to a friend's house at Atlantic Highlands, near Sandy Hook. Still more calming to Wilson's nerves was a week's trip on board his classmate Cleveland Dodge's yacht *Corona*. Wilson, his wife, their daughter Margaret, and a friend sailed through New York harbor and into Long Island Sound. Sitting in the peaceful cabin of the yacht, he wrote out in shorthand his six-thousand-word acceptance speech.

On August 7, a large crowd assembled on the lawn at Sea Girt to listen to Wilson's message. The acceptance speech was a serious one, leavened by little humor and no bombast, leaving the well-wishers and dignitaries restless and bored. It read better than it sounded. The nominee generally endorsed the Democratic platform, but did not mention its call for a single term. Nor did he announce that he would destroy the great trusts, promising only to deal effectively with the problem of trust regulation— whatever that meant. But he did stir up the torpid throng by one palpable hit at Roosevelt—"There is," he declared, "no indispensable man."[46] A few hours later, the indispensable man himself would stand before the crusading Progressives gathered in Chicago to accept their nomination for president.

TEN

The Indispensable Man

I N THE SAME COLISEUM that had been the scene of the Republican conclave in June, the Progressive Party's convention got under way on Monday, August 5. It was unlike any other such gathering. As the *New York Times* wrote, "It was an assemblage of religious enthusiasts. It was such a convention as [the crusader] Peter the Hermit held. It was a Methodist camp meeting done over into political terms."[1]

The 14,000 elected or self-appointed delegates entered the convention hall under a handsome bull moose banner hanging over the entrance. Inside they sang "Onward Christian Soldiers" and the "Battle Hymn of the Republic." The revival hymn "Follow, Follow, We Will Follow Jesus" became "Follow, follow, we will follow Roosevelt." But despite the evangelical atmosphere, the delegates largely consisted of social workers, schoolteachers, and successful-looking young businessmen. There were more immigrants, Jews, and Catholics than had ever been seen at a Republican convention; and there were black delegates from Arkansas, Delaware, Illinois, Indiana, Kentucky, Maryland, Massachusetts, New Jersey, Ohio, Pennsylvania, Rhode Island, Tennessee, and West Virginia; there were, conspicuously, no black delegates from the Deep South.

Above all, this was the first convention by a major political party with women delegates. The professionalism and somber dress of the women contrasted with those who occupied "Purple Row," which reporters called the place where the "millionaires' wives" had sat in June. This row was now filled with "women in shirtwaists."[2]

The woman who was the acknowledged leader was Jane Addams, who had founded Hull House in Chicago, one of the first social settlements. An active supporter of woman suffrage, she was the major figure in Roosevelt's Female Brain Trust, which included the social scientist Frances Kellor, and Florence Kelley, TR's chief factory inspector for New York when he was governor. For well over an hour before the convention officially came to order, delegates paid their respects to Jane Addams, who was sitting in the first row. By now, Roosevelt had fully embraced woman suffrage.[3] As he telegraphed to Addams after the convention, he was for woman suffrage "without qualification or equivocation" and believed that "within a half a dozen years we shall have no one in the United States against it."[4]

Prominent politicians such as Montana's Senator Joseph Dixon, the new party's national chairman and later the Bull Moose campaign manager; former Senator Albert Beveridge of Indiana, whom Mr. Dooley said gave speeches you could waltz to; and California's Governor Hiram Johnson played key roles at the convention. Attending were former cabinet secretaries such as James Garfield, Charles Bonaparte, and Oscar Straus. Hoping for a comeback through the Progressives were William Flinn, the former political boss of Pittsburgh, and "Tiny Tim" Woodruff, the portly political boss of Brooklyn, both of whom had lost power in their states.

Viewing the scene, the Kansas editor and writer William Allen White wrote:

> As a young man I had reported many a Populist convention. These agrarian movements too often appealed to the ne'er-do-wells, the misfits—farmers who had failed, lawyers and doctors who were not orthodox, teachers who could not make the grade, and neurotics full of hates and ebullient, evanescent enthusiasms. . . . But when the Progressive convention assembled in Chicago I looked down upon it from the reporter's stand and saw that here was another crowd. Here were the successful middle-class country-town citizens, the farmer whose barn was painted,

the well paid railroad engineer, and the country editor. . . . Proletarian and plutocrat were absent.[5]

Both publisher Frank Munsey and banker George Perkins, who was prepared to finance much of the Bull Moose campaign, were active, working with Roosevelt and other Progressives in composing the party's platform.[6] Prior to Chicago, TR had also conferred with Gifford Pinchot, the lawyer George Rublee, and Judge Learned Hand. What emerged was a radical compilation of Progressive causes. As editor Fred Warren wrote to Eugene Debs, "My prediction that Roosevelt would steal our platform bodily has been fulfilled. I am also firmly convinced that he is to be the central figure around which the campaign will be waged this year."[7]

The Bull Moose platform, a litany of social justice, included the right of labor to organize in unions, limitation of campaign spending, commitment to conservation, woman suffrage, the eight-hour working day, the six-day week, legislation for safer workplaces, and insurance for unemployment, old age, and sickness.

WHAT WAS MISSING from the Bull Moose platform was any mention of equal rights for African Americans. In this respect, the Chicago convention was one of "lily-white" progressivism, and Roosevelt reluctantly believed it had to be this way. He saw himself in a political dilemma, and there was no safe way out of it. While he privately favored ending lynching and reducing southern congressional delegations where blacks were not permitted to vote—recommended by W. E. B. DuBois, who demanded full civil and political equality for all African Americans—Roosevelt was hopeful that the Progressive Party could at last break the Democrats' stranglehold on the South.[8]

But white southern Progressives were also urging him to permit "lily-white" Progressive Parties in the former Confederate states. John M. Parker of New Orleans, the key strategist for the Progressives in the South, warned Roosevelt that southerners "cannot and will not under any circumstances tolerate the negro."[9] Roosevelt tended to heed Parker's views because he was so eager to attract southern Democrats to his fold. As he told Parker, "Really if I could carry one of the eleven ex-confederate states, I should feel as though I could die happy."[10] He was also still angry about the charges that Taft had paid southern black Republicans to vote against Roosevelt at the Republican convention.

TR did not think that any race was inherently or biologically inferior to any other. Instead, he largely supported the paternalistic views of Booker T. Washington that only through education and self-help training would African Americans become the educational, social, and economic "equals" of whites; at this point white racism would fade away.

As president, Roosevelt had urged equal justice for all and condemned the southern persecution of blacks, but he did little to extend the power of the federal government to protect African Americans against lynching and voting discrimination. He did give blacks more government jobs in the North than had previous administrations. On the other hand, black leaders had criticized him for handing out harsh punishment to black troops accused of starting a riot in Brownsville, Texas, in 1906. TR defended himself on both counts: he said he gave blacks federal appointments because they deserved them; and there was no racial prejudice involved in his Brownsville decision.[11]

Paramount for Roosevelt were his views on American nationalism. He was convinced that Republican sectionalism, by virtually ceding the South to the Democratic Party, had impeded the national goals of breaking down social and racial differences. But even though during his administration he had gained votes from southern Democrats, Roosevelt regarded the winning of the South as the "unfinished business" of his presidency.[12]

Roosevelt tried hard to overcome the contradictions in his thinking. He wanted to find votes among northern blacks, but he did not want to alienate southern whites who could be lured into the Progressive Party. In a lengthy letter to Julian LaRose Harris, editor of *Uncle Remus's Home Magazine,* he wrote that he had received letters from the North urging him to secure black delegates from the South, and from the South asking him to "declare that the new party shall be a white man's party." He did not agree with either proposition: "In the South the Democratic machine has sought to keep itself paramount by encouraging the hatred of the white man for the black; the Republican machine has sought to perpetuate itself by stirring up the black man against the white, and surely the time has come when we should . . . abandon both." His solution was to learn from the lessons of the past. "I earnestly believe," he wrote, "that by appealing to the best white men in the South, the men of justice and of vision as well as of strength and leadership . . . we shall create a situation by which the colored men of the South will ultimately get justice as it is not possible for them to get justice if we are to continue and perpetuate the present conditions."[13]

Roosevelt's strategy was doomed. Most southern editors reminded readers of Roosevelt's African American appointments as president. TR's Progressive Party may have made distinctions between southern and northern blacks, but white southerners did not. When Roosevelt dined with two African American Progressives in Providence, Rhode Island, in August after the convention, southerners simply cited this as final proof that TR was still the man who had asked Booker T. Washington to dine in the White House in 1901.

Moreover, Woodrow Wilson was seen as a true son of the South, and for this reason, too, Southern Democrats would vote for Wilson and not for Roosevelt. Roosevelt did worse in the South than several Republican presidential candidates had done earlier. Wilson, on the other hand, held the South, although that in itself would not give him enough votes for the presidency. Roosevelt's strategy was a failure and flatly contradicted his and the Progressives' stand on issues of social justice.

ON OPENING DAY Indiana's Albert J. Beveridge, slim, boyish, and handsome, strode to the rostrum to give a keynote speech that would be one of the best of his oratorical successes. He fiercely attacked the "special interests" that played such a central role in both the Republican and the Democratic Parties. They are what he called "the invisible government behind our visible government. . . . And, so acting, this political conspiracy is able to delay, mutilate or defeat sound and needed laws." Such an invisible government must be destroyed before honest men and women could bring about true reform.

"Men and women before him listened with rapt faces," the *New York Times* reported. "Here and there men were seen wiping tears from their eyes. There was little cheering; the men and women were too earnest for it. They sat there, bent forward in their places, many of them with their hands to their ears, anxious to catch every word. When they did cheer, it was always for some sentiment in which Beveridge expressed the aspiration of the new party for a better day for humanity."[14]

In closing Beveridge recited the opening lines of Julia Ward Howe's "Battle Hymn of the Republic"—"Mine eyes have seen the glory of the coming of the Lord"—and the delegates spontaneously burst out in song to complete the Civil War hymn: "He has sounded forth the trumpet that shall never call retreat; / He is sifting out the hearts of men before His judgment seat: / Oh! be swift my soul to answer Him! Be jubilant my feet! / Our God is marching on."

THE FOLLOWING DAY when TR marched onto the platform, responding to Beveridge's simple announcement, "The hour and the man, Theodore Roosevelt," fervent cheers broke out and lasted almost an hour. TR waved his hat as he spied his wife sitting in a box with a smile on her face. At this point the California delegation took a golden teddy bear and carried it up to the platform. TR waved a red bandanna and other delegates who were wearing bandannas waved theirs. Somebody even tied a bandanna around the head of a stuffed bull moose; the Illinois delegation fixed a bandanna to its flag. Delegates tossed hats into imaginary rings for their hero, who had used the phrase "My hat's in the ring." Again and again the crowd sang the "Battle Hymn of the Republic," later even breaking into Roosevelt's speech, and every time that happened TR stood on the platform with a puzzled look on his face. As the *Times*'s reporter put it: "They were crusaders; he was not." But he soon would be.

As historian John Gable described him, Roosevelt had grown "stocky with the years; grey now flecked the stiff, closely cropped hair; but the old energy and platform magic were stronger. Glinting pince-nez sat on a large nose; the drooping moustache framed dazzling white teeth which snapped for emphasis; head and thick neck thrust forward from muscular shoulders and barrel chest as he spoke, broad jaw with flexing muscles, fists cutting the air, a voice that was high-pitched and piercing . . . words that seemed hurled out like projectiles."[15]

Roosevelt was there to give his own keynote address, and it was properly called in that atmosphere "A Confession of Faith." Calling the old parties "husks," he went on to spell out the main elements of the platform that would be adopted the next day. The Progressives should make their platform a "contract with the people: for a modern industrial society." It was the industrial condition of the day that called for many federal reforms: the minimum wage, the end of child labor, the need for insurance to deal with the "hazards of sickness, accident, invalidism, involuntary unemployment, and old age."

Refusing to adopt Taft's program of controlling big corporations by "a succession of lawsuits," he proposed instead business regulation. Nor would he echo proposals to do away with the great trusts, for he deeply believed that it was too late to restore competition on every level, as the most fervid trust-busting Progressives wanted to do. His solution was to attack unfair competition and special privilege. His proposal was to create a "national industrial commission" that would have "the complete power to regulate all the great industrial concerns engaged in interstate commerce—which practically means all of them in the country."

Roosevelt concluded by invoking the idea that the cause was greater than the individual, even himself: "Whatever fate may at the moment overtake any of us, the movement itself will not stop. Our cause is based on the eternal principle of righteousness, and even though we who now lead may for the time fail, in the end the cause itself shall triumph." He ended by quoting himself—"We stand at Armageddon, and we battle for the Lord."[16]

THE NEXT AND FINAL DAY of the convention Comptroller William A. Pendergast of New York City nominated Theodore Roosevelt for president. Judge Ben Lindsey, who represented those Democrats who had joined the new Progressive Party, gave the first seconding speech. But by far the most important seconder was Jane Addams, the first woman ever to give a nominating speech at a major party convention. As a leading figure in the National Association for the Advancement of Colored People (NAACP) and a member of the platform committee, Addams incarnated the social justice program of the Progressives. Despite her reservations over TR's straddle on African American rights in the South, she recognized the need to have TR lead the party because of his commitment to social reform. "Because of that, because the program will require a leader of invincible courage, of open mind, of democratic sympathies, one endowed with power to interpret the common man and to identify himself with the common lot," she "heartily" seconded his nomination.[17]

At the conclusion of her speech, she was handed a "Votes for Women" banner as delegates began marching through the aisles. Former Harvard President Charles W. Eliot, a Wilson supporter, would later tell reporters that her speech was in "very bad taste." As he saw it, "Women have no proper share in a political convention."[18]

After Addams's speech, the convention adopted the "Contract with the People" platform and voted to nominate Roosevelt by acclamation.

TR's choice for vice president was the politically popular governor of California, Hiram Johnson. He, too, was nominated by acclamation, and then the two nominees were escorted to the platform. This was the first time that candidates personally accepted their nominations. (Not until 1932 would this happen again, with another Roosevelt.) As TR and Johnson saluted the cheers of the delegates, in the front row a woman dressed in black waved a red bandanna, and Roosevelt smiled as he recognized his wife. After about ten minutes, the band struck up the favored hymn of the convention, "The Battle Hymn of the Republic," and Roosevelt and Johnson, with Beveridge standing between them, joined in the singing.

Roosevelt, deeply moved by the ideological fervor of the delegates, was uncharacteristically brief, speaking only a little longer than to say "of course I accept." Johnson followed and also spoke briefly and to the point: "I would rather go down to defeat with Theodore Roosevelt than go to victory with any other presidential candidate."

Beveridge then declared that the first national convention of the new Progressive Party was adjourned. At this the delegates sang out the words of thanksgiving from the Doxology: "Praise God, from whom all blessings flow."[19]

A more secular reaction came from Eugene V. Debs, who commented that the Progressives' bandanna had replaced the red flag of socialism.[20]

ELEVEN

To Make a Revolution: Debs and Haywood

F OR EUGENE DEBS, neither the radical left, with its emphasis on direct action, nor the conservative right, with its belief in cooperation with and infiltration of the AFL craft unions, was to be the vital core of the Socialist Party. In the three months preceding the Socialist presidential convention in Indianapolis in May 1912, Debs had not only reaffirmed his unwillingness to compromise his stand against the often reactionary craft unions, but, more important, he had also shown himself willing to break with those ultraleft believers in the fight against the evils of industrial capitalism, the Industrial Workers of the World (IWW).

Controlled by William ("Big Bill") Haywood, the IWW (or "Wobblies") had espoused direct action that included even the acceptance of sabotage to further the cause of an industrial unionism committed to the class struggle and beholden to no political party. In the words of Haywood, an officer of the Western Federation of Miners, the IWW's goal was to put "the working class in possession of the economic power, the means of life, in control of the machinery of production and distribution, without regard to capitalist masters."[1] In essence, Haywood's brand of syndicalism meant that the unions should run the country.

To Haywood, as to Debs, the AFL was not a true working-class movement. Its bylaws prohibited blacks, most immigrants, and unskilled whites from membership. By contrast, Haywood said, "What we want to establish at this time is a labor organization that will open its doors to every man that earns his livelihood either by his brain or his muscle."[2] Debs had agreed with these views when Haywood announced them at the founding of the IWW in 1905. With the presidential campaign of 1912 looming, Debs had to ask himself if he was prepared to break with Haywood. The issue was whether Haywood would denounce direct action to accomplish his ends. And this Big Bill Haywood was not prepared to do.

At the Socialist convention in May 1912, the role of Haywood was central to the future of the party. The outcome of the struggle between reformers and revolutionaries would shape the direction of socialism in America. The conservative Socialists led by New York's Morris Hillquit and Victor Berger, now a congressman from Milwaukee, were aching for a confrontation with Haywood before the rank-and-file delegates at the convention. Debs had to choose sides—a choice he had never wanted to make.

DEBS'S HOPE for a militant labor movement seemed to have been fulfilled when he first met Bill Haywood at the convention of the Western Federation of Miners in 1901. The battles this union had fought against the mine owners in strikes at Coeur d'Alene, Idaho, at Telluride, Cripple Creek, and Leadville, Colorado, were far more savage than similar contests in the East. The mine workers had been met with state militias, private armies, spies, court orders, and starvation; on the other side, the miners had armed themselves with rifles and dynamite. There was no need for Debs to remind the miners that class struggle was a reality. Many members of their union as well as their leaders, President Ed Boyce and Secretary-Treasurer Haywood, had joined the Socialist Party, and they had asked Debs to address their convention in Denver.[3]

Haywood at this time was thirty-one and had already lived a hard life. Born in Salt Lake City in 1869, Haywood remembered only one short visit from his father after the latter had left the city for the Utah mountains to prospect for silver and gold. When Haywood was three years old, his father died of pneumonia in a mining camp. A few years later his mother married another miner and moved to the mining town of Ophir. There he received whatever was available as a formal education, and he also lost the sight in his right eye when he lost control of a knife while whittling a piece of wood. At nine years old he was taken to work in the local mine.

In his autobiography he described Ophir in somewhat romantic prose, a frontier environment where wildlife was plentiful and there were shoot-outs in the streets, and vigilantes to lynch presumed criminals. "These scenes of blood and violence happened when I was seven years old," Haywood wrote. "I accepted it as a natural part of life."[4]

By 1880, the family had moved back to Salt Lake City, and within a year he left school forever to work, first on a farm, which he hated, then at odd jobs back in the city, and finally at fifteen leaving his family for good to join a mining camp in Nevada. For the next decade Haywood went from mining camp to mining camp in Utah, Colorado, and Nevada. He probably also worked as a surveyor, and as a real estate agent in Salt Lake City.

In 1889 at the age of twenty he married a woman named Nevada Jane Minor, a classic frontier woman who bore him two daughters. But it was not a close marriage, and when she became sickly, they drifted apart. He did not desert her, however, bringing her to Silver City, Idaho, in 1896, where he was working in the Blaine Mine as an underground digger for $3.50 a day. That same year he met Ed Boyce, the president of the Western Federation of Miners, who had come to Silver City to organize the local miners. Two days after he heard Boyce, Haywood became a charter member of the WFM. 1896 was also when Boyce's union had affiliated with the AFL. It was a marriage that could not last.

Not long after, Boyce confronted Sam Gompers of the AFL, who was abandoning his preaching about the abolition of "wage slavery" and talking of the possibility of a more benevolent capitalism through craft unionism. The WFM, for its part, would accept any member without an initiation fee. It demanded jobs for all, not just for the highly skilled few. "Open our portals to every working man," Boyce declared, "whether engineer, blacksmith, smelterman or milkman."[5]

Later that year the miners in Leadville, Colorado, came into ferocious conflict with the "Cloud City" mine owners. Boyce asked Gompers for material aid. He was rebuffed; he then traveled to the 1896 national convention of the AFL to appeal to the delegates for solidarity. Again, he lost. On his way home he stopped in Terre Haute to see Eugene Debs, whose appeal for help during the great Pullman strike had also been refused by Gompers. Debs was fully sympathetic to Boyce's needs. In January 1897, Debs visited Boyce in Leadville, at which time they decided to create a new national labor federation as an alternative to the AFL.

At his own union's convention later that year, Boyce urged delegates to buy and operate their own mines; and he called on them to arm themselves in self-defense against the use of military force by their capitalist enemies. The miners listened and voted not to pay dues to the AFL and waited for Boyce to found a new western labor organization.[6] In 1898, the Western Labor Union, an offspring of the WFM, was born. "There can be no harmony between organized capitalists and organized labor," Boyce declared. "There can be no harmony between employer and employee."[7]

In 1900, the WFM endorsed the Socialist Party's presidential ticket, and the following year asked Eugene Debs to speak at its convention. By now, Haywood had joined Boyce in the union leadership and was a respected official organizing union shops in all the local mines of Silver City, where he seemed a model union official. In 1900, WFM convention delegates, admiring his combative spirit, elected him to the executive board. This was the man that Debs would embrace at the Denver WFM convention of 1901.

It was a grand occasion for both men. Haywood had been inspired by Debs at the time of the 1894 Pullman boycott, which had marked his commitment to trade unionism. As he declared later: "Here, I felt, was a great power. It was not the fact that produce had been removed from the cars and the strikers were that much ahead. The big thing was that they could stop the trains."[8] Debs's speech to the convention was greeted with great enthusiasm by the delegates, who then recommended that all miners join the Socialist Party.

For Haywood the most memorable event came later. Debs and he drank into the night in Debs's room at the Imperial Hotel, Haywood sprawled in an armchair and Debs sitting on the bed, a glass in one hand and a pipe in his mouth. They talked for hours about a campaign for an eight-hour day for miners, and shared stories of their lives in the labor movement.[9]

By 1900, the labor movement had almost 900,000 members, and its enrollment had doubled in four years. But it was still very difficult for any trade union to win a strike against a major corporation; for this reason, Gompers believed that he should continue with his policy of conciliation and back only the cause of skilled, white workers. This was a policy encouraged by John D. Rockefeller, August Belmont, and J. P. Morgan, as well as other prominent figures in the financial world.

The more conservative Socialist leaders were troubled by Debs and Haywood, believing that their harsh rejection of the AFL and their absolute commitment to industrial unionism was a tactical error. The Western Federation of Miners seemed to be prospering, and when Ed Boyce retired in 1902 his successor, Charles Moyer, expected further growth.

In 1903, there was a brutal strike at the Cripple Creek mines in Colorado, where the power of the state was aligned with the mine owners. The governor used the state militia to break the will of the strikers, substituting martial law in place of civil law in most mining districts. "To hell with the Constitution," one militia officer said, "we aren't going by the Constitution."[10] Both Moyer and Haywood were arrested. When Haywood struck Colonel Bulkeley Wells, allegedly in self-defense, he was savagely beaten. The Western Federation of Miners had gone into Cripple Creek expecting victory; it came out scarred and battered. As Haywood's biographer described him, "Haywood entered the conflict as a full-time unionist, part-time agitator and equivocal revolutionary; he left as a part-time union official, full-time agitator and dedicated revolutionary."[11]

THE LESSONS OF CRIPPLE CREEK taught Haywood that traditional trade unionism, as well as the ideological doctrines of the Socialists, were not enough to win labor's war. On a hot day in June 1905, 203 delegates filled Chicago's Brand Hall for what Haywood called the "Continental Congress of the Working Class." At this time he declared that a new organization was needed, "based and founded on the class struggle," that would be willing to engage in direct action, "having in view no compromise and no surrender."[12]

The new revolutionary organization that emerged was named the

Industrial Workers of the World. It was the first American labor group to open its membership to all wage-earning workers, regardless of skill, nationality, race, sex, or age. Neither Haywood nor Charles Moyer chose to be elected head of the IWW, as both preferred to continue working mainly for the Western Federation of Miners. Debs wholly supported the IWW and urged unity with the new organization. For Debs and the IWW, their common enemy was Gompers and the AFL.

After the convention Debs was widely attacked in the Socialist press. The editors of Congressman Berger's paper, the *Social Democratic Herald,* wrote that Debs might be an excellent fellow but implied that he was also somewhat of a fool. They basically accused Debs of becoming allied with an organization that would split the labor movement. Debs was incensed by these attacks, declaring that the IWW convention "was in many respects the most representative proletarian gathering I have ever seen." He labeled theoreticians like Berger and the editor of the *Herald* as men who "probably never worked for wages a day in their lives, have no trade, never had on a pair of overalls and really have no excuse to be in a trade union at all, and yet they…tell me to what particular union I must belong under penalty of being visited with their displeasure."[13]

Despite the divisiveness that the IWW seemed to bring upon the labor movement, Debs remained its ally. Soon enough, however, there was a cause that could unify, at least temporarily, all the factions of labor. On December 30, 1905, former Idaho Governor Frank Steunenberg was killed by a bomb as he opened the gate to his home in Caldwell. Harry Orchard, a drifter who was a member of the Western Federation of Miners, was arrested and confessed to the crime.

But Idaho's Governor Frank Gooding was convinced that a so-called Inner Circle controlled by the WFM had plotted the assassination. His aim was to get a confession from Orchard that would implicate Haywood and his circle in the crime. To achieve this end, Gooding approached James McParland, the manager of the Pinkerton Detective Agency in Denver, where he coordinated antilabor espionage. Under Pinkerton's threats and inducements, Orchard claimed that Haywood, Moyer, and George Pettibone, a former WFM official and now a Denver businessman, had hired him to kill Steunenberg. The reason: revenge against the ex-governor for his calling out the militia to crush the strikers at Coeur d'Alene in 1899.

With the connivance of Governor Jesse McDonald of Colorado and railroad officials, McParland arranged for a special train provided by the Union Pacific, loaded with beer, sandwiches, and cigars, to be ready to pick up the "criminals," who were now in Denver, and bring them directly to Boise. The abduction would be clearly illegal. Since none of the three men had been in Idaho at the time of the murders, they could not be considered fugitives and therefore they could not be legally extradited. It would be extradition by kidnapping.

On Saturday night, February 17, 1906, Moyer was arrested when he was found fast asleep in a Pullman berth on a train scheduled to leave at 1:30 A.M. the next morning for Deadwood, South Dakota. Earlier that night Haywood had telephoned his wife that he would be spending the night in a Turkish bath, but in fact he was going to a brothel near his office. At 11:30 P.M., he heard a knock on the door of his room. A voice called out, "I want to see you, Bill." Naked, Haywood opened the door and saw a local deputy sheriff, who told Haywood that he had come to arrest him. "If you're arresting me," Haywood retorted, "why didn't you come with a warrant?" The deputy explained that he had no warrant but he had called Edmund Richardson, one of the union's lawyers. Haywood was satisfied.

The deputy was lying. At the jail, Haywood learned that he was being taken to Idaho because he was "mixed up in the Steunenberg murder." When Haywood protested that the authorities could not arrest a man without a warrant and send him to another state without extradition papers, the sheriff simply said, "It looks as though that's what they're preparing to do."

At dawn, Haywood, Moyer, and Pettibone, who was arrested at home, were loaded aboard the three-car train, and the blinds on the windows were drawn. The train steamed toward Boise, carefully avoiding mining towns, where a sheriff might try to serve a writ of habeas corpus. No stops were made until the train crossed the border into Wyoming, and then only to take on water and coal. It was a fast ride, and early Monday morning the captives reached Boise, were loaded into separate carriages, and taken to the penitentiary. In Denver James McParland was pleased with himself: "They will never leave Idaho alive."[14]

On March 6, 1906, Haywood, Moyer, and Pettibone were indicted for murder.

THE ARRESTS BROUGHT waves of protest across the country, and from writers ranging from Jack London to Russia's Maxim Gorky, who was visiting New York. Even Sam Gompers protested the manner of the arrests and asked for contributions from the AFL for the labor leaders' defense.

Within twenty-four hours after he heard of the indictments, Debs sent his reaction to the case to the *Appeal to Reason*. The article was so inflammatory that even Fred Warren hesitated to publish it. But print it he did. The front page contained Debs's response to the statement that the indicted men "will never leave Idaho alive." "Well, by the gods, if they do not," Debs wrote, "the governors of Idaho and Colorado had better prepare to follow them. . . . If they attempt to murder Moyer, Haywood and their brothers, a million revolutionaries at least will meet them with guns."[15]

Debs's rhetoric shocked many people, including President Theodore Roosevelt, who later called Haywood, Moyer, and Debs "undesirable citizens." Nor did it seem that the accused could get a fair trial in Idaho. In March, both the Idaho Supreme Court and the Federal District Court denied a petition for a writ of habeas corpus. Then, in December 1906, the United States Supreme Court followed suit: acknowledging the illegality of the arrests, the Court nevertheless ruled that the prisoners were now within the borders of the state that indicted them and remanded the case to a trial court in Boise. Only a jury could save their lives.

The prosecution then decided that it needed a second witness. Under Idaho law a defendant could not be convicted on the uncorroborated testimony of an accomplice. McParland found one in Steve Adams, a former Kansas City butcher and Cripple Creek miner. Once again, McParland went to work on the "witness." He was told he would be hanged if he did not cooperate; but if he were willing to do so, he would be treated well.

Adams cracked and confessed his connection to Orchard and the crime he had committed.

Meanwhile, Clarence Darrow had joined the defense team. His reputation had grown to heroic proportions in the years following his defense of Debs against the Pullman strike conspiracy charge. Recognizing that Adams's confession was crucial to the prosecution's case, Darrow found the prisoner's uncle on a ranch in Oregon. Darrow learned that Adams was innocent and that he had confessed out of fear he would be hanged. Darrow therefore offered to defend Adams against any charge the state might level against him. The uncle passed this on to Adams, who promptly repudiated his confession. The state then hurried to prosecute Adams. It was Adams's testimony versus McParland's. After several ballots, the jury announced it was deadlocked, with seven to five for acquittal. The state decided to hold Adams for retrial.

Sharing a cell in prison now for over a year, Haywood and Moyer were becoming quarrelsome. They argued bitterly over the rhetoric that should be employed during the trial: Haywood saw the proceedings as an opportunity to spread the gospel of revolutionary unionism; Moyer thought this approach would hurt their chances for acquittal. When McParland heard of their differences, he thought that he might be able to separate Moyer from Haywood, and use Moyer to corroborate Orchard's story. For that reason, the prosecution decided to try Haywood first.

Debs himself wanted to go to Boise as a correspondent for the *Appeal* but Darrow did not want him to come, fearing his presence there would prejudice the jury.

ON MAY 9, 1907, the trial opened, with Haywood's wife, Nevada Jane, sitting in a wheelchair behind the defense attorneys, her two daughters, seventeen-year-old Vernie and nine-year-old Henrietta, by her side. When the defendant was led in, he smiled at Nevada Jane and lay his fingers gently on Henrietta's head.

Celebrities stopped off at Boise to witness the trial—the novelist Upton Sinclair, the muckraking journalist Lincoln Steffens, and even the actress Ethel Barrymore, who was in town for a one-night stand with her hit play, *Captain Jinks of the Horse Marines*. Referring to Darrow as he delivered his opening statement to the jury, she said: "He has all the props, an old mother in a wheelchair and a little girl with curls draped around Haywood."[16]

Edmund Richardson, one of Haywood's lawyers, took the lead in a pitiless cross examination of Harry Orchard, who finally confessed that he had been a paid informant for the Mine Owners Association. This led to his further admission of various lies he had told, and that his cooperation with McParland had yielded amazing privileges for a man in a penitentiary—a private bungalow, new clothes, and spending money. Nonetheless, he did not repudiate his confession. The prosecution brought forward other witnesses to bolster Orchard's confession as the trial dragged on.

Darrow, unlike Richardson, spoke in a confiding tone of voice; as the *Idaho Daily Statesman* put it, "much in the same manner that the good old deacon in the little Methodist church you used to attend led the class meeting."[17] To Darrow, Haywood was simply a "plain, blunt, courageous fighting man." Even when Haywood used strong language or threw some angry punches, that only meant that he was not a devious or secretive person—"That's Haywood." There followed eighty-seven defense witnesses. Charles Moyer, it turned out, was a good witness for the defense.

Finally, Bill Haywood himself took the stand. At first he spoke in such low tones that Darrow had to ask him to speak up. Then his voice grew stronger and more confident. He gave an oral autobiography, denied any close connection to Orchard and the assassination. When Idaho's Senator William E. Borah, who was leading the prosecution team, attacked Haywood in a merciless cross-examination, Haywood did not give way.

When Darrow rose to give his summation to the jury, he was fearful that he was losing the case. He thought only his oratory might save Haywood from the gallows now. He approached each juror, one after another, and told them that "if this man, sitting in his office in Denver, 1500 miles away, employed this miserable assassin to come here and do this cowardly work, then for God's sake, gentlemen, hang him by the neck until dead." But to do this, he said, the jurors had to accept the testimony of a confirmed liar, Harry Orchard. Darrow tore apart Orchard's words. Then when Darrow continued his summation the next day, he spoke of Bill

Haywood, citing his mental courage, and his love for the poor and the weak.

In the unbearably hot afternoon Darrow's voice grew hoarse, his suit sagged with sweat. Finally, after eleven hours of oratory, he appealed to the jurors' class sentiments: "If you should decree Bill Haywood's death, in the railroad offices of our great cities, men will applaud your names. If you decree his death, among the spiders of Wall Street will go up paeans of praise for these twelve men good and true." On the other hand, "thousands of men, and of women and children—men who labor, men who suffer, women and children weary with care and toil—these men and these women and these children . . . are stretching out their helpless hands to this jury in a mute appeal for Bill Haywood's life." Darrow was now in tears and many of those crowding the courtroom sobbed with him.

On Saturday morning the judge gave the case over to the jury. Then, at seven o'clock, Sunday morning, the defense team learned that the jury was ready with its verdict. Haywood, without his family present, was led into the courtroom. "We, the jury . . . find the defendant, William D. Haywood, not guilty." Haywood, at first stunned, leapt to his feet and shook first Richardson's hand, then Darrow's. "God bless you."[18]

Both Moyer and Pettibone also won their freedom. Orchard was sentenced to life imprisonment; he would continue to live in his private bungalow in the penitentiary until his death at eighty-eight years old. He always claimed he told the whole truth.

THE LENGTHY INCARCERATION of Haywood had badly affected the IWW. It had virtually ceased to act as a trade union, and Haywood's antagonists in the Western Federation of Miners withdrew from the IWW. Although a hard core of strike leaders and organizers remained, the IWW did not provide moral and intellectual guidance on a sustained basis to the working men. In no small part because of the Haywood trial, the IWW's radical leaders turned against the government itself as well as the capitalist leadership. In the spring of 1908, the last reference to political action was dropped from its constitution.

For Debs, the dual tracks of trade unionism and the Socialist Party were vital, and in 1906 he quietly resigned from the IWW. But he did not denounce Bill Haywood, who was still a leader of the Socialist Party. Debs could not but admire the IWW leader's honesty and militant vitality.

Haywood became increasingly remote from his family and some of his old friends. Within a year after his release from prison he was elected to the National Executive Committee of the Socialist Party and in 1910 attended the Congress of the Second International in Copenhagen. He traveled to England and France and met with leaders of the European left—Jean Juarès, Keir Hardie, Rosa Luxemburg, and apparently even Lenin. When he returned to America he seemed more committed to socialism than ever, but he also was drawn to the IWW and sought the means to revive it. At last the opportunity came most dramatically in 1912 at a strike by the textile workers of Lawrence, Massachusetts. By that time IWW organizers were usually present at struggles for free speech, for migratory workers, for the unskilled immigrants in the steel mill towns of Ohio and Pennsylvania, and always among timber workers in the forests of northwest. Haywood more than ever saw parallels between the IWW and the radical workers in France, Italy, and Wales, who saw little value in the ballot box and were committed to direct action against their oppressors.[19]

Ironically, after riding on his reputation as an advocate of violence, Haywood told a reporter during the Lawrence strike that he had "turned his back on violence. It wins nothing. When we strike now, we strike with our hands in our pockets." He added that he considered hunger strikes an "action more violent than the discharge of bombs in St. Patrick's cathedral." He looked forward to a "bloodless revolution" in which "our dynamite is mental and our force is organization at the point of production."[20] The tactic of the bloodless revolution was to be the general strike. Unlike the revolutionary Marxists who demanded the seizure of state power by workers, however, the Wobblies were at a loss to explain how their use of the general strike would displace capitalism.

In any case, Haywood was greeted as a secular savior when he appeared in Lawrence to join the textile mill workers in their strike against the capitalists. The strike had begun spontaneously in early January when a group of Polish immigrants, finding out that their wages had been cut, slashed drive belts in the mill in revenge. What made the strike in Lawrence unusual was the makeup of the labor force—Irish, Italian,

French-Canadian, Polish, Russian, Syrian; Roman Catholic, Eastern Orthodox, Protestant, and Jewish. As a matter of course, there were serious tensions among these groups, but now they joined together in a show of solidarity.

The AFL union affiliated with the textile industry, the United Textile Workers of America, had shown little interest in assisting the minimally skilled Lawrence workers. The IWW, on the other hand, did respond and mobilized the mill workers to form a solid front. After an IWW organizer was killed by the police, Haywood immediately returned to Lawrence to assume the leadership of the strike. In response to public officials who were condemning the IWW for its tradition of violence, Haywood replied, "Can you weave cloth with the bayonets of your militia, or spin with the clubs of your policemen?"[21] Yet he still urged the workers to keep their hands in their pockets.

Haywood's approach took hold. But the strike dragged on, and funds to support it were low. The turning point came when Italian Socialists suggested that the children of the strikers should be cared for by families outside Lawrence, and the IWW publicized the offer. Within three days four hundred New Yorkers offered to take care of the children, and in early February children began leaving Lawrence for foster families in New York, and later in Philadelphia, Newark, and Vermont. When the police stepped in to prevent the scheduled departure of some children from the railway station, violence broke out and officers clubbed down women and children. The publicity that resulted led to a state and congressional investigation, and soon the employers started negotiating in earnest. In March the strike was settled favorably for the workers. "The victory at Lawrence," Debs declared, "was the most decisive and far-reaching ever won by organized workers."[22]

FLUSH WITH HIS SUCCESS in Massachusetts, Haywood arrived in Indianapolis for the May 1912 Socialist presidential convention. He had no idea that there was a plot against him. Speaking at Cooper Union in New York City six months earlier on December 21, 1911, Haywood had challenged his Socialist comrades by asserting that he knew nothing that would "bring as much satisfaction to you and as much anguish to the boss as a little sabotage in the right place at the proper time." Parliamentary politics were useless, and he went on to conclude: "It is our purpose to overthrow the capitalist system by forcible means if necessary."

Socialist Morris Hillquit responded to Haywood by debating him at Cooper Union on January 12, 1912. But Haywood then showed his moderate side, which characterized his behavior at the Lawrence strike, saying that "industrial unionism comprehends all that socialism comprehends and that industrial unionism is socialism with its working clothes on." That was no apology as far as Hillquit was concerned. He dismissed the IWW as any viable alternative to the AFL, which Hillquit believed Socialists should infiltrate and influence.[23]

From this point on, Haywood's critics on the National Executive Committee of the Socialist Party of America organized a campaign to remove Haywood from serving on the committee. In their view, it was vital to make sure that the Socialist Party was at a far distance from the IWW's espousal of direct action. Within days of his first speech at Cooper Union, Denver Socialists had introduced a resolution calling for the party to expel him. But the motion did not take hold until March 1912, when Haywood, angry at the beating of children in Lawrence, said, "I will not vote again." To many Socialists this assault on parliamentary politics seemed the words of an anarchist; the Socialist chapter in Yuma, Arizona, moved that Haywood be forced off the National Committee. The New York chapter, led by Hillquit, seconded the motion. (A few days later, with the victory of the strikers in Lawrence, New York withdrew its support for the Yuma motion.)

No matter what Haywood's posture was during the Lawrence strike, no matter that his inflammatory statements were often outweighed by his moderate behavior, the Socialist reformers were not ready to give up. To this faction, the IWW—with Haywood as their Messiah—would scare off potential supporters of socialism. To the revolutionary Wobblies, the reformers were "Slow-cialists" only too ready to sell out their principles for a few votes.

Moreover, by 1912 the Socialists were seen as an increasingly reasonable alternative to the two major parties. In the 1911 elections, American voters had elected some 450 Socialist officials, including 56 mayors

and 305 aldermen and city councilmen, and 1 congressman. The party
had 5 English dailies and 262 English weeklies as well as a good number
of foreign-language journals. If Big Bill Haywood stood in the way of
broader acceptance of socialism by the American people, then he had to
go. And the excuse his critics would use to force him out were his
remarks on sabotage.

HAYWOOD SAW NONE OF THIS. When the labor plank of the Socialist
platform for the first time in the party's history embraced the needs of the
unorganized, unskilled immigrant workers and urged all unions to abolish
"artificial restrictions to the membership," Haywood was overjoyed; he
even endorsed political action. With this new labor policy, he said to the
delegates, "I can go to the working class, to the eight million women and
children, to the four million black men, to the disenfranchised white
men . . . and I can carry to them the message of socialism."[24] Smiling
broadly, he opened himself to the audience, saying that he could now
"shake hands with every delegate in this convention and say that we are a
united working class."

Haywood's words were not good enough for Hillquit, Berger, and their
allies, who remembered the phrases Haywood had employed at his first
Cooper Union speech. They recalled his use of the term "coercion" as the
best way to achieve industrial socialism. They knew of his contempt for
them—he had once said in a clear reference to Berger that he would
much prefer it if the workers could elect a factory superintendent rather
than a congressman. They remembered that he had shown his disrespect
for lawyers such as Hillquit, calling them "the mouthpieces of the capitalist class."[25]

The eventually successful effort to remove Haywood from the party's
ruling machinery did not occur at the convention. Debs, preferring to
remain in Terre Haute to see if the delegates would call on him once
again to lead the party in the general election, was unwilling to fight for
Haywood. He was equally unwilling to attack him. By his absence from
the scene, and in his reluctance to confront Hillquit or Berger in the
months preceding the convention, he had effectively encouraged Hay-

wood's dangerous rhetoric. But by refusing to attempt to influence the IWW, Debs showed that he would not try to prevent the conservative Socialists from going ahead in their plan to get rid of Haywood. Debs had written in the *International Socialist Review* in February that he hoped that at the convention in May, the meeting would "place itself squarely on record . . . against sabotage and every other form, of violence and destructiveness suggested by what is known as 'direct action.'"[26] This was Debs's only statement on the most explosive issue the delegates would confront.

On the day following the adoption of the labor plank, Haywood's joy was shattered. The reformers offered an amendment to the party's constitution that would expel "any member of the party who opposes political action or advocates crime, sabotage or other methods of violence as a weapon of the working class."[27]

Victor Berger, in endorsing the amendment, gave a speech that became a virulent denunciation of Haywood's IWW. He accused members of the IWW who were "in our councils" of using the Socialist Party "as a cloak for direct action, for IWW-ism, sabotage and syndicalism. It is anarchism by a new name." He went on to say that "I, for one, do not believe in murder as a means of propaganda, I do not believe in theft as a means of expropriation. . . . the IWW can go to hell."

Haywood was in a rage at these accusations—Berger "knew that the IWW had never advocated murder as propaganda, he knew that it had never advocated theft as a means of acquiring the capitalists' property."[28]

Although the debate that followed the motion was bitter, the amendment passed, and later the conservatives used it to get rid of Haywood altogether. The Socialist Party of New York passed a resolution calling for the ouster of Haywood from the National Executive Committee. In December 1912 the party mailed ballots to all its members so that they could vote on the recall motion. Thirty-seven prominent Socialists, including Walter Lippmann and Margaret Sanger, signed a petition against the recall, but in February 1913 the general membership voted Haywood out. The one Socialist who might have saved Haywood was Eugene Debs. But Debs tried to have things both ways. He claimed he had opposed the amendment but that, once adopted, it should be obeyed.

After the recall vote, Bill Haywood left the party he had embraced ten years earlier and went off to join the thousands of textile workers on strike in Paterson, New Jersey.

The absence in Indianapolis of Eugene Debs, the one Socialist with a national reputation, inevitably meant that the conservative wing of the party would control the convention. Debs had made clear his opposition to violence by striking workers, for violence often seemed to justify the harsh tactics used to break a strike by the employers. Moreover, he believed, individual direct action was not the way Socialists should behave; it was the method of the anarchist, not the trade unionist.

Following the convention, Debs backtracked. Writing in the *Review* in July, he commented that he would like to have reduced "to the minimum the offenses punishable by expulsion from the party" and while he still opposed "anarchist tactics," he would have preferred that the party condemn them "on moral grounds." Then in a private letter to Berger, Debs wrote that he disagreed with Berger's assertion that there was any "immediate danger from the alleged anarchist element," but that he nonetheless favored after the election "a thorough house cleaning . . . and the expulsion from the party of any who prefer violence to the ballot."[29] To break definitively with Bill Haywood was extremely painful to Debs, and his contradictory statements reflected that.

By not appearing at the convention and knowing the control that Berger and the conservatives would almost surely exert there, Debs did not act as one might have expected he would by trying to enfold Haywood in support of industrial unionism and thus prevent an open breach in the labor movement. It would not be until Franklin D. Roosevelt presided over the Great Depression that a strong industrial union would arise.[30]

BERGER FROM MILWAUKEE and Hillquit from New York would surely have liked to deny the presidential nomination to Debs. At one point, Berger suggested that Debs's health might interfere with his campaigning, and cited Debs's absence from the convention even as a delegate. But Debs had said publicly that he was in fine physical shape for a presidential run, and Berger's ploy went nowhere. Had Berger's and Hillquit's followers united, they might have been able to see their hopes fulfilled, but each group nominated its own man. When Debs's name was put in nomination, he was easily chosen on the first ballot by three-fifths of the votes.

Berger's candidate, Emil Seidel, who had been recently mayor of Milwaukee, was chosen as his running mate; and later Hillquit's choice, J. Mahlon Barnes, was named campaign manager. Even though Debs did not like Barnes's politics, he gave in and accepted his appointment.

The platform was predictably radical, among other things calling for collective ownership of all means of transportation and communication and of all large-scale industry; for collective ownership of land; and for collective ownership and management of the banking and currency system. For the workers, it demanded shorter working hours, adequate insurance and safety rules, and an end to child labor. It favored woman suffrage and direct election of the president and vice president. It further proposed to abolish the Senate and to deny the president the veto over legislation. It would also deny the Supreme Court the right to declare laws unconstitutional, and eliminate federal district and circuit courts. (Of course, to put through these structural changes, there would have to be a constitutional convention.)

All these measures were but "a preparation for the workers to seize the whole powers of the government." These goals would have easily satisfied Haywood, but the way to achieve them was to be exclusively through the ballot box.[31]

Despite the desire of Berger and Hillquit to see Debs become, at fifty-seven, a kind of elder statesman, they also knew that Debs's fame offered the Socialists their only means for presenting themselves as a national movement. Debs in turn preferred the role of a national champion of labor. He may well have also felt inadequate in the face of Berger's theoretical gift and his combative, autocratic nature. By crushing Haywood, the conservative forces were now fully in control of the party's political machine. Nonetheless, the rank and file might well have supported Debs in a showdown with his antagonists.[32]

Paradoxically, it was also Debs's strength that he did not engage in a possibly lethal struggle for control of the party. He was first and foremost a trade unionist. He always preferred to include all those who supported industrial unionism. He was also a democrat, who identified with Lincoln and the revolutionary tradition that he viewed as the bedrock of American exceptionalism. To campaign across the nation would allow Debs to present himself as the democratic embodiment of socialism.

PART THREE

The Contenders

TWELVE

The New Freedom vs.
the New Nationalism

D ESPITE HIS TRIUMPH at the Baltimore convention and his
growing mastery of the politics of the Democratic Party,
Woodrow Wilson could not rid himself of the tortured feelings
of self-doubt that assailed him throughout the sultry days of August.
From Sea Girt he wrote to Mary Peck revealing his dread that he could
not attract the voters by the strength of his personality:

> I feel that Roosevelt's strength is altogether incalculable. The
> contest is between him and me, not between Taft and me.... But
> just what will happen, as between Roosevelt and me, with party
> lines utterly confused and broken, is all guesswork. It depends
> upon what people are thinking . . . and I am by no means confi-
> dent.[1]

Wilson was certainly right about Taft, who had written as early as July
22, "I think I might as well give up so far as being a candidate. There are
so many people in the country who don't like me."[2]

Wilson was also beset by worries about his campaign managers.
William McCombs, who had revealed his instability during the convention, was now a sick man, whose frail constitution was suffering from the
strain of managing events. In mid-August McCombs collapsed and left to

recuperate in the Adirondacks. William McAdoo quickly stepped in to take over the direction of the campaign, though Wilson, fearful of seeming ungrateful as he had in his earlier treatment of Colonel Harvey, did not name McAdoo as McCombs's replacement. He simply let McAdoo take over, and an effective campaign staff emerged by the autumn.

The central problem for Wilson was his inability to come up with a plausible alternative to Roosevelt's Progressive program. It was not enough for him to call for returning government to the people. His rhetoric was empty, and a wholesale attack on tariff protection failed to stir the three audiences he spoke to in August. It is not surprising that Wilson wanted to avoid a classic campaign swing around the country, speaking to well-wishers from a platform on the caboose of a train. "Are the people interested in personalities rather than principles?" he asked his daughter. "If that is true they will not vote for me."[3] He knew that his strength was in attacking TR on issues—but what issue would prove most effective, and how should he mount the attack?

Wilson soon found a savior, the man who would draw up the plan of attack he so badly needed if he were to defeat Roosevelt. On August 28, the famous Boston lawyer Louis D. Brandeis, sometimes known as the "people's attorney," met with Wilson at Sea Girt. He came for lunch and stayed for three hours. By the time he left he had persuaded Wilson to base his campaign on the issue of monopolies. Roosevelt's view that regulating trusts was the best way to deal with big business, which he believed was here to stay, simply made government an instrument for trying to prevent monopolies from doing evil, a thing that cannot be done, Brandeis explained. Wilson should, instead, seek to restore competition by destroying monopolies. This "New Freedom" would give Wilson an answer to Roosevelt's "New Nationalism."[4]

Louis Brandeis would become one of America's most distinguished and influential jurists. In 1916 he would be appointed to the Supreme Court, where he remained until his retirement in 1939. Born in 1856, he grew up in Louisville, Kentucky, of a German-Jewish family that had immigrated to the United States in 1849. Louisville had a large German community, and by the 1860s had reached a population of 100,000, about one-third of whom were German immigrants or descendants of German immigrants. While Jews were often persecuted in Europe, in

Louisville they prospered. The Brandeises were not practicing Jews, but they did not disavow their Jewish heritage.

Brandeis's father did well in the wholesale grain business, and young Louis attended good schools, in which German was also taught. Industrious, determined, a gifted student, Brandeis was able to enter Harvard Law School directly from high school a few weeks before his nineteenth birthday in 1875. Money was tight in the family at this time, and Brandeis had to borrow from his older brother to pay the tuition; he also tutored to earn pocket money.

When Brandeis entered the law school, its dean, Christopher Columbus Langdell, was instituting the case system of instruction. In essence, this meant teaching the law from the principles involved in its application. Years later Brandeis described the process by pointing out that "the law was to be learned only by going to the original source."[5] At the law school, Brandeis was the leader of his class, one of his classmates describing him as "tall, well-made, dark, beardless, and with the brightest eyes I ever saw. . . . The Profs listened to his opinion with the greatest deference, and it was generally correct."[6]

After spending an extra year doing graduate work, he soon joined his classmate Samuel D. Warren Jr. in starting a law practice of their own in Boston. Sam Warren came from an old Boston family, and doubtless this connection smoothed Brandeis's acceptance by the Brahmin circles he now traveled in. Warren had initially worked in the firm of Oliver Wendell Holmes, who later served with Brandeis on the Supreme Court. Holmes became quite friendly with the two younger lawyers, appearing at the new law office to celebrate its opening. "Warren and Holmes talked and I lay outstretched on a ship's chair," Brandeis recalled.[7]

Brandeis grew rich in his practice, but he lived an austere, frugal life, not marrying until his late thirties. When Warren finally left the firm to take over his father's business, Brandeis took in other partners as the firm thrived. He was known as a man who worked hard for his clients; he was described by a New York lawyer who did a good deal of business with the firm as a lawyer who "always got all he could and never gave any favors to anybody."[8] This approach made him respected, even feared, but eventually made him resented by the Bostonians he had to deal with.

This became apparent when he came out in 1908 against a merger of the transportation facilities in New England. Steam railroads, trolleys, and steamboats within the region to the south and the west would be controlled permanently by the New Haven railroad company, under the aegis of J. P. Morgan's banking house. Despite Brandeis's opposition to it, the merger was approved in 1909. The Boston Brahmins were either owners or closely connected to owners of New Haven company stock. A few years after the merger fight, however, Brandeis got into another struggle with the New Haven. This time his formidable documentation of mismanagement was so telling that the railroad failed. Rather than blaming the managers, the Bostonians blamed Brandeis.

Brandeis came to detest the notion that bigness was becoming an end in itself. "Under the trusts capital hires men; under a real corporation, men hire capital."[9] The great monopolies interfered with the freedom of the individual, and a wide distribution of stock was, to Brandeis, "absentee landlordism of the worst kind" because it resulted in "a sense of absolute irresponsibility on the part of the person who holds the stock."[10]

As Brandeis grew more wealthy he could afford to spend more time with reform groups and came to endorse woman suffrage. Though his family and he were Republicans, he supported many Democrats for higher office. By the time he met Wilson, he was recognized by his peers not only as a man who would support worthy causes, but also as a daunting lawyer whose "Brandeis briefs" incorporated sociological and economic facts into his argument.

After Brandeis was named to the bench of the Supreme Court, Dean Acheson, his clerk in 1919, described him as having a "Lincolnian cast and grandeur, the same boldness and ruggedness of features, the same untamed hair, the eyes of infinite depth and bushy eyebrows, which in moments of emotions seemed to jut out." In later years, law clerks would refer to him as Isaiah, the stern moralist and Old Testament prophet. For Brandeis, Acheson wrote, "Perfection was the norm and you went up from there." He possessed "an almost stultifying sense of perfection."[11]

This was the man who told Wilson at lunch on August 28, 1912, that "the system must be changed."[12] Brandeis, the Jeffersonian who had always been an enemy of bigness, realized that the trusts could probably not be destroyed. But he believed there had to be a better way to deal with them than TR's plan for regulating the inevitable. After his first meeting with Brandeis, Wilson spoke with new fervor. "Both of us have as an object the prevention of monopoly," he said. "Monopoly is created by unregulated competition, by competition that overwhelms all other competitions, and the only way to enjoy industrial freedom is to destroy that condition."[13]

Wilson launched his crusade against Roosevelt in a Labor Day speech before ten thousand workers in Buffalo. After praising the Progressive Party platform's commitment to aid labor and to strive for social justice, he said that there was "a central purpose in that platform, from which I very seriously dissent." He went on to spell out the lessons he had learned from Brandeis: "As to the monopolies, which Mr. Roosevelt proposes to legalize and to welcome . . . I do not look forward with pleasure to the time when the juggernauts are licensed and driven by commissioners of the United States." "What has created these monopolies?" he asked. "Unregulated competition."

How did he propose to deal with it? "We can prevent these processes through remedial legislation, and so restructure the wrong use of competition that the right use of competition will destroy monopoly. Ours is a program of liberty; theirs is a program of regulation." For Wilson, Roosevelt was a "self-appointed divinity" who would make people the puppets of a National Board of Guardians.[14]

Thus was born the "New Freedom," and Wilson spent much of September repeating the mantra of the need for competition in order to make men free. But it was one thing to assert that monopolies came about because of unregulated competition and another thing to explain how the federal government could regulate competition to prevent monopoly. He needed more help from Brandeis, and he sought it on September 27 when he conferred with him in Boston. He wanted Brandeis to "set forth as explicitly as possible the actual measures by which competition can be effectively regulated."[15]

The articles that Brandeis dispatched to Wilson were too detailed to be of much use in the campaign. Wilson, however, did come to see that major reforms in banking, along with reduction of the tariff, were ways to restore competition and the functioning of the free market. He fully embraced the Brandeis view that the "difference in the economic policy of the [Democratic and Progressive] parties is fundamental and irrecon-

cilable. It is the difference between industrial liberty and industrial absolutism, tempered by governmental (that is, party) supervision."[16]

Wilson sounded the tocsin that Roosevelt's approach to big business
was the denial of freedom. He flayed the Progressives for their alleged
addiction to paternalism—"a government of experts"—in contrast to Wilson's model of listening to the people and then speaking for them. If the
people themselves did not "understand the job, then we are not a free
people."[17]

ROOSEVELT DID NOT take long to strike back. His attack centered on
Wilson's past endorsement of limited government and his recent and possibly insincere conversion to progressive ideas. On September 9, Wilson
gave his opponent an opening when he declared in New York, "The history of liberty is a history of the limitation of governmental power, not the
increase of it."[18] These words harked back to Wilson's southern roots, to
his Jeffersonian commitment to states' rights.

Before an audience of ten thousand people at the Coliseum in San
Francisco on September 14, TR seized the day. Quoting the damning
sentence, he called it "the key to Mr. Wilson's position" and labeled it "a
bit of outworn academic doctrine which was kept in the schoolroom and
the professional study for a generation after it had been abandoned by all
who had experience of actual life. It is simply the laissez-faire doctrine of
English political economists three-quarters of a century ago." Such a doctrine, he said, was utterly inadequate to the conditions of American
industrial capitalism. Nowadays, Roosevelt said, "the limitation of governmental power, of governmental action, means the enslavement of the
people by the great corporations who can only be held in check through
the extension of governmental power."

TR recounted the problems of the nation that demanded social justice—occupational disease, factory working conditions, industrial acci-
dents, and general living conditions—all of which required "an extension
of government control" on a national scale, and all of which, according to
Wilson, were matters for the states to deal with.

The issues between them, between the New Nationalism and the
New Freedom, were clearly drawn: "The people of the United States,"

TR said, "have but one instrument which they can effectively use against the colossal combinations of business—and that instrument is the government of the United States." Roosevelt's Progressives intended "to use the whole power of government to protect those who, under Mr. Wilson's laissez-faire system, are trodden down in the ferocious scrambling rush of an unregulated and purely individualistic industrialism."[19]

Despite the exaggerated rhetoric of both candidates, and the often unfair descriptions that the one gave of the other's positions, they touched the core of their respective beliefs. Wilson, like Brandeis, distrusted the great combinations that had come to dominate or destroy the Jeffersonian America of small business and community life. He came to believe, however, that he could not rid the country of that evil except by restoring full competition. Roosevelt saw in the industrialized America that Hamilton had foreseen the ills visited upon the working class and knew that industrial capitalism could only be moderated, not erased.

THIRTEEN

_____

The Crusader

WHILE WILSON WAS initially a reluctant campaigner, Roosevelt quickly took the bit between his teeth, invigorated by the prospect of touring America and reminding audiences of a commanding president. His young cousin Nicholas Roosevelt found him looking "younger by ten years than when I had last seen him. . . . In such wonderful spirits that he behaved like a boy."[1]

TR was convinced that this was to be a two-man race: Wilson and he could ignore poor Taft, and they would try to put aside Debs, whose platform dangerously resembled in so many ways their own. At one point when someone in the crowd shouted, "Tell us about Taft," TR retorted, "I never discuss dead issues."[2]

Taft remained bitter and despondent. Writing to his wife in late August, he confessed his anger: "As the campaign goes on and the unscrupulousness of Roosevelt develops, it is hard to realize that we are talking about the same man whom we knew in the presidency. . . . it is impossible to conceive of him as the fakir, the juggler, the green-goods man, the gold brick man that he has come to be." He claimed that he had no "feeling of enmity against Roosevelt or any feeling of hatred. I look upon him as an historical character of a most peculiar type in whom are embodied elements of real greatness," but now "I look upon him as I look upon a freak, almost, in the zoological garden, a kind of animal not often found. So far as personal relations with him are concerned, they don't

exist—I do not have any feeling one way or the other."³ Despite this dis-
claimer, Taft profoundly regretted their broken friendship; his was a constant sadness that he was determined to conceal.

Taft believed that Wilson would probably win because of the split in
the Republican Party but he also thought that he had been right to deny
the nomination to TR. He knew he had the support of the leading figures
in the party, but even Elihu Root, the man who had guaranteed his nomination at Chicago, promised to give only one speech for him, and Taft
knew that was because of Root's attachment to Roosevelt. He sympa-
thized with poor Nick Longworth, TR's son-in-law who had remained
faithful to the Republican Party and was caught between loyalty to his
wife, Alice, whose own fidelity to her father was legendary, and to his
father and mother, who were conservatives.

Taft had a poor opinion of Wilson, considering him a man who had
changed his views so often that he seemed "an utter opportunist."⁴ He
had determined over the summer that he would make no speeches during the campaign, though he nonetheless complained that Wilson and
Roosevelt were getting reams of publicity, "and there is no news from me
except that I played golf. I seemed to have heard that before. It always
makes me impatient, as if I were running a P.T. Barnum show, with two or
three shows across the street, and as if I ought to have as much advertising as the rest."⁵

Taft knew his limitations, declaring that he must cling to his presidential dignity. "I have been told that I ought to do this, ought to do that . . .
that I do not keep myself in the headlines," he told a newspaper reporter.
"I know it, but I can't do it. I couldn't if I would, and I wouldn't if I
could."⁶

ROOSEVELT, on the other hand, opened his campaign on August 16 in
Providence, Rhode Island, where ten thousand people crowded the railroad station to hear him, and then on Boston Common, where twenty
thousand people cheered him. Before the campaign was over he would
visit thirty-four states and travel ten thousand miles. After touring New
England, he headed west to the Pacific Coast, whistle-stopping through
Arizona, Colorado, Nebraska, Kansas, and other states, and then com-

mitted himself to a six-state swing through the South, from surprisingly welcoming New Orleans to hostile Atlanta (where the Atlanta *Journal* attacked him as a political adventurer: "You stand at Armageddon and you battle for the trusts.").[7] He delivered more than 150 speeches. At one point, TR characteristically climbed over a coal tender into the engine room of a transcontinental express and ran the train for a time, jarring the passengers in their seats.[8]

On the state fair grounds in St. Paul, Minnesota, an estimated 50,000 people turned out to welcome him; in Portland, Oregon, the path from the train to his waiting automobile was covered with roses; in Los Angeles, businesses closed and traffic was halted as TR was greeted by 200,000 people lining the streets from the railroad station to the Shrine Auditorium. No matter where he spoke—from the rear of a train, from automobiles, to crowds in big cities and to groups of well-wishers in small towns—throngs saluted him with a fervor reserved for a national hero.[9] In his journey from Fargo, North Dakota, to Helena, Montana, he covered about the same number of miles as Taft would in his whole campaign.[10]

TR's running mate, Hiram Johnson, rivaled him in enthusiasm and exhausting campaigning, giving hundreds of speeches during a twenty-two-state tour. The two men often appeared with state, congressional, and local Progressive candidates to demonstrate that theirs was a broad-gauged crusade. Along with repeating the national platform's calls for democracy and social justice, the state and local candidates addressed the particular needs of the states and districts, demanding, for example, free schoolbooks in Indiana and an end to the severe restrictions on suffrage in Rhode Island.

But were the crowds that turned out for TR going to translate into enough votes for victory? Or were they just turning out because of curiosity, to see the great hero one last time? Because his likely electoral votes were largely in the East and the upper Midwest, Roosevelt may have wasted valuable time in the Southwest and the solidly Democratic South, whose 140 electoral votes were almost surely going to Wilson. (New York, Pennsylvania, and Illinois together would have given TR 112 electoral votes.) His campaign managers thought such extensive campaigning was a mistake.[11]

As the *Providence Journal* observed in conservative Rhode Island, the state that had sent Nelson Aldrich again and again to the Senate: "He will draw crowds, of course—[the prize-fighter] Jack Johnson draws crowds."[12] With the Democratic Party now calling itself the party of progressive reform and the Republican Party machine in full command, especially in New York and Indiana, Roosevelt knew that the odds of winning were not in his favor. On the other hand, if he were destined to lose, he could not resist showing himself as a continental figure, waving the banner of the New Nationalism.

So he went on, basking in the adulation he was receiving from the people. In New Haven, thousands struggled just to shake his hand and could not bear to see his train depart. In St. Louis, TR was demagogic at the state fair grounds, but temperate and judicious addressing businessmen, doctors, and lawyers at the City Club. When he spoke before twenty-five thousand listeners in Minneapolis/St. Paul, one excited admirer struggled through the crowd just to touch the former president's foot; the reporter for the *New York Times* commented: "He had touched the hem of the garment of Moses." The next day the editorial page of the *Times* wrote in horror that this incident "typifies the unreasoning affection these people have come to bear for an audacious, emotional, self-contradictory, scarcely scrupulous but forcible and picturesque leader."[13]

Never was Roosevelt happier than in the Far West, in the countryside where he believed he had achieved his manhood. In Montana, where some of his old ranching crowd had moved from the Dakotas, he showed by his language that he was one of them—"a middling old settler . . . just at the end of the buffalo days." Yes, "I was always in the short grass country, and I worked among the cows."[14] He generally did well with women in the audience, claiming that he was a "natural democrat" who desired equality for all. (In North Dakota, however, he did not do so well with some young girls, offering them the same advice he gave to the boys: "Don't flinch, don't squeal, and hit the line hard.")[15] In New Mexico, he lectured the Indians in sign language, and in "Roosevelt-crazy Oklahoma" a mob tore his suit and destroyed his hat.[16]

· · ·

WILSON ON THE STUMP could not compete with Roosevelt, but he was nonetheless often effective in repackaging the Democrats' old approach to trust-busting, which, by adopting Brandeis's idea of restoring competition, would be brought about by expanding antitrust law. "Government by experts" was also Wilson's way of ridiculing Roosevelt's preferred method of regulating trusts and trade, and reducing tariffs. On social welfare and labor reform, Wilson's New Freedom challenged TR's New Nationalism. Although Wilson declared he was sympathetic to the Progressive goal of social and industrial justice, Wilson disagreed with the specific proposals of the Progressives, claiming that the abolition of child labor and the regulation of working hours, as well as many other labor issues, should be handled at the state level; he contended that minimum wage acts would harm laboring men and women by driving down their wages to the minimum level.

As he put it at a workers' dinner on September 4, "No government has ever been beneficent when the attitude of the government was that it could take care of the people. Let me tell you that the only freedom exists where the people take care of the government." The reformers who believed otherwise, Wilson declared, were badly misguided. Wilson spoke about change without radical measures, reform without fundamental, albeit risky, innovation. As he had assured his listeners in his acceptance speech in early August, he was not seeking destruction of any kind.[17]

To some degree, Roosevelt was put on the defensive. The Progressive campaign had begun with evangelistic fervor, Roosevelt declaring in mid-August in a speech in Revere, Massachusetts, that the Progressive platform was a bold new covenant "where the voice of the people strives to utter the biddings of divine right and where the soul of the people is bent on realizing the brotherhood of man."[18] But soon Wilson's attacks mired TR in the old politics, and he abandoned lectures on moral uplift and returned to the classic rhetoric that he was always most comfortable with.

Appealing to voters in the moderate center had in the past been Roosevelt's preferred political strategy. In 1912 he was determined to put Wilson and the Democrats in the same boat with the reactionary Republicans, and to signal the dangers of that Socialist revolutionary, Eugene V.

Debs. But this approach was not persuasive, given that Wilson had assumed the guise of a progressive reformer and the press was eager to point out the many parallels between Roosevelt and Debs. Nor could Roosevelt retreat from the radical social values he now espoused. As always, TR was never one to back away from a fight, and his 1912 campaign remains one of the most radical ever waged by a major American political figure.

BOTH THE DEMOCRATS and the Progressives were eager to demonstrate that they received much of their financial support from the average voter. Up to a point this was true, but both Wilson and Roosevelt needed big money that only the rich and the organized party machinery could produce.

The Democratic National Committee spent the most, $1,110,952, topping the Republican National Committee's $904,828. Along with Jacob Schiff, a Republican financier who backed Wilson and gave $12,500, Wall Street speculator Bernard Baruch and the party organization of Kentucky each gave the same sum, while the Jones brothers of International Harvester donated a total of $20,000. Taft's campaign war chest came to $904,828, which included Andrew Carnegie's $35,000 and J. P. Morgan's $25,000.

TR's Progressives spent a relatively modest $596,405, including publisher Frank Munsey's $135,000 and banker George Perkins's $130,000. The Roosevelt family put in a total of $77,500. Smaller contributors supplied $163,657. There was no way that the new party could compete with the party machines and patrons of the Democrats and Republicans without the major contributions of Munsey and Perkins, whose loyalty was to Roosevelt alone.[19]

ATTACKS ON ROOSEVELT in the press painted him in the image of an imperial Caesar. George Harvey once again proved his Wilsonian credentials by headlining his editorial in his *North American Review,* "Roosevelt or the Republic," declaring that "Roosevelt was the first President whose chief personal characteristic was mendacity, the first to glory in duplicity, the first braggart, the first bully, the first betrayer of a friend who ever occupied the White House." Harvey concluded the editorial by writing: "It is not the foreign war so commonly anticipated as a consequence of Roosevelt's accession to the dizzy height of unrestrained authority that makes for dread; it is the civil strife that would almost inevitably ensue from patriotic resistance to usurpation by a half-mad genius at the head of the proletariat."

Harvey's old ally, "Marse Henry" Watterson, in the Louisville *Courier-Journal,* wrote of Roosevelt that he was "half-mad," and even if "he be not of disordered mind, the record would show him a monster of depravity and turpitude." His election would mean "the end of the Republic and the beginning of a Dictatorship."[20]

More serious were the misrepresentations of the Progressive Party's cause that were written anonymously by Brandeis and appeared as a series of editorials in *Collier's* magazine. As *Collier's* had previously supported Roosevelt and the Progressive Party, the editorials were especially damaging. Once the journal's publisher discovered who the author of the editorials was, he fired the editor, Norman Hapgood, who had become an ardent Wilson supporter, and brought the magazine back into the Roosevelt camp by late October. But the hour was late, and it was not until the November 9 issue that readers were told that five of the editorials had been written by one of Wilson's advisers.[21]

The Progressive Party organizers struck back at the Democrats with more modern techniques of electioneering. They called on celebrities to further their cause. Actress Lillian Russell, whose husband was a prominent Pennsylvania Progressive, was photographed buying Bull Moose buttons; William Gillette, who played Sherlock Holmes on the stage, agreed to go out on a speaking tour. Perhaps most impressive was the party's securing the endorsement of Thomas Alva Edison. The party also published an illustrated magazine, the *Progressive Bulletin,* with copy provided by famous correspondents, including Richard Harding Davis and William Allen White. Campaign literature appeared in Italian, Yiddish, and other languages, and the poet George Silvester Viereck wrote to members of the National German-American League in praise of Roosevelt, who was of Dutch and English ancestry. Viereck described TR as "the only candidate in the race in whose veins flows German blood, who has received part of his education in Germany and who refuses to tie this country to the apron strings of Great Britain."[22]

Roosevelt, however, refused to accept letters purportedly linking Wilson to an extramarital affair. "Those letters would be entirely unconvincing," he said. "Nothing, no evidence could ever make the American people believe that a man like Woodrow Wilson, cast so perfectly as the apothecary's clerk, could ever play Romeo."[23]

WHILE ROOSEVELT REMAINED on the defensive in his responses to Wilson's and Brandeis's attacks on his proposed commission to regulate monopolies, he was more sure-footed in his attacks on Wilson's calls for a low tariff to reduce the cost of living and repair other economic problems. He saw the tariff as a "red herring" that both traditional parties were using to avoid dealing with the far more troubling question of social justice. It was not, he believed, simply a question of protection versus free trade. Instead, Roosevelt preferred a commission that would regulate the tariff and business; Wilson's criticisms reminded him of similar attacks against the Interstate Commerce Commission.

As for Wilson's opposition to the minimum wage, Roosevelt contended that the New Jersey governor did not know the working conditions that existed in the United States. A minimum wage, he said, would not depress wages; the companies were already paying the lowest wages the labor market would allow. Trust-busting—"restoring competition"—would not by itself create good working conditions. In Colorado, TR highlighted the practices of the Colorado Fuel and Iron Company, which was owned by the Rockefellers and was not a trust; its working conditions, he declared, were the most deplorable in the industry.[24]

Eventually, however, Roosevelt concluded that he had to shift his view on competition. Just before the election, he asserted in *Collier's*: "I am not for monopoly. We intend to restore competition." For Roosevelt, competition would follow the regulation of monopoly, but the Brandeis-Wilson position of promoting free competition continued to hurt him. Perhaps if he had linked competition to regulation earlier in the campaign, he might have blunted the assault on his own views of trust-busting. If expediency won the day, it may have come too late in the game.

Confronted by the reluctance of Democratic progressives to quit their party and come over to his side, Roosevelt had to attract Republican progressives to his new party. But there were not enough of those Republicans. Moreover, Republican progressives were to be found largely outside the cities, and Roosevelt's paternalistic approach to government did not generally appeal to farmers but rather to voters living in urban centers. Regulating monopolies, opposing low tariffs, urging reforms in the working conditions of industrial capitalism—these were not positions that stirred rural America. Nor did Roosevelt's passionate commitment to conservation help his cause in the Far West.[25]

To reach beyond the ranks of urban voters, Progressives had to rely on the heroic stature of Roosevelt the man.

FOURTEEN

The Moralist

COLONEL EDWARD HOUSE believed that the split in the Republican Party guaranteed a Democratic victory. There was thus no need for him to cut short his European vacation, which included Sweden, Finland, Russia (as far east as Moscow), Germany, France, and of course England. Nonetheless, he was eager to join the campaign and returned in late August to see what had to be done. Soon enough, he realized that he was sorely needed.

Upon arriving in the United States, House wrote Wilson that he wanted to do everything he could to ensure Wilson's election. Wilson wrote him back immediately, saying that he was delighted to learn this and would run up to House's summer place in Beverly, Massachusetts, were it not so far away. House soon advised Wilson to follow a strategy that would avoid disharmony among Democratic leaders. To organize properly in Maine and Vermont, House wrote Wilson, they should try to get a committee in every precinct that would be composed of "a Taft Republican who is supporting you for one reason or another, a progressive Republican who does not want to vote for Roosevelt and cannot vote for Taft, and the best Democratic organizer that can be obtained." If this method were followed, "not only in Vermont and Maine, but in every State of the Union, there will be nothing left of your opponents that will be worth while."[1]

What was becoming quite evident to both Wilson and House was the

effect of the continuing struggle between McCombs, who had been chosen chairman of the National Committee, and McAdoo, the vice chairman, for control of the campaign. This was the first news that House
received after landing in Boston. McCombs traveled from the Adirondacks to see House and told him, in House's words, "A tale of perfidy that
was hardly believable. McAdoo was the ringleader and he, McCombs,
was the victim."[2] Such enmity alarmed House, who was determined that
harmony should prevail during the election campaign and, indeed, in
what he hoped would be the first Democratic administration in twenty
years.

Upon learning that McCombs was seriously thinking of resigning,
House decided to go to New York in early September and see Woodrow
Wilson. He told the candidate about the feud between McAdoo and
McCombs and indicated his sympathy for McCombs. Wilson was very
aware of the rivalry and urged him not to make up his mind about the
rights and wrongs of the situation until he knew more. In two weeks, the
Colonel did learn that there was another side to the story and concluded
that "it was almost wholly McCombs' fault and that McAdoo was
scarcely to blame at all." McCombs, House noted in his journal, "was
jealous, was dictatorial. . . . He was not well enough to attend to the campaign itself, and he could not sit by and allow McAdoo to carry on the
work and get a certain amount of newspaper publicity."[3] (It was on this
day, September 25, 1912, that House began dictating daily memoranda
that recorded the events of the day, a task that he followed for the next
seven years, leaving a journal of more than two thousand pages.)

While House was convinced he would have to mediate between the
two men, a more pressing problem loomed. This was the predictable conflict between the National Committee and Tammany Hall. Having
already fought against Wilson's nomination at the Baltimore convention,
Tammany's Charles Murphy threatened not to work to turn out voters for
Wilson unless the candidate actively supported his New York ticket. As
Wilson knew, there was always the danger that Murphy would be willing
to trade his support for Wilson in return for Republican willingness to let
Tammany's candidate win New York's City Hall the year following. This
seemed even more likely when Wilson refused to support the renomination of John H. Dix, Tammany's choice for governor.

In addition, a small group of New York state progressive Democratic legislators had been successful in 1911 in thwarting Murphy's efforts to elect his candidate to the U.S. Senate in favor of one of their choosing. Led by a young, somewhat arrogant Democratic state senator, Franklin D. Roosevelt—Theodore's fifth cousin, who had married TR's niece Eleanor—the group threatened to bolt from the regular Democratic organization and nominate a full slate of candidates for the November 1912 election and so rid New York of Tammany's control.[4] Murphy was determined to renominate Governor Dix and was enraged at Wilson's refusal to approve his plan.

This was the situation Wilson confronted when he went to Syracuse in September as a guest of the New York state fair committee. The afternoon he spent there was farcical. When Wilson mounted the stairs to the rostrum at the fairgrounds, Murphy, who had remained with the crowd below, climbed to the platform after Wilson had begun his speech. Later, when the Democratic politicians went to their clubhouse in Syracuse, Murphy, who was already on the scene, hid in the bushes until Wilson passed. Then, after two hundred politicians had sat down for lunch with Wilson on the porch, the fair commissioner went outside and brought Murphy in, seating him very close to Wilson. There was plenty of food, but Wilson ate only a piece of bread and left the table before Murphy had begun his meal.

If that wasn't enough, Wilson, after being taken to an auditorium where he was to address state and county politicians, discovered that the doors were locked behind him. He found himself alone with Governor Dix and an ex-prizefighter guarding the door. Wilson listened to Dix make his pitch but remained cold and silent, and when the Democratic committeemen were finally allowed to enter the room, they found Wilson sitting alone in a corner.

His brief speech fully reflected Wilson's anger. He mentioned neither Dix nor Murphy, yet clearly implied that New York Democrats must shed their connections to bossism. As a result of Wilson's snub of Dix and Murphy, progressive Democratic leaders soon urged Wilson to openly denounce the whole Tammany machine. After conferring with McAdoo on September 23, Wilson agreed "to put his foot down and put it down hard against boss control of the New York State situation."[5]

House wrote in his journal that his own "dislike of Tammany and its leaders is perhaps stronger than that of Governor Wilson." Yet, "having more political experience, I am always ready to work with the least material at hand. My idea is to have them decide upon some unobjectionable Tammany man for Governor of New York."[6]

A few days later, House met with Wilson to urge him not to make an open break with Murphy, and Wilson saw the wisdom of House's advice. Murphy, in turn, capitulated to the National Committee's demand that no one should dictate to the state nominating convention what it must do. Quietly, Murphy let it be known that Dix need not be renominated. At the convention in Syracuse, October 3, according to one reporter, "Boss Murphy . . . said nothing, gave no orders—when nominations for Governor were called reported himself 'present, not voting!'" The delegates, "freed from the despotism of the bosses," nominated Representative William Sulzer, who came out of the New York City organization, and Franklin Roosevelt's protest Democrats withdrew their counter ticket and endorsed Sulzer and the regular Democratic nominees. The newspaperman commented that the "advocates of the bossless convention had won and nominated a Tammany brave."[7]

House had saved Wilson from making a grave tactical error, while persuading Murphy to seemingly yield to Wilson. Later, according to the editor of the House papers, "When the leadership of Wilson in the party had been assured, House urged a vigorous assault upon Tammany; but a less propitious moment than the autumn of 1912 could not have been selected."[8]

By the end of October, House had succeeded in mediating the conflict between McCombs and McAdoo. According to the colonel, McAdoo was "not in evidence at all, and has almost effaced himself to secure harmony."[9]

To counter further accusations that he was a prisoner of the bosses, Wilson also had to intervene in New Jersey politics to prevent his old enemy, James Smith, from winning the Democratic state primary for U. S. senator.[10] Breaking his campaign stride on September 21, Wilson went to Hoboken and Jersey City to plead for his own candidate, William Hughes. Linking James Smith to the policies of the Republican Party, Wilson declared that Smith thereby "excludes himself from any consideration as a Democratic candidate."[11] The voters followed Wilson's advice: Hughes won the nomination by such a great margin that Smith retired from politics.

WILSON'S ATTEMPTS TO include and appeal to minorities among the voting population centered on two issues—immigration and racism. His racist statements on "new" immigrants from Italy, Hungary, and Poland, which he had written in his history of the American people, could never be fully explained away. Neither Taft nor Roosevelt brought up the immigration issue. But the president of the American Association of Foreign Language Newspapers, a man who was close to the Republican Party managers, did. His organization claimed twenty million readers and he unstintingly attacked Wilson: "No man who had an iron heart like Woodrow Wilson, and who slanders his fellowmen, because they are poor and many of them without friends when they come to this country seeking honest work and wishing to become good citizens, is fit to be President of the United States."[12]

Although Wilson wrote dozens of letters to leaders of the Polish-, Hungarian-, and Jewish-American communities defending the Democratic Party's commitment to an "open door" to immigrants, most of the time he simply repeated what he had said during the weeks preceding the Democratic convention. It is difficult to know what effect this had on the final vote, but a survey in mid-October found that some 90 percent of Italian-American priests and 78 percent of the Polish-American priests were supporting Roosevelt.[13]

Most American blacks were also justifiably suspicious of Woodrow Wilson, viewing him as a southern white supremacist. At Princeton, he had maintained the university's ban on admitting blacks. As a Democrat Wilson believed that to ensure the "Jim Crow" South remained loyal to the party he had no intention of offending white southerners.

African Americans in the South expected little or no commitment to racial justice when they read an editorial on October 1, 1912, by Josephus Daniels, publisher of the *Raleigh News and Observer* and a Wilson manager. The South is solidly Democratic, Daniels wrote, because of "the realization that the subjection of the negro politically, and the separation of the negro socially, are paramount to all other considerations in the South short of the preservation of the Republic itself. And we shall recognize no emancipation, nor shall we proclaim any deliverer that falls short of these essentials to the peace and the welfare of our part of the country."[14] The African American editor of the *New York Age* wrote that his paper "does not see how it will be possible for a single self-respecting Negro in the United States to vote for Woodrow Wilson. . . . Both by inheritance and absorption, he has most of the prejudices of the narrowest type of Southern white people against the Negro."[15]

Wilson's way of addressing the plight of black Americans was to tell an African American delegation from New Jersey at the end of July: "There is no place where it is easier to cement friendship between the two races than [in the South]. They understand each other better there than elsewhere. You may feel assured of my entire comprehension of the ambitions of the negro race and my willingness and desire to deal with that race fairly and justly."[16] This view of race relations in the South showed Wilson to be, as his biographer Arthur Link admits, "largely a Southerner on the race question." Both he and his wife were "opposed to social relations between the races."[17]

A month after the Baltimore convention, Wilson met with Oswald Garrison Villard, one of the white founders of the National Association for the Advancement of Colored People and the editor of the *New York Evening Post*. He assured Garrison that he would be the president of all the people, and in his appointments, merit, not race, would decide the issue. He said he would gladly speak out against lynching, but he didn't want the blacks to think he could actually help them in this matter.

Earlier that month he had also met the Reverend J. Milton Waldron, and after the meeting Waldron put down on paper what Wilson had told him. The result was a statement in which Wilson is said to have promised to veto any legislation passed by the Congress that would hurt the interests of black Americans. Waldron's statement was printed in *Crisis*, described by Villard to Wilson as "a monthly devoted to the colored people," of which he was one of the editors. When Villard sent him a copy of Waldron's statement, Wilson was enraged. On August 23, he wrote Villard, saying that he had been stunned by the Waldron statement and had never promised to veto any such laws, "if by accident such legislation should be passed."[18]

The farthest Wilson would go to satisfy the fears of African Americans was to declare that "they could count upon me for absolute fair dealing and for everything by which I could assist in advancing the interests of their race in the United States."[19]

ON THE ROAD, however, Wilson could avoid for the most part having to answer his critics. Searching for a way to explain away his contradictory pronouncements on immigration and race, he insisted on speaking of great principles and portrayed himself as a moralist. One observer described Wilson's approach as fulfilling "the popular idea of a philosopher who confers honor upon the sordid concerns of political life by bringing to them high thoughts and ideals. . . . On the other hand, his philosophy is not too high for human understanding, and is not withheld from the admiring multitude."[20]

As Wilson reluctantly began campaigning in early September, he had not yet mastered the tricks of oratory that later characterized his whistle-stop campaign. He eventually learned the value of repetition, vagueness, and incantation. As political scientist Charles Merriam put it, Wilson's "astounding gift of statement . . . enabled him to attract support to a general spirit rather than a specific program, to avoid unpleasant commitments in dubious cases, and to arouse intense enthusiasm for a specific cause." He was not, in Merriam's view, "primarily profound" but "was extraordinarily gifted with hypnotic power of expression."[21]

In his first swing into the West in mid-September, Wilson traveled in an old wooden railway car, the *Magnet,* which was attached to local trains. The candidate had no choice but to appear on its rear platform to address the folks who showed up to listen to him. Through Iowa and South Dakota, he had not yet gained control of his speaking voice or overcome his seemingly academic style. But when he reached Minneapolis, he was determined to reach out to the masses. In a speech to eight thousand people there, he dropped his philosophical tone by telling them that the best answer to Roosevelt's policy for regulating trusts was "Rats."[22]

By contrast, he was especially courteous toward the incumbent president. In Minneapolis, a bastion of anti-Taft voters, he said: "I do not believe that any man in the United States who knows his facts can question the patriotism or the integrity of the man who now presides at the executive office in Washington."[23]

Wilson began warming to his audiences, and the crowds grew as he continued on through Michigan and Ohio. In Columbus, he urged rapt listeners to take up the torch and run a "race of freedom," a race that would finish only when "the torch is lifted high upon those uplands where no light is needed, but where shines the brilliancy of the justice of God."[24]

THE FIRST PHASE of Wilson's campaign came to a climax in Boston at the end of September, when Boston Brahmins joined with the Democratic Irish from South Boston to give him an overwhelming reception. He had chosen a political march through New England in order to demonstrate to the bastion of American conservatism that he was indeed the chief conservative candidate. He would explain that his economic proposals would strengthen legitimate businesses and that his modest calls for political reform would not threaten the bedrock structure of American political institutions.

Before arriving in Boston, however, he spoke at Springfield and Barre, and then to the factory workers of Fall River, at that time the largest cotton-spinning city in the world. Wilson had to demonstrate his concern for the needs of the working class: "The right to organize on the part of labor is not recognized by the laws of the United States," he said. "I believe we ought to hold a brief for the legal right of labor to organize."[25]

At Tremont Temple in downtown Boston Wilson assured the audience, "We are not fighting the trusts, we are trying to put them upon an equality with everybody else." On this occasion, however, Wilson made an important change from his earlier political agenda. Until Boston, Wilson had mocked Roosevelt's proposed industrial commission to regulate trusts and had criticized what Wilson called his "government by experts." Responding to Brandeis's proposal that a federal trade commission be set up to regulate competition, Wilson now put forward his own suggestion for an industrial commission to regulate business enterprise.[26]

Wilson returned to New York via Bridgeport, Connecticut. The crowds had swelled, and he reacted to their support by throwing campaign buttons from the rear platform of the train to the bystanders waiting to greet him. Adopting a somewhat similar program to Roosevelt's for regulating trusts had apparently not damaged him with the voters. He continued to send forth his message that free competition was the way to curb the excesses of the monopolies. At last, Wilson had made contact with those who turned out to see and hear him. He might have preferred to portray himself as a moralist, but now his eloquence was in the service of economic matters. He would avoid the more dangerous political and social questions that his principal opponent so easily embraced.

FIFTEEN

The Authentic Conservative
and the Red Prophet

WITH TAFT SPURNING a rough contest with Roosevelt and Wilson, TR soon labeled him "a dead cock in the pit."[1] Taft was convinced that he had already accomplished the most important task—defeating Roosevelt in Chicago. He was more cheerful than ever, now that he had decided not to embark on a nationwide speaking tour that would surely exhaust him. Nonetheless, he was determined to define himself in opposition to Roosevelt, Wilson, and certainly Debs, viewing all three as radicals while knowing that he had "no part to play but that of a conservative, and that I am going to play."[2] The occasion he chose to articulate this position came on August 1 at the official notification ceremony in Washington confirming his nomination as the standard-bearer of the Republican Party. This was one of only two major speeches he was to give in the months from August to election day in November.

Five hundred guests crammed into the East Room of the White House while the Marine band played. Mrs. Taft sat with a small group on a raised platform to hear her husband offer a defense of his policies. Elihu Root, in his role as permanent chair of the convention, introduced Taft after first assuring the audience that Taft's right to the nomination was "as clear and unimpeachable as the title of any candidate of any party since political conventions began."[3]

Taft may have felt uncomfortable with Root's assertion of rectitude, but he was determined to define himself as the party's presidential candidate in exhausting detail. He clearly pleased his audience by reciting the conservative creed of individualism coupled with the dangers of socialism: "[T]he fruits of energy, courage, enterprise, attention to duty, hard work, thrift, providence, restraints of appetite and passion will continue to have their reward under the present system, . . . and laziness, lack of attention, lack of industry, the yielding to appetite and passion, carelessness, dishonesty, and disloyalty will ultimately find their own punishment in the world here."

Both Roosevelt and Wilson, though not officially Socialists, in calling for change invited a "condition in which the rich are to be made reasonably poor and the poor reasonably rich by law," said Taft. He went on to declare that "the equal opportunity which those seek who proclaim the coming of so-called social justice involves a forced division of property, and that means socialism."

But Taft did not repudiate the reformist strains in his own party, citing the Interstate Commerce Act, the Sherman Anti-Trust Act, the Pure Food and Drug Act, the Mann Act against interstate transportation of women for immoral purposes, and other laws that furthered "equality of opportunity in respect to the weaker classes in their dealings with the stronger and more powerful." The trouble with his opponents was that they chased phantoms. The only safe route to prosperity for all was to be found in the policies of the Republican Party.[4]

Four hundred guests stayed for lunch, and as soon as possible the president was off to Massachusetts for a day of golf before making a brief visit to the Centennial at Columbus, Ohio. After another trip to Washington, and a conference with the chairman of the Republican National Committee, Charles Hillis, on a yacht sailing from New York to New London, it wasn't until September that Taft happily ensconced himself in Beverly for golf on the Myopia course and motoring around the North Shore. (According to TR, Beverly was "principally noted for its baked beans and rheumatism."[5])

Throughout September, Taft would occasionally have to go to Washington, where he continued to fight for a stronger executive role in the making of the federal budget, but otherwise he played golf, often with his amiable son Charlie, and avoided public appearances whenever he could. From Washington, Hillis kept him informed of the progress of the campaign. Without a live candidate to preach the gospel of Republican virtue to the voters, Hillis created a broad advertising campaign in the press, on billboards, and on streetcars.[6] The Republican chairman constantly encouraged him to believe all was going well, with most of the western states along with the solidly Republican eastern states expected to bring success to the party.

At the end of September, Taft temporarily abandoned his mood of resigned serenity and mercilessly attacked Roosevelt and the Democrats at a gathering of Republican clubs from Beverly's Essex County. About 2,500 persons listened to the president as he spoke facing the veranda of the cottage where Mrs. Taft, his young son Robert A. Taft, and a number of other guests sat. Although Taft was applauded politely when he attacked the Democrats, loud applause came when he castigated the third party, and while he did not mention Roosevelt by name, the happy Republicans knew whom he meant. Taft said:

> A third party has split off from the Republican Party, not for any one principle, or indeed on any principle at all, but merely to gratify personal ambition and vengeance, and in the gratification of that personal ambition and vengeance, every new fad and theory, some of them good, some of them utterly preposterous and impractical, some of them as Socialistic as anything that has been proposed in the countries of Europe . . . have been crowded into a platform in order to tempt the votes of enthusiastic supporters of each of these proposed reforms. . . . The new party is not united on any cohesive principles, and is only kept together by the remarkable personality of its leader. Were he to die the party would go to pieces [due to the] crazy-quilt character of the platform.

"A National Government," he warned, "cannot create good times. It cannot make the rain to fall, the sun to shine, or the crops to grow, but it can, by pursuing a meddlesome policy, attempting to change economic conditions, and frightening the investment of capital, prevent a prosperity and a revival of business which otherwise might have taken place." Taft had become an apostle of the status quo, urging the "negative virtue"

of reelecting a Republican Party that promised to take "no step to interfere with the coming of prosperity and the comfort of the people."[7]

With little or no hope of winning, Taft had permitted himself to speak
the naked truth to his constituency: that the Republican Party that had
once elected Theodore Roosevelt, and which he had served so ably and
so loyally, was no longer the party of activist government.

Two days later, before three hundred cheering Republicans at the Beverly Republican Club, Taft hardened his stance against any Republican
who had left the GOP to join the Progressives. Should such activists
want to return to the fold, Taft declared, they would have to come back
on their knees. "In the not distant future," he said in a talk made on the
spur of the moment, "these gentlemen who have deserted us in the hope
of enjoying office on the one hand or a millennium on the other, will find
themselves without office, millennium, or party." And "when they come
back to the Republican Party, as they will come back, let them come back
as Republicans, but show repentance."[8]

DEBS NEVER ABANDONED the key objectives that he had held for more
than a decade—industrial unionism and revolutionary politics. He knew
that he was caught between the anarcho-syndicalist left wing of the party,
symbolized by Big Bill Haywood, and the right-wing reformers who
stressed machine politics. His goal was socialism, and in the 1912 campaign he believed that those who would vote for TR's Progressive Party or
for Wilson—whose Democratic Party had undergone a late conversion
to reform—were voters starting to head down the road to embracing
socialism.[9]

In mid-June when Debs opened his campaign in Riverside Park,
Chicago, he warned his audience of 100,000 or more that "never for a
moment [mistake] reform for revolution and never [lose] sight of the ultimate goal," which he defined as "revolutionary industrial unionism" that
would allow workers to develop their abilities and their knowledge, which
in turn would prepare them "for mastery and control of industry."[10]

Debs never believed that his party would be victorious in 1912.
Rather, he saw his task as preparing the way to a utopian future in which
the promises of the founders of the nation, the abolitionists, the Pop-

ulists, all those dissenters who were at the very core of American exceptionalism, would be realized.[11] Debs saw *his* Socialists as squarely within the American tradition.

Although true revolution might be a long way away, Debs believed that when the people saw that the piecemeal reforms that the Progressives and the Democrats offered were grossly insufficient, voters would flock to the Socialist Party. As he wrote in an article for a Socialist review in August, "All the votes of the people would do us no good if our party ceased to be a revolutionary party, or came to be only incidentally so, while yielding more and more to the pressure to modify the principles and program of the party" simply for the sake of "swelling the vote and hastening the days of its expected triumph."[12]

AFTER WILSON WAS NOMINATED, Debs gave him no quarter: "Wilson is entering this campaign as a 'progressive,' a great friend of the workers. He has as rotten a labor record as any man possibly could have." Even before Roosevelt returned to Chicago for the Bull Moose convention, Debs labeled him a "servile functionary to the trusts" and dismissed "his empty promises as [those of] a ranting demagogue and a vote-seeking politician."[13]

Nonetheless, Debs feared Roosevelt's candidacy, which he knew would take votes away from him. In an interview with the *New York World,* Debs asserted that the Progressive Party's platform, while aiming at "some of the flagrant evils and abuses of capitalism," in its essence "supports and strengthens the existing system."[14]

While the conservative Socialist congressman Victor Berger could speak of Socialists accepting reforms and supporting the "peaceful, orderly transformation of society,"[15] Debs called on workers "to destroy all despotisms, topple over all thrones, seize all scepters of authority . . . tear up privilege by the roots, and consecrate the earth and all its fullness to the joy and service of all humanity." Their mission was "not only to destroy capitalist despotism but to establish industrial and social democracy."[16]

THE CAMPAIGN DEBS WAGED was backbreaking, yet he was invigorated by the cheering crowds. He started off by going north, to Fergus

Falls, Minnesota, then west, to Montana, Washington, and California, where the bitter miners rallied to his cry, then through the Southwest to Texas and Oklahoma, which, along with Nevada, would give him 16.61 percent of their votes, a larger proportion than he received anywhere else in the country. After barnstorming through Kansas and Kentucky, he rested in Terre Haute, then went east via Iowa and Wisconsin, then through Indiana and Ohio to Philadelphia, where eighteen thousand people crammed into Convention Hall. On September 29, he ended the first phase of his tour at Madison Square Garden in New York, where people paid from twenty-five cents to a dollar to hear him speak and raised an estimated $10,000 for the campaign.

His speaking manner was more inspired than ever. His purity of character came through, as did his evangelical devotion to principles, coupled with what historian Arthur Schlesinger Jr. described as his "sweetness of temper, his generosity and kindliness, his sensitivity to pain and suffering, his perfect sincerity, his warm, sad smile and his candid grey eyes." He was truly "irresistible."[17]

A member of Bill Haywood's IWW saw Debs at one of his campaign stops and recorded her impressions:

> Debs paced back and forth on the platform, like a lion ready to spring, then leaned far over the edge, his gaunt tall frame bending like a reed, his long bony finger pointing—his favorite gesture. . . . Debs' voice was strong and clear and could be heard in the largest hall and outside places. He spoke with imagery and poetry of expression, drew word pictures of the lives of the workers, of child labor, of men in prison, or at war. He was full of loving kindness to those who are heavily laden, and had a searing contempt for "gory-beaked vultures" who fatten on their exploitation.[18]

Neither Roosevelt nor Wilson would appear on a platform to debate with him. TR did not want to draw voters' attention to the fact that many of Debs's proposals resembled his own. Wilson said that since none of the "minor parties" was going to win, he had to confine himself to dealing with the "serious" contenders.

·   ·   ·

The climax of Debs's first tour was the Madison Square Garden rally. The *New York Times* summed up the great occasion with the headline—"Socialists Cheer Debs 29 Minutes." Fifteen thousand men and women gathered inside, and three thousand more were outside jammed against police lines. The predominant color was red: red handkerchiefs, red hats, red cloths, red aprons, and red flags waving in unison. The audience had waited for Debs for two hours while other candidates—Emil Seidel for the vice presidency and Charles Russell for the governorship—tried to warm up the crowd. Debs's appearance on stage brought the proceedings to a halt for half an hour. In between frequent outbursts of "La Marseillaise" and the "International," Debs threatened the capitalist class with his predictions that thirty thousand shirtwaist workers would soon strike in New York, and that if the Lawrence strike leaders were convicted of murder, there would be an uprising of the whole working class.

Each of his opponents came in for a scalding. He called Taft "a former more or less celebrated jurist who was a specialist when it came to issuing injunctions to keep working men in subjugation." Wilson was "a kid glove on the paw of the Tammany tiger." As for Roosevelt, "He is today the champion of the oppressed and the downtrodden of the Nation. . . . Just think of it. Theodore Roosevelt, who stands on a platform that four years ago he denounced as anarchist."[19]

The gentle Debs became, in Madison Square Garden, the red revolutionary who could call for uprisings by the working class while holding fast to the democratic tradition of consent.

SIXTEEN

"To Kill a Bull Moose"

VEN THOUGH WILSON knew that he hadn't "a Bull Moose's strength, as Roosevelt seems to have,"[1] he actually gained in force as the campaign pushed into its second phase. In early October he spoke before a boisterous crowd of some twenty-five thousand people in Indianapolis, where he used the phrase "the New Freedom," which became the emblematic description of his domestic program. "I tell you frankly," he said to his listeners in the baseball park, "there will be no greater burden in our generation than to organize the forces of liberty . . . in order to make a conquest of the new freedom for America."[2]

After campaigning in a dozen towns in Indiana, Wilson reached Gary to speak to an audience of steel workers. There he accused the steel monopolies of allying themselves with the Progressive Party because its leader favored trusts. When Roosevelt heard of the speech, he demanded that Wilson take back his accusation that the trusts were behind his campaign. Later in his midwestern swing, Wilson explained away his position by saying that he had not meant that TR had received financial backing from U.S. Steel, but he did mean that "the kind of control which [Roosevelt] proposes is the kind of control that the United States Steel Corporation wants."[3] Even the *New York Times*, which strongly favored Wilson, admonished him for going too far and advised unless he had proof of his charges, "it is probably better not to say these things."[4]

After campaigning in Chicago, Wilson then proceeded to Nebraska to meet with William Jennings Bryan. On the overnight trip to Omaha, Wilson's freight car slammed into his Pullman sleeper, tearing the guardrail off and smashing the observation platform. Miraculously, Wilson was unhurt and was able to make six speeches in seven hours in Omaha. While crowds there were wildly enthusiastic, their reception was nothing compared to what awaited him when he met Bryan in Lincoln.

Nine brass bands, at least a dozen marching clubs, and, of course, thousands of Democrats greeted Wilson as he stepped from his car into the arms of Bryan, their first meeting since the convention. With bands playing, factory whistles blowing, and car horns honking, they rode together to a hotel where Wilson addressed the Democratic state committee. "We are free to serve the people of the United States," Wilson said, "and in my opinion it was Mr. Bryan who set us free." To which Bryan responded: "Let me ask you to do twice as much for Wilson as you ever did for Bryan. For I have as much at stake in this fight as he has, and you have as much as I have."[5]

Wilson was utterly exhausted and was able to take the next day, Sunday, to attend church and rest.

The time Wilson and Bryan spent together was marked by genuine expressions of friendship. Coming out of an auditorium, Wilson had lost his hat. Bryan offered him his, saying, "I suppose you cannot find yours because it is in the ring." Wilson happily donned Bryan's "immense sombrero."[6]

AFTER THE BRYAN INTERLUDE, the candidate was off to Colorado, where he spoke in Denver, now linking his theme of the New Freedom to the need to free the nation from the grip of monopolistic trusts: "This is a second struggle for emancipation. . . . If America is not to have free enterprise, then she can have freedom of no sort whatever."[7] He felt it was far better to reach the people by stressing his crusade for economic equality of opportunity, which would make possible the preservation of political liberty, than to delve into the arcane issues of the high tariff and the essential meaning of monopoly.[8]

In Kansas City, Wilson's reception was somewhat muted; after all, this was the stronghold of Champ Clark. Worse yet, Wilson's voice was almost wholly gone, and many in the audience left early rather than try to understand his all-but-inaudible remarks. Things were marginally better in St. Louis, but in Chicago, Wilson found 100,000 people waiting for him in a cold rain. Ticker tape flowed from the windows overhead, businesses were closed or suspended, and street car traffic was blocked. But once again, Wilson's speaking voice was weak. Despite his heroic efforts, there was little left of his voice when he reached Cleveland, and he was grateful to return to Princeton on October 12. He had spoken thirty times in seven states, and he was both tired and proud that he had been able to campaign with such vigor.

As he wrote to Mrs. Peck the day after his first night back home, "It is wonderful how tough I have turned out to be, and how much I can stand—for the physical strain of what I went through this time is all but overwhelming; and yet I lost nothing but my voice—and not all of that."[9]

EVEN ROOSEVELT was growing hoarse as he resumed campaigning in the Midwest in the early weeks of October. In Michigan he was dogged by a squad of Democratic "Truth Tellers." In Marquette, when a heckler took issue with his praise for Governor Hiram Johnson's achievements in California and his own support for the minimum wage for women, his young cousin Philip Roosevelt recalled that as soon as Roosevelt discovered that the man was a local Republican, "He tore the hide off the man's words."[10]

Roosevelt knew he could not continue giving twenty speeches a day until November, but otherwise he was beginning to believe that he might be able to beat Wilson after all. By the time he reached Chicago on Sunday, October 13, he had to take the day off to rest. But he insisted on going on to Milwaukee the next day, where he was scheduled to deliver another address, even though his voice was barely above a whisper. Dr. Scurry Terrell, the throat specialist who was traveling with him on the campaign, warned TR that he would not be able to continue unless he stopped speaking. Of course TR insisted that he fulfill his engagement in Milwaukee; even if he could not speak, at least the audience would witness his good intentions.[11] But in Milwaukee a gunman was waiting to kill him.

After leaving Racine in the afternoon for Milwaukee, on the afternoon of October 14, Roosevelt decided to dine in the railroad car and then go directly to the auditorium where he was to deliver the speech. On arrival, however, a large civic committee begged Roosevelt to go to the Gilpatrick Hotel for dinner. Dr. Terrell objected, as he wanted TR to save his strength for the big event. Roosevelt asked the chairman of the committee whether it would be too great a disappointment if he did not go to the hotel. Told that it would be, Roosevelt surrendered to the pleas of the committee, saying, "I want to be a good Indian." Dr. Terrell, worried about the strain on Roosevelt if he had to push through the crowd, insisted that he would give his consent only if there were extra police protection. With that assurance, TR said he would go.

Indeed, there was ample police protection as Roosevelt rode a mile or so through streets lined with well-wishers who gave him a rousing reception. Because of the police fewer people were on the sidewalk in front of the hotel and in the corridors than might have been expected. After he entered the hotel, Roosevelt went to his room for a short nap, later going down to the dining room and back to his suite before walking to the automobile that was waiting at the door of the hotel.

Roosevelt got into the car, followed by Elbert Martin, one of his secretaries. The crowd on the street began to stir. TR, wearing a big brown army overcoat, sat down for the ride to the auditorium. But hearing the people break into a cheer, he stood up, faced the rear of the car, and raised his right hand to salute them. A stocky man who had been standing at the edge of the sidewalk only a few feet from Roosevelt pushed his way forward. TR looked at him and smiled. The man then pulled out a Colt revolver and fired one shot at the candidate.

Martin, a former New Hampshire farm boy, coal stoker, and football player, sprang directly over the car and caught the would-be assassin, wrapped his right arm around his neck, and threw him to the pavement. Roosevelt sank back in his seat, hardly aware that a bullet had struck him. Harry Cochems, the local Bull Moose leader, threw his arm around TR and asked him if he were hurt. Roosevelt called to Martin, saying, "Don't hurt him, bring him to me."

Martin pulled the man up, handed the revolver to Roosevelt, and then twisted the man's head around so that TR could see him. "Here he is," said Martin, "look at him, Colonel." "Why did you do it?" Roosevelt asked. "What was your reason?" And without waiting for an answer TR told Martin to hand him over to the authorities. The police meantime were struggling to keep back the mob, which was now shouting, "Lynch him! Kill him!" But Roosevelt motioned the people to fall back. "Stop, stop!" he cried. "Stand back. Don't hurt him!" Martin then pulled the gunman back into the hotel and handed him over to the police.

It was later learned that the man who shot Roosevelt was John Schrank of New York City, that he had been following Roosevelt on the campaign trail, and was obsessed with the fact that TR was seeking a third term. He claimed he had had a dream of McKinley, and that the martyred president had told him that Roosevelt had to be slain. (Schrank was later confined to an insane asylum and died in 1940, the very year that Franklin Roosevelt sought and won a third term.)

At first Roosevelt was not sure he had been wounded, but when one of his secretaries pointed to a hole in his overcoat, Roosevelt unbuttoned the coat and put his hand beneath it. When he withdrew it, his fingers were coated with blood. "It looks as though I have been hit," he said, "but I don't think it is anything serious."

Dr. Terrell, who had pushed his way through the crowd, insisted that Roosevelt go directly to a hospital. TR countermanded the order and said they should drive to the auditorium. "You get me to the speech. It may be the last one I shall ever deliver, but I am going to deliver this one."

In the dressing room at the auditorium, Dr. Terrell and two other doctors who were in the audience made a quick examination and determined that the bullet, slowed by the fifty-page speech that had been in Roosevelt's right breast pocket, had punctured his flesh just below the nipple. The wound was bleeding slightly, making a stain about the size of a man's fist on TR's shirt. All three doctors urged Roosevelt to go to a hospital because they could not gauge the full extent of his injury. "I will deliver this speech or die, one or the other," Roosevelt replied. Under these circumstances, the doctors bandaged him up with a handkerchief and Roosevelt walked on stage.

Harry Cochems, who was presiding at the meeting, stepped forward. "In presenting Colonel Roosevelt . . . you should know that . . . as we were leaving the hotel a few minutes ago a dastardly hand raised a revolver and fired a shot at him, and the Colonel speaks as a soldier with a bullet in his breast—where we don't know."

There were cries of "Oh, Oh," as Roosevelt stepped forward, and taking his notes out of his vest pocket, he turned to those near him and showed them the bloody shirt. This brought sympathetic cheers. "Friends," he began, "I shall have to ask you to be as quiet as possible. I do not know whether you fully understand that I have just been shot. But it takes more than that to kill a Bull Moose." He explained that the manuscript of what was to be a long speech had probably saved his life. "The bullet is in me now, so that I cannot make a very long speech. But I will do my best."

He nonetheless talked for almost an hour. He called his would-be assassin a "coward," but added that "it is a very natural thing that weak and vicious minds should be inflamed to acts of violence by the kind of foul mendacity and abuse that have been heaped upon me for the last three months."

It was not "insane ambition" that had made him run for president again. Instead, he was running "to stand for the sacred rights of childhood and womanhood . . . to see that manhood is not crushed out of the men who toil by excessive hours of labor, by underpayment, by injustice and oppression." Above all, he defended the right of labor to organize but urged the laborers to denounce crime and violence, and to repudiate all forms of discrimination.

His speech at an end, Roosevelt finally allowed his doctors to rush him to the Milwaukee Hospital for further inspection. The operating room had been readied to receive him, and six of the leading surgeons of the city were waiting for his arrival. The examination revealed a deep bullet wound in the chest wall, but the doctors needed to get an X-ray machine to assess further damage. While waiting for the machine, Roosevelt sat up and talked politics with the physicians. He joked to one physician, "I do not want to fall into the hands of too many doctors and have the same experience that McKinley and Garfield had."[12] (Both died of their gunshot wounds.)

After the X-ray, which showed the bullet had fractured and lodged along the fifth rib, less than an inch from his heart, the doctors insisted that he be sent to Chicago to enter a hospital there for his recovery. At 12:45 A.M. Roosevelt boarded the train for Chicago, but even then he insisted that he would simply spend the night in the railroad car and after a few hours in Chicago would go on to Indianapolis to fulfill a speaking engagement the following night.[13] The doctors, however, overcame his objections and brought him to Chicago's Mercy Hospital. There, Roosevelt was somewhat more docile. He allowed the attending physicians to inject him with a tetanus antitoxin, and a decision was made not to try to remove the bullet unless infection set in. Dr. John Murphy, chief of the surgeons, suggested, "You were elected last night. It was the turn of the tide in your favor."[14]

Roosevelt quickly recovered, and as the recipient of so much favorable publicity as a result of the attack and his spirited reaction to it, he began to believe that victory in the election would at last be his. Oddsmakers, who had rated Roosevelt's chance of winning at four to one before the attempted assassination, soon improved his chances to almost two to one.[15]

EDITH ROOSEVELT was at a theater in New York when she was notified about what had happened. Though stunned by the news, she stayed for the rest of the play, after learning that Theodore had been "scratched but had kept on with the speech." She avoided reporters who were waiting outside the theater by leaving through a side door and took a car to the headquarters of the Progressive Party to obtain further news. She remained there until midnight, and then went to TR's cousin Laura Roosevelt's for a few hours' sleep. On Tuesday morning, after she found out that her husband was safely in a hospital room in Chicago, she boarded the 4 P.M. train to Chicago, accompanied by her son Ted, her daughter Ethel, and Dr. Alexander Lambert.[16]

Roosevelt had telegraphed his wife before he left Milwaukee that the wound was superficial and that she should not come out: "I am not nearly as hurt as I have been again and again with a fall from my horse," he said, adding that he would go on with his campaign engagements. This only caused Edith to say, "That's just the sort of thing that was said when Mr.

McKinley was shot."[17] She knew she had to join her husband because no one else could persuade him to obey doctor's orders.

On Wednesday morning she arrived in Chicago, where her stepdaughter Alice was waiting. Once she saw Theodore, she was able to write to her sister-in-law Anna Roosevelt Cowles (Bamie), that "Theodore looks splendidly." In fact, when Edith arrived she found he was having trouble breathing because of the broken rib, which also caused a sharp pain in his side. The doctors insisted that he must have "absolute quiet; must cease from talking; and must see no one until we give permission."[18]

For the next five nights, Edith slept in a furnished room next to Theodore's, spending much of that time reading cables from all over the country and the world. As one reporter wrote of Mrs. Roosevelt's role in the hospital: "Up to her advent [TR] was throwing bombshells into his doctors. . . . The moment she arrived a hush fell on TR. . . . he became as meek as Moses. Now and then the Colonel would send out secretly for somebody he knew and wanted to talk to, but every time the vigilant Mrs. Roosevelt would swoop down on the emissary. . . . No such tyrannical sway has ever been seen in the history of American politics."[19]

To his supporters, Roosevelt sent a melodramatic message through former Senator Albert Beveridge: "It matters little to me, but it matters all about the cause we fight for. If one soldier who happens to carry the flag is stricken another will take it from his hands and carry on. . . . Tell the people not to worry about me, for if I go down another will take my place."[20]

Virtually all the newspapers, even those vehemently opposed to Roosevelt, praised him for his courage and his "pluck." In the lead editorial in *Collier's*, Norman Hapgood wrote that people should not cast their votes for Roosevelt simply because a would-be assassin had shot him, but nonetheless "no amount of argument, no amount of reflection concentrated in many months, could have influenced as many Americans as were stirred by the shot of a madman."[21]

Taft, deeply shaken, learned of the attempted assassination at the Hotel Astor in New York where an official dinner was being given for the president, members of his cabinet, and the naval officers of the Atlantic fleet. In a message to Roosevelt, Taft recorded his shock "to hear of the outrageous and deplorable assault made on you, and I earnestly hope and pray that your recovery may be speedy and without suffering." Declaring that he would cease any campaigning until TR recovered, Taft also issued a personal statement to the press: "I cannot withhold an expression of horror at the act of the maniac who attempted to assassinate Colonel Roosevelt."[22]

Wilson, too, sent a message of sympathy to the wounded ex-president, but he was initially uncertain as to whether he should halt campaigning while Roosevelt recuperated. Colonel House telephoned Wilson at Princeton and urged him "to cancel all engagements until Roosevelt was able to get out again." The Democratic campaign committee opposed House's advice, but as House wrote in his diary, "My thought was that if he continued to speak after TR had been shot, it would create sympathy for TR and would do Wilson infinite harm. The generous, the chivalrous, and the wise thing to do, so it seems to me, is to discontinue speaking until his antagonist is also able to speak."[23] Wilson, though insisting on making a few speeches that he was already committed to deliver, generally, if reluctantly, took House's advice. Debs, too, sent his wishes to TR for a speedy recovery and curtailed his speech making.

Roosevelt, however, was soon on the mend and got back to New York a week after the shooting, determined to make his big speech on October 30 at Madison Square Garden. As his special train bore him east, crowds lined the tracks, silent, and often bareheaded in reverence.

THE CAMPAIGN RESUMED. From Beverly, Taft issued a statement on October 19, replying to Wilson's charge that Taft's party was one of drift. Lincoln, Taft recalled, was also accused of letting the nation drift: "It drifted—yes—with Lincoln at the helm, from the reefs of secession and slavery into the placid waters of union and liberty."[24]

At the end of his vacation, Taft traveled a bit—to Maine and to Boston, and to Washington. His train stopped off in New York and three times in Pennsylvania, where he repeated his litany that he had been administering the existing laws in order to regulate the trusts, and that under his stewardship the nation was growing ever more prosperous. At the very end of October, Taft's vice president, James ("Sunny Jim") Sherman, died in Utica, New York, after an illness that had gone on for most of the summer. Although Taft quickly named Nicholas Murray Butler, the president of Columbia University, as his new running mate, Sherman's death seemed a further ill omen for his faltering campaign.[25]

In the Midwest Debs was making his final appeal to the voters, evoking Ralph Waldo Emerson, who had said that when God turns a thinker loose on the world, the earth trembles. Once again, Debs put himself squarely in the middle of the American tradition and predicted—rightly as it turned out—that the size of the Socialist vote would be "a surprise to the country."[26]

On October 30, the day after Sherman's death, Louis Seibold of the *New York World* met with Taft in the White House for an interview on the president's relationship with Roosevelt. Seibold believed that the publicity resulting from the interview might help Taft to at least best Roosevelt in the four-way race for the presidency. The interview went well, but later that day Seibold learned that Taft wanted to make some changes in the statements he had given. Seibold therefore agreed to accompany Taft on a train from Washington to New York and to go over Taft's suggested revisions; Taft would then proceed to Utica for Sherman's funeral.

Space was being saved in the *World*'s Saturday edition for the interview; the election would take place the following Tuesday, November 5. Taft went into his stateroom to make changes in the interview. After a good hour, the president came out and told Seibold that he had had second thoughts about some of what he had said and wanted to get advice about the advisability of publishing the text from leaders of the party after arriving in New York. But that would be too late to make the Saturday edition, Seibold told him. At this, Taft revealed his tortured feelings for TR. "But Roosevelt was my closest friend," he said, using the same words he had used when speaking to Seibold after attacking Roosevelt in Boston earlier that year. That time Taft had been unable to contain his tears.[27]

Although Taft eventually ordered all copies of the interview to be destroyed, one copy was filed with his private papers. Taft had said nothing insulting about Roosevelt to Seibold, but he did describe TR's way of thinking:

> Mr. Roosevelt is not a logician, and he never argues. His power of concentrated statement is that of a genius. His power of making a

statement in such phrases as to give them currency is equal to that of any man I know. He never makes a sustained argument that appeals to you. He is not looking for an argument. Each blow he strikes is a hard one, because it calls attention to some defect in his enemy's armor, or some great claim to right on his part, but he does not establish a conclusion by one step and then another and another. He has not either patience or power to do that. He once said to me, "When I fight I like to get close up to a man." Well, by that he meant—he could not mean otherwise—that he fought not only the man's argument but the man himself.[28]

Taft had depicted TR accurately, but it was a portrait seen through the eyes of a jurist, which was all Taft ever wanted to be.

FOR ROOSEVELT the Madison Square Garden speech was an apotheosis. As it was the first time he had appeared before a large audience since the shooting, Roosevelt had to show that he was well again. And except for his inability to lift his right arm in his characteristic, fist-pounding gesture, he was back in form. After he was introduced, the sixteen thousand people who crowded the Garden would not let Roosevelt speak for forty-five minutes. Their cheering went on and on, even as TR signaled for them to stop. Those in the audience were aware of his weakness—the bullet was still lodged in his ribs—and they cheered as though their very hysteria would give him strength.

His speech was vigorous but thoughtful, less aggressive than reflective. On this occasion, he rarely referred to himself in the first-person singular; instead, he almost always used the words "we Progressives" or just plain "we." He sounded the themes not only of his campaign but also of his past presidency: it was time to prevent the division of America between the haves and the have-nots and therefore to insist on the rights and duties of all men and women. He referred to Wilsonian appeals for formulas of states' rights as "the dead dogma of a vanished past" and denied that the history of liberty was the history of the limitation of governmental power.

"It is idle to ask us not to exercise the power of government when only by the power of government can we curb the greed that sits in high places," he declared. Once again he repeated his litany: "In the long fight for righteousness the watchword of all of us is spend and be spent. It is of little matter whether any one man fails or succeeds; but the cause shall not fail, for it is the cause of mankind."[29]

The next day Wilson spoke to Democrats from the same rostrum. Determined to outdo Roosevelt's supporters, the Democrats gave Wilson an ovation that lasted more than an hour. The wild cheering so stirred Wilson that he discarded his prepared speech. His remarks were therefore rambling as he tried to summarize the issues of the campaign. He accused the Republicans of being poor servants of the people and, in a reference to the Progressives and Roosevelt, declared that they were adventurers who proposed to change "all the centers of energy and organization in the Government of the United States . . . to the discretionary action of the executive."[30] For Wilson the presidential campaign was over. By his presence, more than his words, he had sought to reassure his supporters that he would win.

AND WIN WILSON DID, receiving 6,293,454 votes. Roosevelt came in second, with 4,119,538 votes, then Taft with 3,484,980. Debs came in last, as expected, with 901,873 votes—more than double his total in 1908. At 6 percent, this was the largest share of the popular vote won by a Socialist candidate for president before or since.

What did it all mean? Although there was no breakdown of the vote by class interest, the tallies reveal a strong commitment by the voters to reform, both progressive and radical. Wilson had embraced reform even while he was reluctant to provide much in the way of specific programs. Yet the South, and even the border states, came through for a man who was seen by conservative southerners as one of them. Taft held on to the regular Republican vote thanks to the powerful Republican political machine. In a two-man race against Taft, Wilson almost surely would have won.

The vote totals for Roosevelt and Taft together indicate a Republican victory over Wilson had TR received the Republican nomination in Chicago. Even those of the party faithful who would have preferred Taft would have had nowhere to go. The party organization would have backed TR. And Roosevelt himself would have tacked to the center. Nonetheless, Roosevelt would not have shed the bulk of his progressive credentials. After his radical stance at Osawatomie in August 1910, there could be no wholesale turning back.

Wilson carried forty states and 435 electoral votes, leaving TR with six states and 88 electoral votes, and poor Taft with only two states—Vermont and Utah. But Wilson's sweeping victory allowed the Democrats to take control of the Senate for the first time in twenty years, with a majority of fifty-one seats (ten more than in the previous Congress), leaving the Republicans with forty-four seats, and the Progressives with one. Nonetheless, despite the overwhelming electoral vote for Wilson and the decisive Democratic majority in the Senate, Republican regulars and the Progressives had together garnered 50.5 percent of the popular vote, Wilson less than 42 percent. In 1912, 100,000 fewer people had voted for Wilson than had voted for Bryan in 1908.[31]

The problem for the Progressive Party was that the vote was a personal one for Roosevelt (as to a large degree the Socialist vote was a personal endorsement of Debs). Progressive state and congressional candidates ran well behind TR, and indeed in many cases behind both the Democratic and Republican contenders. As Roosevelt said later, with scarcely any Progressives in Congress, there were few "loaves and fishes" to hold the party together.[32]

As for Debs, the magnitude of his vote seemed to promise ever greater rewards for the Socialist Party in the future. But strains within the party surfaced soon after the election. Although the Socialist vote in the 1920 presidential election would rival that of 1912, the vote was almost wholly a show of solidarity with Debs. Without him as the candidate in the 1916 election, the party's total was about 300,000 votes less than it received four years earlier. The 1912 election thus marked the apogee of the Socialist movement in America.

TR came to believe that his greatest misfortune—as president and in 1912—was in not having had a war that called for heroic leadership. He looked back to Lincoln and understood that Lincoln's greatness rested upon his confronting and resolving a great national crisis like the Civil War. As a wartime leader he could have roused the people to self-sacrifice, to renounce the materialism he so hated, and to rise above the class divisions that had been growing so apparent in the early years of the twentieth century.[33]

Theodore Roosevelt's 1912 campaign anticipated the industrial and social service state that came into being under another President Roosevelt later in the century, along with its use of executive power on behalf of its citizens.[34] To this day, TR's New Nationalism remains one of the most radical covenants for idealistic reform ever offered in American history.

PART FOUR

The Consequences of Victory

SEVENTEEN

The Ironies of Fate

I T WOULD BE an irony of fate if my administration had to deal chiefly with foreign affairs, for all my preparation has been in domestic matters," Woodrow Wilson remarked as he left his home in Princeton for his inauguration in March 1913. That, however, was precisely the irony fate had in store for the century's first Democratic president. Wilson sent troops on frequent forays into Latin America, especially into Mexico; led the United States into World War I; and finally destroyed his health in an effort—ambitious in its goals but marked by a fatal rigidity—to shape the war's aftermath. Behind all these actions was his belief that America's historical mission was to establish a universal peace rooted in American moral values. Believing that the American way had prospered because it had shunned revolutionary change, he became what one historian has called "the greatest military interventionist in U.S. history."[1]

Wilson's most enduring achievements, therefore, came in the realm of domestic policy. In his first term in the White House—indeed, in the first year of his administration—his allegiance to the Brandeis-inspired New Freedom paid off. He fought off bitter attacks of special-interest groups and made progress toward dismantling Republican protectionism.

But he bought the support of the conservative southern Democrats by offering them patronage and filling half his cabinet with resident or expatriate southerners. Only too willing to further solidify his southern constituency, Wilson presided over a policy of draconian segregation in the federal government, resulting in a significant loss of black patronage jobs and the extension of Jim Crow laws into federal agencies.[2]

With consummate skill, he pursued a number of sweeping reforms: the Underwood-Simmons tariff, which lowered rates; the first graduated income tax; the creation of the Federal Trade Commission, which intensified government regulation of business; the Clayton Anti-Trust Act, which strengthened the Sherman Act of 1890; the popular election of U.S. senators; and, most important of all, the Federal Reserve Act, which reformed the banking system by creating a European-style central bank that could monitor the nation's money supply and smooth out dangerous fluctuations.

While Wilson, like Roosevelt, believed in strong executive leadership and even admitted that "the trust was no longer an ogre . . . to be bludgeoned into submission," he nevertheless emphasized the principles of the New Freedom as "the restoration of free competition," and thus "the application of Jefferson's principles to our present-day America."[3]

In foreign affairs, Wilson's commitment to self-determination as the key to a peaceful world contrasts with TR's fundamental belief in the ability of the great powers to establish a global balance of power. Although both men sought to achieve common interests among peoples through the establishment of an international body of nations, Roosevelt was always more disposed than Wilson to seek a means of military enforcement to ensure peace. Their argument over the purposes of foreign policy as well as of domestic politics remains with us still.[4]

WILSON, though masterly in getting through so much significant legislation, was never able to match the appeal of Roosevelt's rhetoric of inclusion and reconciliation, the denial of self-interest that had always been TR's goal; instead, Wilson was able to ride a tailwind of reform with a Democratic Congress that allowed him to press ahead with measures designed to curb the excesses of big business.

In retrospect, what seems remarkable was Wilson's ability to work well with members of Congress. He saw no need to massage, pressure, or threaten the forces on Capitol Hill. His governing approach in the first two years of his first administration therefore resembled his success early in his presidency of Princeton. His careful collegiality reflected his view that he should appear "impersonal," and he likened himself to a driver leading a team of horses, willing to take advice, and adapting himself to the conditions required to get things done. But his impersonality also gave the impression of aloofness, particularly as contrasted with Roosevelt's exuberance and willingness to attract talented and lively individuals to serve him.

Wilson never established close relations with the men in his cabinet, nor did he enjoy an inner circle comparable to TR's "tennis cabinet" (which even included the French ambassador). Colonel House alone enjoyed the intimacy that Wilson had shown to Mrs. Peck, and at times to his family. Thus, House could write to Wilson on May 20, 1913, "My faith in you is as great as my love for you—more than that I cannot say."[5] If House did not stint in flattering Wilson on almost every occasion, it was surely because he knew that Wilson required continual reassurance—"I nearly always praise at first in order to strengthen the President's confidence in himself which, strangely enough, is often lacking," he wrote in 1918.[6] At the same time, House's supple mind knew that Wilson could turn on those who were once close to him, as he had on those who contested his belief that what he wanted to do at Princeton had a moral as well as an intellectual or social purpose.

In his diary, House described Wilson's intense "prejudices against people. He likes very few and is very loyal to them, but his prejudices are many and often unjust. He finds great difficulty in conferring with men against whom, for some reason, he has a prejudice and in whom he can find nothing good."[7]

The Wilson historian Arthur Link notes the "curious limitations in Wilson's intellectual processes." As he told a reporter in 1916, he hadn't read a serious book through in fourteen years after accepting the presidency of Princeton. Link writes that Wilson was able to grasp ideas quickly, but his interest in them was "chiefly to the degree to which they could be put to practical use." A man of "limited interests and narrow reading," he had "almost no interest in political developments abroad before he entered the White House. . . . Indeed, even in his own specialties of political science, constitutional law, and English and American history, Wilson was surprisingly poorly read."[8]

Once convinced of the rightness of a decision, Wilson was usually
unwilling to change his mind. If someone too strongly urged him to do
something contrary to his conviction, he would often cease to have any
regard for that person. His tendency to view opposition to his policies as
personal antagonism was relatively unimportant as long as he had a
Democratic majority in Congress to carry out his wishes. But after 1918
when the Republicans won control of Congress, it was fatal.

AT THE VERY MOMENT the chief justice was swearing Wilson into
office, Theodore Roosevelt was viewing "Futurist" paintings at the Sixty-
ninth Regiment Armory in New York City. Some viewers suggested to
reporters that perhaps there was something in the word *Futurist* that
appealed to TR at this particular hour. It was certainly characteristic of
Roosevelt to want to keep up with the current art scene; not surprisingly,
he was taken aback by the display of cubist paintings, most notably Mar-
cel Duchamp's *Nude Descending a Staircase,* which were featured in this
display of modernism that had arrived from Europe to astonish and dis-
may much of the viewing public. After looking long and hard at a painting, which someone described as resembling "a Bull Moose argument
put into concrete form," Roosevelt remarked, "The only things I have
seen that resembled some of these pictures were certain animals in
Africa."[9]

Despite TR's early doubts that he could win against an entrenched
party system, defeat was bitter, above all because so many of his oldest
political allies turned their backs on him. But he was constitutionally
incapable of lengthy depression. He answered thousands of letters and
spent some of his own money to keep the Progressive Party alive. As Wilson implemented a reformist program in Washington, TR continued to
maintain what he called "a sane and temperate radicalism."[10] In the
meantime, he was working hard on his *Autobiography,* finishing it by May
1913.

None of this was enough for Roosevelt. He needed adventure, and
that also meant distance from the political scene in the United States and
his role as a party politician. This time it was to explore the River of
Doubt (later to be named the Rio Roosevelt), an uncharted tributary of

the Amazon. "It was my last chance to be a boy," he later explained to a friend. He was to set sail on October 4, 1913, to begin a speaking tour in South America, and then head an expedition into the Brazilian wilderness.

Unlike his African safari, the Brazilian expedition, which included twenty-four-year-old Kermit, was a disaster, rife with fevers, malaria, and in TR's case an abscessed leg. Both he and Kermit nearly died. But in *Through the Brazilian Wilderness,* his account of the expedition, Roosevelt played down his deadly illnesses, and portrayed himself as a man who could deal with his weaknesses without heroic efforts. He never fully recovered from the toll that the River of Doubt took on his body, which surely hastened his death.[11]

By MID-MAY, home at last, Roosevelt did what he could to campaign for candidates in the 1914 congressional elections. Despite his lingering illness, he gave over 110 speeches in fifteen states. As usual, he was greeted by enthusiastic crowds, but it was difficult to know how many had turned out to see a charismatic figure from the past and how many intended to support the Progressive Party. At the same time, the country was suffering from the recession in 1913 and 1914, and the Republicans promised a return to the good old days of the "Full Dinner Pail." The Progressives were overwhelmingly defeated, losing every state but California.[12]

Roosevelt gave his analysis of the causes of defeat to William Allen White right after the election: "The fundamental trouble was that the country was sick and tired of reform. . . . They felt the pinch of poverty; they were suffering from hard times; they wanted prosperity and compared with this they did not care a rap for social justice or industrial justice or clean politics or decency in public life." He was nonetheless sure that the "revulsion is only temporary" and vowed "to fight on for every one of our principles as long as I live."[13]

Waves of social reform seemed to come when there was a social surplus and voters were willing to pass prosperity around. By contrast, in a period of clear economic disaster, such as the Great Depression of the 1930s, economic and social reforms became the prescribed medicine for cure.

· · ·

By now Americans were also becoming fixated on the Great War that had broken out in Europe in August 1914. Roosevelt was surprised at the breadth of the conflict—that it would spread beyond the Balkans, which he had earlier believed could unsettle the affairs of Europe. He also did not trust the secretary of state ("our own special prize idiot, Bryan") or the president ("his ridiculous and insincere chief, Mr. Wilson") to effectively manage the foreign policy of the United States.[14]

Roosevelt had always believed that the surest way to prevent great conflicts was for America to play a large part in promoting regional balances of power. With the outbreak of war in Europe, he called for "preparedness" and urged the government to set up a program of universal military training.

In the fall of 1914, after the French had held off the Germans at the Battle of the Marne, ensuring that World War I would be a long one, TR spelled out his grand strategy in a series of lectures and articles. It was a remarkably restrained design. The defense perimeter was to be the Western Hemisphere, but surprisingly he exempted the southern cone of South America from policing by the United States. He also made public his long-held conviction that America should withdraw from the Philippines.

Most significant of all, he reiterated his proposal for the creation of an association of nations, similar to what he had set forth in his 1910 Nobel Peace Prize speech. At that time he had urged "those great powers honestly bent on peace" to create "some form of international police force, competent and willing to prevent violence among nations."[15]

Comparing international affairs with the Wild West before state and municipal law enforcement were in place, he suggested a remedy similar to what then seemed possible—"the action of a posse comitatus of powerful and civilized nations." Even when he urged the creation of an "international judiciary," he believed that for it to be effective, it had to be backed by an "international police force."[16] As John Morton Blum comments in *The Republican Roosevelt*, TR "sought security and peace in concerts of power in Europe and Asia and in power applied to discipline disorder."[17] He always distrusted what George Kennan would later call "legalistic-moralism."

. . .

WITH THE SINKING of the British liner *Lusitania* by a German U-boat on May 7, 1915, killing 1,198 passengers, 128 of them Americans, Wilson was faced with the decision of whether to go to war. But his commitment to neutrality was fixed. Three days after the tragedy, he sounded a cautious note: "There is such a thing as a man being too proud to fight. There is such a thing as a nation being so right that it does not need to convince others by force that it is right." He soon regretted these remarks, which suggested that he had no backbone. TR considered Wilson's words the most shocking display of cowardice he had ever heard.

Wilson sent two notes to Berlin protesting Germany's attack and calling for an end to submarine warfare. At this, Secretary of State William Jennings Bryan resigned. He considered it unjust that Wilson should protest only to Berlin and not to London; he believed, as he had written earlier to Wilson, that "Germany has a right to prevent contraband going to the Allies and a ship carrying contraband should not rely upon passengers to protect her from attack—it would be like putting women and children in front of an army."[18] As a State Department officer later said, the liner carried both "babies and bullets."

Yet Wilson was still determined that the United States should remain neutral. With the 1916 presidential election in the offing, he wanted to tell voters that he should be elected precisely because he had kept America out of the war. Roosevelt's attacks on Wilson grew more vehement.

The greatest problem for Woodrow Wilson was maintaining a watchful neutrality. He could not endorse Bryan's repugnance at America's being drawn into almost any European war. Nor could he easily dismiss Roosevelt's criticism of his reluctance to embrace a full-bodied policy of "preparedness." By November 1915, the president had reversed his previous position and announced a program of military and naval readiness. His growing skill at finding a middle way by initiating preparations for war but at the same time keeping his commitment to neutrality seemed to reflect a more confident man, one who was finding new happiness with a new wife.

· · ·

THE SUMMER OF 1914 had brought not only the outbreak of war in
Europe but also the death of Wilson's wife. Her illness, Bright's disease,
an ailment of the kidneys, came over her in March 1914. Five months
later, Ellen was dead.

Wilson struggled against his grief by immersing himself in unrelenting
work, yet by the spring of 1915, he was in love again. He had met Edith
Bolling Galt through his cousin Helen Bones, who was acting as first lady
at the White House. Wilson was soon passionately in love with Mrs.
Galt. Widowed in 1908, she was a stylish woman of forty-two living quietly in a house near Dupont Circle. In post–Civil War Virginia, she had
been raised in modest circumstances and received a sketchy education.
But Edith was a quick-witted woman, and before long Wilson was send-
ing her packets of state papers on which he had scribbled marginal notes,
which he expected her to comment on.

With a likely marriage impending, neither Colonel House nor Treasury
Secretary William McAdoo was pleased. The 1916 presidential campaign was approaching, and they believed that voters would disapprove of
their president marrying so soon after the death of his wife.

McAdoo, fearful of a Democratic loss in the 1916 election and hoping
someday to inherit Wilson's presidency, was active in trying to head off
the marriage. He had found out that Wilson had sent Mary Hulbert Peck
a check for $7,500 to help her out with a loan against two mortgages.
After McAdoo learned this, he made up a story in September that he
knew Mrs. Peck was planning to sell incriminating letters by Wilson that
would damage his reputation. When McAdoo told this to his father-in-
law, Wilson was convinced that such letters would reveal his earlier affair
with Mary.

Wilson decided to tell Edith the story of his relationship with Mrs.
Peck, and of the likelihood of scandal. In the letter that Wilson wrote
early in the morning after his meeting with Edith the night before, he
admitted to her his "folly" and his remorse for what he had done. Edith, in
a letter that crossed his, assured him that she would "stand by him—not
for duty, not for pity . . . but for love."[19]

Their engagement was announced on October 8. Soon after, Wilson introduced Edith to House in New York, a visit that marked the waning of Wilson's dependence on him. The colonel's diary begins to assume a petulant tone that the president was too distracted by his betrothed to pay close attention to business.

The wedding took place on December 18, 1915, at Edith's house. Colonel House had been invited to the ceremony but found himself too busy in New York City to attend.

WITH THE COUPLE settled in the White House, the president was able to focus his energies on the Democratic national convention, scheduled for mid-June. He approved a platform that stressed the Democrats' commitment to progressivism at home and internationalism abroad—which meant neutrality in foreign policy and a continued military and naval buildup. It was Wilson's final shift from the New Freedom to the New Nationalism, from a view that the federal government should act as an impartial mediator in the nation's affairs to a belief that the executive branch of the government should actively promote economic progress and social justice.[20]

At the convention in St. Louis, the keynote speaker, former Governor Martin Glynn of New York (chosen by Wilson and House), repeatedly sounded the patriotic theme of "Americanism." His evocation of a tradition of American neutrality showing that the United States would not be provoked into going to war was greeted with a chorus of chants from the delegates—"What did we do? What did we do?"—and then Glynn would shout back, "We didn't go to war."[21]

Wilson chose to give his acceptance speech at "Shadow Lawn," his new summer home at Long Branch on the New Jersey shore. Before a huge crowd, Wilson declared, "We have in four years come very near to carrying out the platform of the Progressive Party, as well as our own; for we are also progressives."[22]

"IT WOULD BE A MISTAKE to nominate me unless the country has in its mood something of the heroic—unless it feels not only devotion to ideals but the purpose measurably to realize those ideals in action."[23] This is what Theodore Roosevelt was saying in the spring of 1916. And his suspicions were right. The country was far from wanting a new Lincoln to lead the nation into war.

Roosevelt was faced with a dilemma. He knew that the Democratic Party had appropriated much of the Progressive Party policies. He also knew that the Republican Party had to nominate a moderate progressive. If Roosevelt wished to rejoin the Republicans, however, he had to do so before the campaign and be willing to speak out frequently and forcefully for the Republican candidate. This would surely be Charles Evans Hughes, former governor of New York, now a Supreme Court justice, and a man TR never much liked. Regulars, such as Taft, could back him, and reformers could point to his generally progressive record as governor.

The Republican convention was to open in Chicago on June 7, but far from trying to round up supporters, Roosevelt spent the last months before the convention preaching preparedness. The Progressives had decided to open their convention the same day. TR and the Progressive Party leaders had already said they would unite with the Republicans if a candidate could be found that was acceptable to both parties. Both conventions were scheduled for the same time so that it would be possible to join them together in a marriage of convenience.

In any case, the Republicans were determined to nominate Hughes, which they did fairly quickly. The Progressive Party delegates believed that if they nominated Roosevelt, he would have to accept. This was a miscalculation. When TR was nominated only minutes before the Republicans nominated Hughes, he sent a telegram from Sagamore Hill turning down the honor. William Allen White, who was at the conclave, recalled the reaction when the telegram was read: "For a moment there was silence. Then there was a roar of rage. It was the cry of a broken heart such as no convention ever had uttered in this land before." The second Progressive national convention then adjourned.[24]

Candidate Hughes declared that he was committed to preparedness and progressivism, and TR readily endorsed him. Roosevelt also sent a message to the Progressive National Committee, meeting in Chicago later that month, urging them to back Hughes. A majority voted to do so, and most of the leaders followed Roosevelt's lead. In effect TR, after presiding at its birth, buried the Progressive Party.

• • •

BY TEMPERAMENT HUGHES, like Taft, was more fitted for the court-room than the political cockpit. Although he was warm and witty in small gatherings of friends, he appeared austere and aloof in public. In the national campaign, the "bearded iceberg," as TR labeled him, needed the fire that perhaps only Roosevelt could supply.[25] Eventually, the Republican National Committee asked TR to "perform a personal rescue act" on Hughes's campaign.[26]

Journalists caught the spirit of a revived TR. In Kentucky, a reporter wrote that, "to see the Colonel standing bareheaded in the cold mountain rain telling pinch-faced, unnourished moutaineers that their ancestors were 'not too proud to fight' was enough to make you run for a type-writer."[27]

Hughes was unable to dispel the iceberg image even though he tried. In a speaking tour across the country, he not only attended a baseball game in Detroit, but he also actually jumped over the railing to shake hands with the players and to chat with Ty Cobb. He went to the bottom of a copper mine in Montana, climbed to Bear Lake in the Rockies, and kissed every baby he could find. As one Missouri newspaper put it, "He is liked better than his speeches."[28]

Hughes then made a crucial error. On a visit to California, his associates didn't bother to tell him that Governor Hiram Johnson, a paladin of the Progressive movement, was staying at the same hotel. Even though Johnson backed Hughes publicly, there was bad blood between the regular Republicans and Johnson's Progressives. After it appeared to Johnson that Hughes had snubbed him at the hotel, the governor's party organization did little to mobilize support for the nominee. Hughes lost California by some 4,000 votes.

On election day, November 7, early returns from the East showed an overwhelming victory for Hughes. By evening it was clear that he had carried most of the big eastern and midwestern states and had almost certainly won 247 electoral votes. Only 19 more were needed to win the race. At 10 P.M. the *New York Times* gave the election to Hughes, and Wilson went to bed thinking he had lost.

Then, as returns from the West started coming in about 2 A.M., the trend was toward Wilson. At breakfast time, Joe Tumulty called to say that the election was now in doubt. All day long the returns favored the Democrats. Finally, at 11 P.M. the night of November 9, Wilson's reelection was assured. Overcoming Hughes's early lead in California, he had won the 13 crucial California votes. Wilson thus had united the South and the West, which Bryan had failed to do in 1896.[29]

As for the Republican Party, in 1912 it may have voted for the past when it turned aside Theodore Roosevelt, but it was Roosevelt's ability to attract Progressive voters to vote Republican that allowed Hughes to come so close to winning in 1916. Nominating Hughes was an effort to try to bring Progressives back into the Republican camp, and TR was central to this task. Wilson owed his victory to his near total sweep of the West, but the old Progressives actually deprived him of a bigger margin of victory.[30]

WHILE 1912 REPRESENTED the high point of Socialist electoral success, in the next year factional strife destroyed the seeming unity that Debs had provided. After the convention of 1912 when Bill Haywood was expelled from the National Executive Committee, many radicals left the party. Which is just what the conservative Socialists wanted, even at a price of a weakened party.

The European conflict further undermined Socialist unity. To the party leaders, neutrality seemed the best policy; they hoped that the war would cause the collapse of the old order, paving the way for the triumph of international socialism. But many American Socialists were eager to demonstrate their patriotism. As the likelihood grew that the United States might intervene, they started to support the Allies.

Eugene Debs never intended to run for president in the 1916 election. He had collapsed in the spring of 1915. He was in bed for over six weeks with torn leg muscles, congestion, and physical exhaustion. By mid-June he was stronger, but he remained at a sanitarium until he was well enough to go home to Terre Haute.[31]

To save money, the party held no national convention to nominate a presidential ticket in 1916. Instead, a referendum chose Allan Benson, a

Socialist organizer and newspaperman acceptable to the party factions. Like Debs, he was critical of Wilson's new emphasis on preparedness, seeing it as readiness for intervention. He portrayed the slogan "He kept us out of the war" as sheer hypocrisy.

Though Debs could not have undertaken a national campaign, he nevertheless gave in to supporters who begged him to run for Congress from his home district. Characteristically, he worked with great intensity. War-ravaged Europe now fired up his rhetoric, as he saw the horrors of hunger and cold, and the wastage of human lives and resources. He toured the district in an auto caravan, and during the first two weeks of September, delivered over fifty speeches. Often he climbed on the hood of his Model T when the crowd was large.[32]

In his own district, Debs ran well ahead of the Democrats but lost to a Republican. He had one comment about his defeat: "Blessed are they who expect nothing, for they shall not be disappointed."[33] In the presidential race, the Socialist Party did far worse than in 1912, receiving only 585,113 votes. The factionalism in the party, along with divisions over the desirability of a "peace" campaign, had inflicted severe wounds. Worst of all, Debs was not the national candidate.

ON JANUARY 22, 1917, increasingly fearful that the United States would be dragged into the European war, Wilson went to Capitol Hill to outline America's postwar objectives. He uttered his famous call for a "peace without victory," in other words, a peace in which neither side would dictate terms to the other. He also attacked the hallowed concept of the balance of power, which he believed had failed to prevent war and, if restored, would undermine the peace. "There must be not a balance of power," Wilson declared, "but a community of power, not organized rivalries, but an organized community of peace." In saying this, he did not understand that what had caused the war was a breakdown in the European balance of power—when Germany had embarked on a naval buildup that challenged British supremacy—not its existence.[34]

Nine days later, Germany responded by commencing unrestricted submarine warfare. Although the German leaders knew this would almost surely bring America into war, the German naval minister told them: "From a military standpoint, America's entrance is as nothing." The hundred German U-boats, he believed, could shrink U.S. munitions shipments, knocking England out of the war within six months.[35] Two days later Washington broke diplomatic relations with Berlin.

Even if Wilson were still searching for a way to avoid war, another challenge from Berlin narrowed that possibility. In February the British passed on to the American ambassador an intercepted and coded message, dated January 16, sent by German foreign minister Arthur Zimmermann to his ambassador in Mexico. The telegram proposed a military alliance with Mexico. Should war break out between Germany and the United States, Germany would help Mexico "gain back by conquest" the territory lost to the United States in 1848: Arizona, California, and New Mexico.[36] On March 1, Wilson released the Zimmermann message to the press. He then went ahead to arm American merchant vessels. Within three weeks, three American ships had been sunk.

Finally, on April 2, 1917, Wilson addressed a joint session of Congress to ask for a declaration of war against Germany, depicting Germany's "outlaw U-boats" as "warfare against mankind." Once again, he couched his appeal in universalistic terms, declaring that the "world must be made safe for democracy." In his missionary zeal, the immediate causes for war—unrestricted submarine warfare and the Zimmermann telegram—were not in themselves sufficient for Wilson to abandon "armed neutrality." What made him finally willing to send American troops into battle was the opportunity for the United States to imprint its values on the Old World. "We created this nation," he once said, "not to serve ourselves, but to serve mankind."[37]

ROOSEVELT'S FOUR SONS went to war—Ted and Archie as officers in the U.S. Army; Kermit, eager to get into the fight, becoming a captain in the British Army assigned to Mesopotamia (now Iraq); and nineteen-year-old Quentin to flight training with the new air service. "It's rather up to us to practice what Father preaches," Quentin said.

As the war progressed, TR soon became Wilson's most vocal and bitter critic. By early 1918, he had all but called the president a traitor for his tardy failure to aid the Allies, his increasing application of censorship, and his excessive use of executive power. In this respect, TR's attacks often challenged the spirit of the Espionage and Sedition Acts, which Wilson's attorney general was using to forbid criticism of the president in speech or print.

While the Senate debated a sedition bill to silence any Wilson critics, Roosevelt called it "sheer treason to the United States."[38] Congress nevertheless passed the Sedition Act in 1918, and at that point, Roosevelt wrote to his son Archie that he wished Wilson dared to send him to jail, because it "would make my voice carry farther."[39]

EUGENE DEBS did not escape the full effects of the wartime climate of repression. Radicals of every kind and nationality were hunted down as U.S. district attorneys broadly interpreted the Espionage Act to win indictments and convictions on charges of treason and antiwar activities.

In 1918, Debs, at sixty-three, was ailing. His comrades were in jail and the Socialist movement gravely weakened while he was home in bed. For Debs, the situation was intolerable. He would have expected himself to be the standard-bearer of rebellion. Yet when he gave speeches during the first two weeks of July in Indiana and Illinois, he attracted little attention from the authorities. All this would change on June 16, when he spoke at the convention of the Socialist Party in Canton, Ohio.

Nothing he said in his address to over one thousand people gathered to hear him was very different from what he had said before. But this time Justice Department agents were making their way through the crowd, checking draft cards.

Leaning forward on the platform, stretching his hands out toward the people in front of him, Debs defended men who were being labeled murderers and German agents, or just plain hoodlums. Only once did he speak of war—"The master class has always declared the wars; the subject class has always fought the battles. The master class has had all to gain and nothing to lose, while the subject class has had nothing to gain and all to lose—especially their lives."[40]

That was enough. Thirteen days after the Canton speech, a federal grand jury in Cleveland indicted Debs for violating the new Sedition Act. The trial was set to take place on September 9 in Cleveland.

Debs never denied the substance of what he had said. What he did contest was the insinuation that he had favored violent revolution. He therefore based his defense on the right of free speech under the Constitution. His argument was that the Sedition Act violated the First Amendment, and that that question could not be decided in a trial court. "Gentlemen, I am the smallest part of this trial," Debs declared. "There is an infinitely greater issue that is being tried in this court, though you may not be conscious of it. American institutions are on trial here before a court of American citizens."[41]

The judge hearing the case instructed the jury to find Debs not guilty on the counts dealing with ridiculing the federal government, but rather to decide on those counts charging him with willfully and knowingly trying to obstruct the operation of the conscription act. The following day the jury found Debs guilty, and after a final statement declaring his solidarity with those imprisoned or oppressed, Debs asked for no mercy but pointed out that in the struggle between "greed" and "the rising hosts of freedom," the "cross is bending, the midnight is passing."[42]

Debs was sentenced to ten years in prison.

IN APRIL, Debs left Terre Haute to enter prison at Moundsville, West Virginia. The warden, appreciating Debs's eminence, bent the rules to allow his star prisoner liberal visiting privileges. Given a light hospital job, he was allowed a good measure of personal freedom. Almost all the other prisoners, aware of Debs's compassion for them, wanted to see and talk to him.

Soon, Wilson's Attorney General, A. Mitchell Palmer, decided to send Debs to a more restrictive prison, and in June, Debs was transferred to a maximum security prison in Atlanta, Georgia. At this time, the so-called Palmer raids went into full force; any Socialists, who were not citizens, were expelled from the country or otherwise silenced as the Wilson administration began a wholesale crackdown on radicalism.

Debs's health suffered from the severe Georgia climate, but Warden Fred Zerbst was determined that Debs would not die in his jail. He transferred him to a light job in the hospital, where he was given a private room and eventually allowed to entertain visitors in Zerbst's private office. An amnesty committee, headed by Clarence Darrow, was formed to seek freedom for Debs, though Debs himself refused to ask any favors of Washington.

The Socialist Party, recognizing that Debs in prison could make a formidable candidate in the 1920 election, nominated him for president. On election day, the vote of 919,000 rivaled his total for 1912, and significantly exceeded the Socialist vote of 1916. Nevertheless, it was only 3.5 percent of the total vote, little more than half the percentage he had won in 1912. It seemed to Debs that the "people can have anything they want. The trouble is they do not want anything. At least they vote that way on election day."[43]

EIGHTEEN

Endgames

THEODORE ROOSEVELT'S continued criticism of Wilson's preparations for war served him ill in the months running up to the declaration of war against Imperial Germany. If power can lead to unbridled ruthlessness, it can also prove a restraint on bad behavior. Political campaigns often unleash cruel and intemperate attacks on opposing candidates, but once in office the newly elected politician can appear the most moderate of rulers. In TR's case, the responsibilities of power more often than not proved a restraint on reckless behavior; once out of power, however, restraint gave way to excessively belligerent attacks on the president.[1]

This initially hurt his popularity, but as the war went on, dissatisfaction with Wilson grew, and became one of the main factors leading to a Republican takeover of the House and Senate in the 1918 congressional elections (now with Henry Cabot Lodge as both majority leader and chairman of the Senate Foreign Relations Committee). With TR having called for the United States to intervene before 1917, with his support for the draft, along with his willingness to campaign for Hughes, he came to be seen as a righteous warrior. Roosevelt soon regained his popularity and could reasonably expect to be the Republican candidate for president in 1920.[2]

Roosevelt's internationalism had always been rooted in his belief in traditional power politics. Even his support for an association of nations in his Nobel Peace Prize address was tied to the exercise of power. The strongest nations in the world were to have a special role in preserving the peace, and they must be willing to use military force to do so. These views were certainly shared by Elihu Root, Henry Cabot Lodge, and even by William Howard Taft.

But Roosevelt's emphasis on international security was no exercise of cool Bismarckian calculation; instead it was intimately connected to his idealism. Would Americans live up to the highest standards of honor and righteousness? Would they cooperate with other powers for the greater good of mankind? As he had said in his Nobel address, "Peace is generally good in itself, but it is never the highest good unless it comes as the handmaid of righteousness."[3]

TR, as well as Wilson, understood that a successful American foreign policy had to have a moral component. The differences between TR and Wilson were over the nature of that component.[4] Both Roosevelt and Lodge believed that the Founders of the nation knew that a moral foreign policy had to be linked to the national interest. In short, what might be called "practical idealism" had to operate from a base of power.[5]

As Roosevelt wrote Lodge, "[Our] greatest national asset is that . . . we have produced the greatest examples that the world has ever seen in Washington and Lincoln."[6] Thus, in foreign relations, Roosevelt believed that "our chief usefulness to humanity rests on our combining power with high purpose."[7]

The Wilsonians contended that American and indeed global security would come about through a world organization that stressed arbitration, arms reductions, economic sanctions, and the force of public opinion, and only as a last resort the military enforcement of collective security. Roosevelt and his closest colleagues, though they agreed that international law should be strengthened, stressed the use of American power and did not shy away from limited security commitments to a few other nations in time of need. There were, of course, in both parties a significant number of isolationists who disliked American adherence to international organizations and certainly detested security guarantees to temporary allies.[8]

· · ·

THE WAR ITSELF changed things for both TR and Taft. They now had sons in the war, TR's four boys, and Taft's boy Charlie (his other son, Bob, could not get into the service because of poor eyesight). And both Taft and Roosevelt had a common antagonist.

The final reconciliation between the two men came about in Chicago in May 1918—a mere five blocks from the Coliseum where the great conflict between them had taken place in 1912. Taft had arrived at the Blackstone Hotel by coincidence; Roosevelt happened to be dining there before going on to Des Moines to deliver a speech. When Taft learned that TR was in the dining room eating dinner alone, he made straight for that room. It was time to go beyond a rapprochement that had been growing and firmly restore their friendship.

Taft easily located Roosevelt, who was sitting at a little table, and quickly walked up to him. TR was intent on his meal, but a sudden stillness in the dining room made him look up. He saw Taft, threw down his napkin and rose, extending his hand to greet him. They shook hands vigorously and clapped each other on the back. Those in the dining room started to cheer, and at that point both Taft and Roosevelt bowed and smiled at the audience. Then they sat down and talked for a good half hour.[9]

After he returned home, TR wrote Taft: "It was a very real pleasure to see you the other day. When you next pass through New York, do let me know. I will come in town to meet you, or I will get you to come out to Sagamore Hill for lunch, or for dinner and the night if it is convenient."[10] The next time Will Taft came to Sagamore Hill, sadly, was for Theodore's funeral.

BY 1919 ROOSEVELT'S NOMINATION as the Republican standard-bearer for president was, if not assured, very likely. His unremitting criticism of Wilson, his rapprochement with Taft and Root, and the heroic qualities that served him well once American soldiers were fighting in France made him the man to beat for the nomination. In early 1918, even Old Guard Republicans had begun to seek him out as a speaker.

Roosevelt's policies showed him far from being an embryonic isolationist. Not only did he endorse Taft's League to Enforce Peace, backed up, however, by military force, but he also wanted to extend America's ties to the Allies. He repeatedly told British friends that he definitely wanted postwar security pacts with the British and the French. This reflected his view that such security agreements would ensure that America would continue to play a global role as a leading world power.[11]

While Roosevelt was achieving a political resurrection, he was devastated to learn on July 18, 1918, of the death of his youngest son, Quentin. The German government confirmed that he had been shot down behind German lines by seven Fokkers, and had been buried with full military honors where he had fallen.[12] No matter that TR was proud that his sons had gone to battle; the loss of Quentin, the boy who most resembled him, cast him down in the months to come. That August he wrote to Edith Wharton that "there is no use my writing about Quentin; for I should break down if I tried."[13]

Roosevelt nonetheless continued his quest for the nomination, fulfilling as many speaking engagements as he felt strong enough to do. His last public appearance was at Carnegie Hall, November 2, 1918, where he spoke for the Circle for Negro War Relief at the invitation of W. E. B. DuBois, then one of leaders of the NAACP. In that speech, TR called for equal "civil and political rights" and promised to do "everything I can to aid, and bring about, to bring nearer, the day when justice, the square-deal, will be given as between black man and white."[14] (Though Roosevelt's racial views had clearly changed over the years, it is unlikely that he would have decided to make racial equality a central issue in a campaign in 1920.)

TR's health, however, continued to deteriorate. On November 11, 1918, the day on which Germany surrendered, he again entered the hospital, where he remained for seven weeks. At one point rheumatism in his left arm grew so great that the arm had to be bound in a splint. During this time, Republican leaders visited him to see if he would accept the Republican nomination. He responded that he would not actively seek it, but if the party leaders came to him and said they were convinced he was the only man who could be elected and that they were all for him, he would not refuse.

When Roosevelt was finally discharged from the hospital on Christmas Day, the doctors warned him that he might have to use a wheelchair for the rest of his life if he did not slow down. "All right," TR replied. "I can work and live that way, too."[15]

On January 3, Edith believed that Theodore was "so melancholy," but he nevertheless had the energy to write senators, urging their support for the Nineteenth Amendment to the Constitution granting woman suffrage. Two days later he worked on page proofs for an article on postwar reform that he had written. He felt poorly that night as he went to bed, and Edith called the nurse and doctor, who found his heart, lungs, and pulse in good shape.[16]

Around midnight, Roosevelt asked his valet, James Amos, to turn off the light. Edith, who was sleeping in the master bedroom, checked on her husband at 2 A.M. and found him sleeping comfortably, while Amos kept watch by the fire. At four in the morning, however, the nurse woke Edith to tell her that her husband had stopped breathing. TR was dead of an embolism.[17]

On his bedside table was a penciled note he had written to tell Will Hays, chairman of the Republican National Committee, to go to Washington to "see Senate & House; prevent split on domestic policies."[18]

COLONEL HOUSE had never wanted Wilson to go to Paris to negotiate a treaty with the British and French. He believed that if things went awry, Wilson could then insist on revisions in any treaty he disliked. But he should have known that Wilson would never have passed up his great opportunity to impose American values on a broken world.

Had Wilson been more cautious, he would have perceived how serious the opposition to his notion of a "peace without victory" and a League of Nations might prove to be in Britain and France. His speech in January 1918 had contained the famous Fourteen Points, which outlined his view of what the postwar aims of the Allies should be. Briefly, the first six dealt with cardinal principles of diplomacy: no secret engagements, freedom of the seas, and fair settlement of colonial claims. The next few points dealt with the need for self-determination of European peoples. The last point—and by far the most important—called for a "general association of nations" that would guarantee political independence and territorial integrity to "great and small states alike."[19]

By the time the peace conference convened, British Prime Minister Lloyd George had won an overwhelming victory in the so-called Khaki election in which he had promised to work for a brutal peace with Germany. In Paris, Premier Georges Clemenceau appeared before the Chamber of Deputies, declared his support for the "old system of alliances called the 'balance of power,'" and won a strong vote of confidence.[20] For Wilson, the political victories of his Allies meant that a generous peace was out of the question.

Wilson's most formidable antagonist at the conference was Clemenceau, the "Tiger," one of the great political figures of the French Third Republic. In 1917, he had become premier, renewed the morale of the country, and pushed the war relentlessly forward to victory. As the economist John Maynard Keynes saw it at the Paris peace conference, Clemenceau had little use for a League of Nations, but he gave lip service to the "'ideals' of the foolish Americans and the hypocritical British." The principle of self-determination, Keynes wrote, made little sense to him "except as an ingenious formula for rearranging the balance of power in one's own interests."[21]

Wilson, over the objections of Clemenceau and others, persuaded the peacemakers to merge the peace terms with the League into the eventual package that would constitute the Versailles Treaty. At the heart of the document was Article X, designed to curb aggression and war. The League was "to respect and preserve as against external aggression the territorial integrity and existing political independence" of all members of the League.

But how to do so? Here the treaty was equivocal. If aggression, or any threat of it, did take place, the member states would consult and advise on what should be done. One constituency could interpret the article as implying that the League would use military force; another—and as it turned out a much larger one—could see the League possessing such moral influence that the resort to force would almost never arise.

To achieve his heart's desire, Wilson violated the principles he had first set down in the Fourteen Points again and again, especially on the issue of self-determination and reparations from Germany. For example, he supported the creation of the state of Czechoslovakia, which contained millions of Germans. Nor did self-determination bring the benefits that

Wilson had expected. All too often self-determination meant that majorities ruled; the fledgling states contained minorities that could easily destabilize these newly created countries in Europe. There were minorities in Poland, large numbers of Hungarians in Romania; and in Yugoslavia were Albanians, Bosnians, Croatians, Montenegrins, Serbs, and Slovenians, all of which did not produce a more stable continent. But for Wilson, the League would be in place to resolve these tensions.

Wilson also gave in to the Allies on the question of reparations. Before the Paris negotiations began, Wilson had wanted a limited indemnity in order to avoid a harsh peace that might result in deep German resentment and gravely weaken the German economy. Wilson, now more vindictive, seemed to betray the very ideals he had set forth in the Fourteen Points. The victors wrote into the treaty a "war guilt" clause, holding Germany responsible for all the war's damages. (In 1921, the Reparations Commission would present a stricken Germany with an excessive reparations bill of $33 billion, which poisoned international economic relations for more than a decade.)

The French, however, were still fearful of a rearmed and aggressive Germany and made claim to the banks of the Rhine. To avoid this and to assuage French fears, Wilson agreed that the United States would sign a security pact guaranteeing the French border; the British went along by offering a similar guarantee. Should the U.S. Senate refuse to ratify the Versailles Treaty, the security pact would also fall away. This left the French in the position of maintaining the security of the postwar European system; Clemenceau's France, however, was not the France of a Louis XIV, but the France of a weakened Third Republic.

The treaty contained the worst of both worlds. It was neither a Carthaginian peace nor a generous one; it humiliated the Germans without crushing them.[22]

Throughout most of the negotiations, Wilson was very much alone. He rarely consulted with the delegates he had appointed to accompany him to Paris, except with Colonel House. He had not named any prominent Republicans to the delegation, even though the Republicans now controlled the Senate. In addition, his relationship with House in Paris was growing ever more distant. By April, after he returned from a brief visit to the United States, he had lost all confidence in House, who had in his absence discussed with the Allies the possibility of having a preliminary treaty that did not include the Covenant of the League. Convinced that House had overstepped his bounds, he told his wife, who always resented House's primacy, that House had "yielded until there is nothing left," and he would have to start all over again.[23]

That spring Wilson, whose strength was often impaired due to progressive arteriosclerosis, suffered a serious bout of influenza. In fact, he had undergone three earlier strokes, not known to the public; a small one in 1896, another in 1904, and a grave one in 1906 that left some permanent visual loss in the right eye.[24] The influenza that felled him in Paris, combined with the immense task of negotiating without a support staff he could rely on, made Wilson more petulant, angry, and emotional than ever. His break with House was never repaired; he had no one but his wife with whom he could share his deepest feelings or his rationalizations for what he was doing.

After all his struggles with the Allies, Wilson believed, "If I didn't feel that I was the personal instrument of God I couldn't carry on."[25] In contrast, Lloyd George remarked after the peace conference, "I think I did as well as might be expected, seated as I was between Jesus Christ and Napoleon Bonaparte."[26]

LIKE ROOSEVELT, Henry Cabot Lodge was an internationalist, but one who thought that American power and purpose would be ill served by a document that did not rely on military power as the primary means of enforcement. Like Roosevelt, he seriously considered a working alliance with Britain and France in the postwar period. He also realized that fighting a great war merely to restore the balance of power in Europe would never gain the support of the American people. Like Roosevelt, he believed it had to be a righteous war.

Lodge's reservations over the treaty centered on Article X, which he believed would cost the United States too much sovereignty. Would members of the League be obligated to use force? Did the article mean that the United States was committed to uphold the status quo? Did it transfer from the Congress to the president the power to declare war?

But Wilson was determined that there would be no meddling with the treaty. In submitting the 244-page document to the Senate, he took an evangelical tone: "The stage is set, the destiny disclosed. It has come about by no plan of our conceiving, but by the hand of God, who led us in this way."[27] Asked by the French ambassador if he would accept senatorial "reservations," Wilson took a far less holy tone: "I shall consent to nothing. The Senate must take its medicine."[28]

Senator Lodge was fighting on two fronts—to secure Senate support for his positions on foreign policy, and to discredit Wilson in order to prepare for a Republican victory in the 1920 presidential election. Lodge, who detested Wilson, had little respect for his intellect. By trying again and again to force Wilson to explain the practical details of the treaty, he hoped to expose the weaknesses inherent in the Covenant and, in the process, destroy him.

Wilson proved Lodge right. The president refused to discuss the details of the treaty, and decided to bring his case directly to the nation. In so doing, he rejected the opportunity to gain support for the treaty by a sufficient number of senators who were asking only that he accept the Lodge reservations, which were not in fact lethal. Many of the objections restated the obvious: that the Congress would retain its constitutional role in foreign policy. As for Article X, the reservation simply declared that the United States would assume no obligation to preserve the territorial integrity or political independence of another country unless authorized by Congress.[29]

IN SEPTEMBER 1919, Wilson set off on an eight-thousand-mile trip across the country. Accompanied by Edith and Doctor Grayson, he delivered thirty-two major speeches, in addition to numerous rear-platform appearances and other ceremonies.[30] The conditions of the trip were grueling. Dr. Grayson wrote that the steel cars of the special train "held the heat like ovens."[31] Headaches that Wilson had suffered throughout the summer did not abate. In Los Angeles, Grayson noticed little drops of saliva at the corners of Wilson's mouth. His lips trembled, and his pallor grew worse.

By the time the president reached Pueblo, Colorado, he had such a splitting headache that he could hardly see. Yet he gave a long speech, one of his most eloquent, at one point evoking the cemetery at Suresnes: "I wish some of those men who are now opposing the settlement for which those men died could visit such a spot as that. I wish they could feel the moral obligation that rests upon us not to go back on those boys, but to see this thing through to the end and make good their redemption of the world."[32]

It was the last time he would be able to address the American people on this journey. At 2 A.M. the next morning, Mrs. Wilson and Dr. Grayson found the president "unable to sleep and in a highly nervous condition, the muscles of his face twitching, and he was extremely nauseated."[33]

Wilson reluctantly agreed to cancel the rest of the trip, as "tears ran down his face."[34]

On Sunday morning, September 28, the train pulled into Washington's Union Station. Four days later, Mrs. Wilson found her husband on the bathroom floor unconscious. Wilson had suffered a massive stroke through a clot that had formed in the artery to his brain, though there was no rupture. This had paralyzed the left side of his body, though leaving his brain still functioning.[35]

THEN BEGAN one of the strangest and most dangerous episodes in American history. Edith Wilson, with the connivance of Dr. Grayson, concealed from the Congress and the American people the degree of her husband's illness and incapacity.

The president was invisible for weeks. It was not until the end of October that he was taken out of bed and placed in a chair. It was not until Christmas that he could stand and manage a few steps with the help of a cane. When visitors were at last admitted to his bedroom, he was propped up in bed with his body covered, except for his head and right arm. The room was dimly lit with the curtains drawn, and the visitors placed on his right so that his paralysis was not obvious. Mrs. Wilson stood at the end of the bed and Grayson at the doorway, both ready to interrupt if necessary.

His wife and his physician concealed from the president the gravity of his illness, as they believed that his recovery might be hindered if he were presented with anything or anyone that might tax his capacities. If the nature of Wilson's illness were known, he might well have been forced to cede his authority to the vice president. Thus during the first stages of his illness, Wilson saw neither Joe Tumulty nor any members of his cabinet.

When anyone needed to consult her husband over a matter of state, Mrs. Wilson took the message and reported back what her husband had presumably said. Sometimes she answered with a handwritten note. A number of letters went unopened.

Wilson did get somewhat better, but his moral rigidity grew worse. When his supporters dared to suggest any compromise in order to get his beloved League passed, he refused them. On November 19, 1919, the Senate voted, 55 to 39, not to ratify the treaty without the reservations. Then, under strong pressure from Wilson not to ratify the treaty *with* the reservations, Democrats voted with Republicans who were unalterably opposed to the treaty under any circumstances. Again the treaty was defeated. Lodge later commented to Elihu Root that if "Wilson had not written his letter to the Democratic caucus, calling on them to kill the treaty rather than accept the reservations, the treaty would have been ratified on the 19th of November."[36]

Even at this juncture, however, fewer than a score of the senators had declared themselves unalterably opposed to the treaty. But Wilson would not budge. Colonel House from his enforced exile wrote Wilson a letter urging him to let the thing be voted on; reservations could be corrected later. What was essential was to let the president's great work survive. When Mrs. Wilson saw the letter she considered it a counsel of surrender. House then wrote the president again, explaining that he was advising not surrender, but action that could save the treaty. Wilson did not acknowledge either of these letters. Nor is it known if Wilson saw them. House never offered any advice again—but he noted in his diary that he had once thought Lodge the worst enemy of the treaty, but now he believed that first place had to be ceded to Wilson.[37]

In March 1920, the treaty once more came up for a vote, and in this tally many Democrats broke ranks to vote in favor of reservations. Nevertheless, the treaty was rejected 49 to 35, far from the two-thirds required for ratification. At that point, Wilson declared that the election of 1920 would be a "solemn referendum" on the treaty.[38]

• • •

AFTER ELECTING TWO of the most forceful presidents in the twentieth century, both Democrats and Republicans were at a loss to come up with anyone worthy enough to take the place of Wilson and Roosevelt. Both parties then turned to Ohio. In the meantime, Wilson continued to deny the extent of his infirmity and waited at the White House for what he hoped would be a call from the Democratic convention in San Francisco for him to run for an unprecedented third term. It never came. On July 6, with no clear front-runner, on the forty-fourth ballot the exhausted delegates nominated Ohio's Governor James M. Cox, with Franklin D. Roosevelt as the vice presidential candidate.

Cox was a colorless candidate but a shrewd politician, favored by the big city bosses and uncommitted to the League of Nations. The thirty-eight-year-old Roosevelt had made a creditable showing for himself as Wilson's assistant secretary of the navy; he would also balance the ticket and help the Democrats carry New York. And of course he bore the Roosevelt name. Handsome and high-spirited, he looked forward to vigorous campaigning.

THE REPUBLICANS KNEW they had probably lost a sure winner with the death of TR. But they believed that Wilson's unpopularity was such that it would tar any Democratic candidate and would thus be enough to carry them to victory. At their convention in mid-June, they selected the affable Senator Warren G. Harding of Ohio, largely because no one had anything against him.

Running against Wilson's record, Harding proved a strong candidate. The nation had been essentially leaderless after the president was felled by his stroke. Both inflation and unemployment were rising, and Harding, who had been one of the "reservationists," was able to avoid alienating both the "irreconcilables," who would never accept the League, and the Taft wing, which favored it with only mild reservations.

The semischooled, bloviating Harding (the word he used to describe his own oratory) conducted an effective "front-porch" campaign from his house in Marion, Ohio, in the manner of his Ohio political hero, William McKinley. He even arranged to have McKinley's original flagpole brought over from Canton and set up in his yard. Unlike TR, Harding promised "not heroism but healing, not nostrums but normalcy." He wrote to a friend well before his election that the "only thing I worry about is that I might be nominated and elected." To another friend, he later asserted, "I am not fit for this office and should never have been here."[39]

On November 2, Harding was elected president by what was then the largest popular majority ever. Two days later, speaking from the porch of his Ohio home, he declared Wilson's League "now deceased."[40]

ON INAUGURATION DAY at the Capitol, Wilson walked slowly on the arm of an attendant to the elevator and then to the president's room. There, he signed a few remaining bills. Senator Lodge entered. The Sixty-eighth Congress, he declared, was now ready to adjourn. Wilson stared coldly at his great antagonist: "Tell them I have no further communication to make." And then almost inaudibly, he said, "I thank you for your courtesy."[41]

By the time he left office, most people in the Congress, and as well as much of the public, believed Wilson had had a stroke. According to Arthur Link, Dr. Grayson, when questioned, neither confirmed nor denied that the president had suffered a stroke, though he admitted that Wilson was "a very sick man." But at the time of his stroke, Wilson also had a blockage of his urethra, and when a urologist from Johns Hopkins was called in, he immediately saw what had happened. On February 20, 1920, he gave an interview and said, "We all agreed at the time that the President had had a thrombosis in the brain and suffered a stroke." It was hardly news. Vice President Thomas Marshall, fearful of assassination, refused to press the issue. Nor did leading Democratic senators want to see a weak man like Marshall in the White House.[42]

In his retirement Wilson moved to a comfortable brick and limestone house, purchased by admiring friends, on Washington's "S" Street. Edith devotedly attended to his every need; visitors were usually limited to half an hour, and most afternoons Wilson was taken for a drive. It was in many ways a life of prolonged convalescence. Perhaps the most significant visit was from Georges Clemenceau, who had fallen from power as a result of his own compromises at the peace conference. When he spoke of their reunion, Clemenceau reported, "We fully forgave each other for our bitter quarrels at Versailles. That was all in the past; and both of us had lost."[43]

Wilson always hoped he could undo the decision of the Senate on the League of Nations and even thought that he could be called out of retirement to run for president in 1924. Though he grew ever more dour and querulous, he saw his faith restored on Armistice Day, 1923, when a throng of well-wishers gathered in front of his house. He then appeared in the balcony and, emotional and unrelenting, spoke briefly. "I am not one of those that have the least anxiety about the triumph of the principles I have stood for," he concluded. "I have seen fools resist Providence before and I have seen their destruction and contempt. That we shall prevail is as sure as God reigns."[44]

On February 3, 1924, Woodrow Wilson died. He was buried in the National Cathedral.

PRESIDENT WARREN HARDING gave William Howard Taft what he had always wanted. In the summer of 1921, he appointed Taft to be the chief justice of the United States Supreme Court. Before long, the unhappiness Taft had experienced in the White House was forgotten. "The truth is," Taft wrote in December 1925, "that in my present life I don't remember that I ever was president."[45]

EVEN AS HARDING doubted that he deserved the White House, he very much wanted to make his name as a dignified, compassionate president. His opportunity soon came. Only a few weeks after his inaugural, there was pressure put on him to pardon Eugene V. Debs and the other prisoners jailed because of antiwar activities. During the campaign Harding had said that he favored a general amnesty. What could better illustrate getting back to normalcy than wiping the slate clean of the excesses of the Wilson years. Notable figures from all over the world appealed for clemency for Debs, including George Bernard Shaw, H. G. Wells, Clarence Darrow, Upton Sinclair, Lincoln Steffens, and William Allen White. Cautious and calculating, Harding did not free Debs until Christmas Day, 1921.

Harding's response was a marked contrast to Wilson's mean-spirited denial in the months preceding Harding's inauguration. On January 31, 1921, Attorney General Palmer had recommended to President Wilson that he commute Debs's sentence to end on Lincoln's Birthday. Palmer pointed out that Debs, now sixty-five years old, was in poor health, and that his friends were fearful he might die in prison. When Wilson received his recommendation he wrote across it—"Denied."

Later he explained to Joe Tumulty: "I know there will be a great deal of denunciation of me for refusing this pardon. They will say I am cold-blooded and indifferent, but it will make no impression on me. This man was a traitor to his country and he will never be pardoned during my administration."[46]

WHEN DEBS WAS RELEASED from prison, the warden suspended all rules so that 2,300 convicts could crowd along the front wall of the prison to shout their farewells. Debs turned to them, with tears streaming down his face, and held his hat in tribute to them high above his head. Finally, a drawn and terribly thin Debs offered a last good-bye and drove away.

Debs, however, did not return to Terre Haute that day but instead took a train to Washington at Harding's invitation to meet with the president. When he stepped into Harding's office on the day after Christmas, he said quietly, "Good morning, Mr. President."

"Well," said Harding, striding over to shake Debs's hand, "I have heard so damned much about you, Mr. Debs, that now I am very glad to meet you personally."

Debs had promised not to reveal what was said between them, but when he emerged from the interview he was confronted by a group of reporters. "Mr. Harding appears to me," Debs said, "to be a kind gentleman, one whom I believe possesses human impulses. We understand each other perfectly."[47]

The Inheritors

THE FLOURISHING OF American radicalism, was over.[1] The growth of the Communist Party had further split the Socialists; many, particularly those radicals who had fallen away with Haywood, joined the Communists or embraced insurrectionary tactics. Debs had welcomed the Russian Revolution, but became increasingly distressed by Moscow's efforts to dictate policies to Socialists elsewhere. Typically he did little to mediate between the ultraleftists and the traditional Socialists. After the conservative wing purged the Communists, he simply called for a more revolutionary party. As the party never won large support from organized labor, many Socialists sought adherents among the middle-class Progressives.

Debs could never bring himself to abandon the Socialist Party. In 1923, he delivered fifty-three speeches to enormous crowds in major cities. He raised funds for the party, but exhausted himself; even his heroic efforts could not produce a Socialist revival.

In 1924, Debs endorsed Senator Robert LaFollette of Wisconsin and his new Progressive party, which was supported not only by the Socialists but also by the AFL, the Farmer-Labor Party, and most non-Communist left-wing groups. Much of LaFollette's support came from disaffected farmers who were being left out of the general prosperity. It was far from the workers' party Debs had always hoped for.

On October 20, 1926, Debs suffered a massive heart attack and died at the age of seventy. At his funeral, the orator was a young Norman Thomas, who would succeed Debs as the leader of the party and perennial presidential candidate.

DEBS HAD ALWAYS seen his mission as organizing workers into industrial unions. He understood that this was the only democratic response to the excesses of industrial capitalism, but he underestimated the vitality of American business to adjust.

In the decade after his death, Debs's legacy would be lodged in the founding of the Congress of Industrial Organizations. The CIO accepted the Debsian view of industrial unionism, where all the workers in, for example, the automobile or steel industry would belong to one union. So spectacular was its success in creating industrial unions that it soon challenged the dominance of the AFL within organized labor. It was finally the tough, dynamic Walter Reuther, head of the United Auto Workers, who pushed through a merger of the AFL and the CIO in the early 1950s.

The triumph of industrial unionism took place when the United States was suffering from the Great Depression, and Debs in his fight to preserve American democracy against the threats from both the right and the extreme left helped prepare the way for the radical reforms of the New Deal. As an old Debsian comrade in arms wrote, "Those years of education forced on the people, in towns big and little (from pulpit, platform and soapbox, by voice, leaflet and books), saved this country from civil war in the depths of the Depression, and gave Franklin D. Roosevelt . . . the understanding public and trained workers for the immediate job he had on taking over."[2]

THE COMING TO POWER OF FDR in 1932 also fulfilled the promise of TR's radicalism in 1912 and expanded Wilson's achievements in his first administration. In foreign policy as well, FDR adopted the "practical idealism" that Theodore Roosevelt had espoused, while avoiding the pitfalls of Wilson's messianic internationalism.

The hiatus between Wilson and Franklin Roosevelt was relatively brief. Even the election of Herbert Hoover seemed to many at the time a return to a dynamic, former Progressive, who had worked to improve wages and working conditions while secretary of commerce under Harding and Coolidge. By appointing Henry Stimson to State, Hoover chose an avowed disciple of Theodore Roosevelt, a man who, he thought, was "more of a warrior than a diplomat."[3]

Stimson soon opened contacts with the League of Nations. But as the United States could participate only as an observer, he was frustrated that he could not pressure member nations to take strong measures against Japan when it seized Manchuria in 1931. Nor could he persuade the Hoover administration to take military action to curb Japanese aggression. The collapse of the stock market and the coming of the Depression necessarily focused the White House on the grave problems at home. In the end, the Hoover administration was not marked by governmental energy and direction in either its foreign or domestic policy.

By contrast, Franklin Roosevelt's election to the White House brought to the fore the vigor and ambition that had characterized his illustrious cousin. In many respects, the extraordinary display of government action in the first months of the New Deal—the famous Hundred Days—was a clear reminder that a president who believed in executive power now headed the United States once again. For FDR as for TR, reform meant strong federal powers wielded by the White House in the pattern of the New Nationalism.

Roosevelt, a pragmatist to the core, committed himself to endless experimentation to see what would work to alleviate the Depression. "I have no expectation of making a hit every time I come to bat," Roosevelt declared in one of his early radio Fireside Chats. As he later said, "The country needs . . . bold, persistent experimentation. It is common sense to take a method and try it: if it fails, admit it frankly and try another. But above all, try something."[4]

What resulted was government regulation and compulsory national planning. As for social legislation, more was passed in the first two years of the New Deal than in the administrations of Theodore Roosevelt and Woodrow Wilson combined. And when FDR decried "the falsity of material wealth as the standard of success," he was echoing TR's patrician contempt for the Newport crowd, the new money that put greed ahead of social responsibility. Like "Uncle Ted," FDR believed that nationalist leadership would transcend self-interest; happiness, he said, "lies not in the mere possession of money; it lies in the joy of achievement, in the thrill of the creative effort."[5]

In FDR's second term, on the other hand, a Wilson-like New Freedom tended to predominate, in part as a reaction to overregulation. In 1935, the Supreme Court had declared unconstitutional the National Recovery Act (NRA), which set forth a program of cooperative planning with business, suspension of anti-trust laws, and control of production and working conditions. In so doing, the NRA overreached by attempting to write codes for hundreds of industries.

In response to that and other rebuffs from the bench, in 1937 Roosevelt tried to enlarge the Supreme Court with appointees who would be more sympathetic to the new legislation. This mirrored TR's demands for judicial recall when decisions went against his legislative efforts. In effect, what FDR wanted to do was to guarantee a New Deal majority in the Court by forcing conservatives into retirement or to offset their votes by adding new justices. His plan—which even his opponents agreed was probably constitutional—was to provide retirement at full pay for all federal judges over age seventy; if a Supreme Court justice refused to retire, an "assistant" with full voting rights was to be appointed. In no case could there be more than fifteen justices.

After the 1936 election, in which Roosevelt won more than 60 percent of the popular vote and carried every state but Maine and Vermont, the Supreme Court began approving New Deal legislation while the Congress killed the "court-packing" plan. Roosevelt quipped that he had lost a "battle" but won the "war."[6]

The indications that the New Freedom was now in the ascendancy came with the 1936 Wagner-Connery Act, which included strong anti-corporation legislation. In response to a severe recession in 1937 to 1938, which FDR's advisers attributed to price-fixing by monopolistic combines, Roosevelt beefed up the anti-trust division of the Justice Department. He sent a powerful message to Congress urging "a thorough study of the concentration of economic power in American industry and the effect of that concentration upon the decline of competition."[7]

The New Freedom, however, could never be fairly tested. Not only was there a Republican resurgence in the 1938 congressional elections, but the looming threat of a military conflict in Europe also focused the energies of the president on preparing the nation for war, which, when it came, demanded the centralization of power that the New Nationalism had encouraged.

Between 1935 and 1938, as historian John Milton Cooper observed, "Roosevelt completed the task Wilson had begun. He aligned a majority coalition of disadvantaged interest groups—economic, social, and sectional—behind the Democratic party."[8] Even in 1938, the Democrats retained control of both houses of Congress by comfortable, if not overwhelming, margins. Most important, Roosevelt had put together a coalition of ethnic and poorer voters in the Northeast and Midwest that, together with southern Democrats, would give the Democrats a majority status for the next four decades. (During that time, Democrats gained the presidency five out of eight times and lost control of Congress for only four years).[9] The prospect of American entrance into the Second World War then allowed Roosevelt to run for and win a third term, and to assume the Theodore Rooseveltian mantle of a national leader.

TO DO SO, Roosevelt built up a bipartisan support for his foreign policy. This was done initially by appointing Henry Stimson as secretary of war in 1940, and Frank Knox as secretary of the navy. Both men's credentials stemmed from their association with Theodore Roosevelt. FDR cooperated heartily with the Committee to Defend America by Aiding the Allies, headed by Republican and TR admirer William Allen White, and after the 1940 election, he sent Wendell Willkie, who ran against him in 1940, to Great Britain as his special emissary.

Meeting with Winston Churchill in August 1941 on the battleship H.M.S. *Prince of Wales* in Argentia Bay, Newfoundland, Roosevelt and the British prime minister set forth an eight-point, broad statement of war aims—the Atlantic Charter, reminiscent of Wilson's Fourteen Points. They reaffirmed the principles of collective security, national self-determination, freedom of the seas, and liberal trading practices. They also denied themselves any further territorial expansion and pledged economic collaboration leading to "social security." At this point Roosevelt would not back any new League of Nations, as Churchill suggested, but did agree to a statement accepting "the establishment of a wider and permanent system of general security."[10]

Once America entered the war, Roosevelt thought more carefully about what kind of program would be acceptable to the American people, and how to avoid Wilson's errors of relying so heavily on the power of public opinion and international law to assure a durable peace. For FDR, the portrait of Wilson that hung in the cabinet room was not only a reminder that Wilson had aspired to a system of collective security, but also a warning not to fail here as Wilson had.

In drawing up his plans for the United Nations, Roosevelt looked to traditional notions of great-power leadership. In this sense his inspiration in foreign affairs was the model that Theodore Roosevelt suggested. FDR wanted a steering committee headed by the great powers that would provide the means to enforce the peace. He saw such a committee as the "Four Policemen" made up of the United States, Britain, the Soviet Union, and China. This was the template for the United Nations Security Council, the four great powers (plus France) as having permanent veto power over substantive questions such as economic and military sanctions, and thus central control over peace enforcement.

In contrast to Wilson, Roosevelt included prominent Republican senators to assist in drawing up the plans for the United Nations, a move that helped him immeasurably in presenting his case for collective security to the American people.

Even though the Cold War severely hobbled the ability of the Big Five to cooperate in preserving the peace (the absence of military conflict between America and the Soviet Union was the result of the nuclear balance), FDR's vision still offers hope for a more just global system. A half century after the rendezvous in Newfoundland, cooperation among the five permanent members of the Security Council could and did authorize peacekeeping and peace enforcement missions in war-torn parts of the world. As FDR once reminded Americans, "The retreat to isolationism a quarter century ago was started not by a direct attack against international cooperation but against the alleged imperfections of the peace."[11]

With FDR's death the last direct link to Theodore Roosevelt and

Woodrow Wilson came to an end. But more than either of his predecessors, this Roosevelt understood how best to strike the right balance between idealism and power.[12]

THEODORE ROOSEVELT and Woodrow Wilson invented the activist modern presidency. TR's commitment to use Hamiltonian means to achieve Jeffersonian ends was not unlike Wilson's use of executive power to promote free competition that would prevent big business from stifling local economies. Their legacy was the use of centralized power to create greater democracy. For TR, as for Wilson, Hamilton's strong government had to be united with the "one great truth taught by Jefferson—that in America a statesman should trust the people, and should endeavor to secure each man all possible individual liberty, confident that he will use it right."[13]

NOTES

Prologue: The Defining Moment

1. The description of Wilson's arrival in France, and the quotation from Bolitho, are taken from Gene Davis, *When the Cheering Stopped: The Last Years of Woodrow Wilson* (New York: Time special edition, 1964), 33–36.

2. See Davis, *When the Cheering Stopped*, 37–39.

3. *Kansas City Star*, November 26, 1918, quoted in Alexander L. George and Juliette L. George, *Woodrow Wilson and Colonel House: A Personality Study* (New York: Dover Publications, 1964), 205.

4. Letter from Wilson to Mary Hulbert Peck, August 25, 1912, quoted in Ray Stannard Baker, *Woodrow Wilson: Life and Letters, Governor, 1910–1913* (London: William Heinemann, 1932), 3:390.

5. Henry Pringle, *Theodore Roosevelt* (New York: Harcourt, Brace, 1931), Arthur Krock and Bellamy Partridge to the author, 602.

6. *New York Times*, January 8, 1919.

7. Taft to Corinne Roosevelt Cowles, July 26, 1921, quoted in Pringle, *Theodore Roosevelt*, 11:913.

8. Taft to Helen Taft, January 9, 1919, quoted in Pringle, *Theodore Roosevelt*, 2:914.

9. Sylvia Jukes Morris, *Edith Kermit Roosevelt: Portrait of a First Lady* (New York: Coward, McCann & Geoghegan, 1980), 436–37; see also William Manners, *T.R. and Will: A Friendship That Split the Republican Party* (New York: Harcourt, Brace, 1969), 311–13.

10. Quoted in Walter LaFeber, *The American Age: United States Foreign Policy at Home and Abroad*, 2nd ed. (New York: W. W. Norton, 1994), 2:328.

11. Ray Ginger, *The Bending Cross: A Biography of Eugene Victor Debs* (New Brunswick, N.J.: Rutgers University Press, 1949, reprinted by Thomas Jefferson University Press, 1992), 359.

12. Eugene V. Debs, *Writings and Speeches of Eugene V. Debs* (New York: Hermitage Press, 1948), Statement to the court, September 14, 1918, 437; see also Nick Salvatore, *Eugene V. Debs: Citizen and Socialist* (Urbana, Ill.: University of Chicago Press, 1982), 295.

13. See John Morton Blum, *The Republican Roosevelt* (Cambridge, Mass.: Harvard University Press, 1954 [paper]), 145.

14. See Richard Hofstadter, *The American Political Tradition and the Men Who Made It* (New York: Vintage Books, 1974), 318.

15. See John Milton Cooper, *The Warrior and the Priest: Woodrow Wilson and Theodore Roosevelt* (Cambridge, Mass.: Belknap/Harvard, 1984 [paper]), xiii.

1. "Back from Elba"

1. Quoted in Henry Pringle, *The Life and Times of William Howard Taft* (New York: Farrar and Rinehart, 1939), 1:543.

2. Letter to Taft, June 8, 1910, in *The Letters of Theodore Roosevelt* (Cambridge, Mass.: Harvard University Press, 1954), vol. 7, *The Days of Armageddon, 1909–1914,* selected and edited by Elting E. Morison, 88–89.

3. Quoted in Manners, *T.R. and Will,* 160.

4. Taft to Roosevelt, Feb. 25, 1909, quoted in Henry F. Pringle, *Taft,* 1:392.

5. Roosevelt to Taft, Feb. 26, 1909, TR *Letters,* 6:1538.

6. Mark Sullivan, *Our Times* (New York: Charles Scribner's Sons, 1932), vol. 4, *The War Begins, 1909–1914,* 331–32.

7. Letter to Theodore Roosevelt Jr., May 17, 1909; letter to Anna Roosevelt Cowles, May 19, 1909, in TR *Letters,* 7:10–11.

8. See Tweed Roosevelt, "Theodore Roosevelt's African Safari," in *Theodore Roosevelt: Many-Sided American* (Interlaken, New York: Heart of Lakes Publishing, 1992), 413–32.

9. Theodore Roosevelt, in foreword to *African Game Trails* (New York: Charles Scribner's Sons, 1910).

10. *Selections from the Correspondence of Theodore Roosevelt and Henry Cabot Lodge, 1884–1918* (New York: Charles Scribner's Sons, 1925), 2:360.

11. TR *Letters,* 7:45.

12. Gifford Pinchot to TR, December 31, 1909, in Gifford Pinchot, *Breaking New Ground* (New York: Harcourt, Brace, 1947), 498–500.

13. H. W. Brands, *T.R.: The Last Romantic* (New York: Basic Books, 1997), 613; see also Edmund Morris, *Theodore Rex* (New York: Random House, 2001), 227, 246.

14. Roosevelt-Lodge *Letters,* vol. 2, Lodge to TR, January 15, 1910, 358; TR to Lodge, March 1, 1910, 361; TR to Lodge, March 4, 1910, 361–62.

15. Citations on the European tour in Henry F. Pringle, *Theodore Roosevelt: A Biography* (New York: Harcourt, Brace, 1931), 516–18.

16. See Manners, *T.R. and Will,* 138.

17. Ibid., 148.

18. Quoted in Nathan Miller, *Theodore Roosevelt: A Life* (New York: William Morrow, 1992), 501.

19. Ibid.; see also George E. Mowry, *Theodore Roosevelt and the Progressive Movement* (Madison, Wisconsin: The University of Wisconsin Press, 1946), 125.

20. Quoted in *New York Review of Books,* April 11, 2002, 10.

21. Letter from TR to Lodge, April 11, 1910, in TR *Letters,* 7:69–74.

22. Archibald Willingham Butt, *Taft and Roosevelt: The Intimate Letters of Archie Butt, Military Aide* (Port Washington, New York: Kennikat Press, 1971 [first published 1930]), vol. 1, Letter to Mrs. Lewis F. Butt (Clara), April 12, 1910, 327.

23. Butt's letter in *Taft and Roosevelt,* April 19, 1910, 1:332.

24. Quoted in Manners, *T.R. and Will,* 153.

25. Quoted in Miller, *Theodore Roosevelt,* 507–08; see also *Letters of Theodore Roosevelt,* fn., 75.

26. Quoted in Manners, *T.R. and Will,* 156.

27. For the homecoming, see Butt's letter in *Taft and Roosevelt,* vol. 1, June 19, 1910, 393–405.

28. Ibid., 1:396.

29. Pringle, *The Life and Times of William Howard Taft,* 3.

30. Quoted in "William Howard Taft," by Mark C. Carnes, in *"To the Best of My Ability": The American Presidents,* James M. McPherson and David Rubel, eds. (New York: Dorling Kindersley/Agincourt Press, 2000), 188.

31. Quoted in Pringle, *Taft,* 45.

32. For a good portrait of Hanna, see Matthew Josephson, *The Politicos: 1865–1896* (New York: Harcourt, Brace, 1938), 640–41.

33. Ibid., 641.

34. Quoted in Carnes, *"To the Best of My Ability,"* 172.

35. Quoted in Pringle, *Taft,* 82.

36. Charlie Taft anecdote, quoted in Manners, *T.R. and Will,* 47; Taft statement to Roosevelt, from the *War Secretary Diaries,* quoted in Pringle, *Taft,* 315.

37. Quoted in Pringle, *Taft,* 313.

38. See Louis Auchincloss, *Theodore Roosevelt* (New York: Times Books, 2001), 21; see also Silvia Jukes Morris, *Edith Kermit Roosevelt: Portrait of a First Lady,* 3.

39. Butt, *Taft and Roosevelt,* 181.

40. See Manners, *T.R. and Will,* 8–14; Pringle, *Taft,* 392–93.

41. Lawrence F. Abbott, *The Letters of Archie Butt* (New York: Doubleday, 1924), 390.

42. Quoted in Pringle, *Taft,* 394.

43. See Mrs. William Howard Taft, *Recollections of Fall Years* (New York: Dodd, Mead, 1914), cited in Pringle, *Taft,* 398.

44. Quoted in Pringle, *Taft,* 399.

45. Ibid., *Taft,* 400–01.

46. Manners, *T.R. and Will,* 84.

47. For a description of Nellie Taft's illness, see Butt, *Taft and Roosevelt,* 1:86–91; 99–100.

48. See George E. Mowry, *Theodore Roosevelt and the Progressive Movement* (Madison, Wisc.: University of Wisconsin Press, 1946), 17, 18, 19, 44, 45.

49. *New York Times,* January 31, 1908.

50. See Mowry, *Theodore Roosevelt and the Progressive Movement,* 34–45; for the appellation "advance agent of progressivism," 34.

51. Quoted in Pringle, *Taft,* 425.

52. Ibid., 454.

53. TR *Letters,* vol. 7, Roosevelt to Pinchot, June 28, 1910, 95–96.

54. Quoted in Manners, *T.R. and Will,* 171.

55. For the description of the meeting in Beverly, see Butt, *Taft and Roosevelt,* 417–31; for Mrs. Taft's reaction, see Manners, *T.R. and Will,* 172.

2. "The Ruthlessness of the Pure in Heart"

1. Quoted in August Heckscher, *Woodrow Wilson* (Newtown, Ct.: American Political Biography Press, 2000), 145.

2. See Louis Auchincloss, *Woodrow Wilson* (New York: Penguin/Viking, 2000), 17–18.

3. Arthur S. Link, *Wilson: The Road to the White House* (Princeton, N.J.: Princeton University Press, 1947), 98–100.

4. Ibid., 102–06.

5. For Wilson's quotes, see John Milton Cooper Jr., *The Warrior and the Priest* (The Belknap Press of Harvard University Press, 1983 [paper]), 20–21.

6. On Wilson's desire to dominate and for the quote by Wilson's daughter, see Alexander L. George and Juliette L. George, *Woodrow Wilson and Colonel House: A Personality Study* (New York: Dover Publications, 1964 [paper]), 8, 11–12.

7. Ibid., 12.

8. See Auchincloss, *Woodrow Wilson,* 6.

9. See Cooper, *The Warrior and the Priest,* 17–19.

10. George, *Wilson and House,* 21.

11. Quoted in Heckscher, *Woodrow Wilson,* 69.

12. Quoted in Auchincloss, *Woodrow Wilson,* 14.

13. Quoted in Heckscher, *Woodrow Wilson,* 75.

14. See Auchincloss, *Woodrow Wilson,* 20.

15. The most persuasive account of the affair with Mary Hulbert Peck can be found in August Heckscher's *Woodrow Wilson,* 185–88.

16. Quoted in Auchincloss, *Woodrow Wilson,* 22.

17. Edmund Wilson, *The Shores of Light: A Literary Chronicle of the Twenties and Thirties* (New York: Farrar, Straus and Young, 1952), "Woodrow Wilson at Princeton," 314–17.

18. Quoted in Link, *The Road to the White House,* 84.

19. For the controversy over the graduate college, see Cooper, *The Warrior and the Priest,* 102–05; George, *Woodrow Wilson and Colonel House,* 39–47; see also Link, *The Road to the White House,* chap. 3, "The Battle of Princeton."

20. Cooper, *The Warrior and the Priest,* 120.

21. Link, *The Road to the White House,* 127.

22. See Hofstadter, *The American Political Tradition,* 323–24.

23. Link, *The Road to the White House,* 141.

24. Ibid., 142.

25. Ibid., 149–50.

26. Quoted in Joseph P. Tumulty, *Woodrow Wilson As I Know Him* (New York: Doubleday, Page & Company, 1921), 15.

27. Tumulty, *Woodrow Wilson As I Know Him,* 21.

28. For Wilson's speech, see Link, *The Road to the White House,* 162–68.

29. Hofstadter, *The American Political Tradition,* 327.

3. The Heirs of Hamilton and Jefferson

1. See Mowry, *Theodore Roosevelt and the Progressive Movement,* 135–40.

2. Butt's letter in *Taft and Roosevelt,* August 17, 1910, 2:479–82.

3. Letter to Henry Cabot Lodge, August 17, 1910, in TR *Letters,* 7:117.

4. Butt's letter in *Taft and Roosevelt,* August 19, 1910, 2:485.

5. Miller, *Theodore Roosevelt,* 515.

6. For Osawatomie speech, see Theodore Roosevelt, *Works,* nat. ed. (New York: Charles Scribner's Sons, 1925), 17:5–22.

7. All of Croly's quotes are taken from *The Promise of American Life* (Boston: Northeastern University Press, 1989, reprinted from the 1909 edition), 12, 20, 22, 23, 24, 32, 34, 40, 42, 43, 44, 45, 168, 169.

8. Theodore Roosevelt, *Autobiography,* 28.

9. Butt, *Taft and Roosevelt,* September 1910, 529.

10. Cooper, *The Warrior and the Priest,* 127, 123–24.

11. See Joseph P. Tumulty, *Woodrow Wilson As I Know Him* (New York: Doubleday), 44–45.

12. Quoted in Link, *Wilson: The Road to the White House,* 212.

13. George, *Wilson and House,* 63.

14. Ibid., 64.

15. Ibid., 65.

16. Cooper, *The Warrior and the Priest,* 169.

17. Ibid., 173.

4. The Debs Rebellion

1. Quoted in Ray Ginger, *The Bending Cross: A Biography of Eugene Victor Debs,* 293.

2. Quoted in Nick Salvatore, *Eugene V. Debs: Citizen and Socialist,* 225.

3. Quoted in Ginger, 266.

4. Ibid., 10.

5. Quoted in Salvatore, 11.

6. Ibid., 17.

7. Ginger, 16.

8. For citation on manhood, see Salvatore, 19. For childhood of Eugene Debs, see Ginger, chap. 1; see also Salvatore, chap. 1, "An Earthly Paradise."

9. Quoted in Ginger, 19.

10. Quoted in Salvatore, 49.

11. See Salvatore, chap. 2, "The Blue-Eyed Boy of Destiny."

12. Quoted in Ginger, 44.

13. Quoted in Salvatore, 55.

14. Ibid., 58, 60.

15. Ginger, 217–18.

16. Quoted in Salvatore, 125.

17. Ibid., 127.

18. Ginger, 114.

19. *New York Times,* June 27, 1894, quoted in Salvatore, 129.

20. See "Grover Cleveland," by Vincent P. De Santis, in *To the Best of My Ability,* James M. McPherson and David Rubel eds. (New York: Dorling Kindersley, 2000); see also Ginger, 137.

21. On the Pullman strike, see Ginger, 108–52; Salvatore, 126–37.

22. For a descripton of Debs in the Cook County jail, see Ginger, 152.

23. Ginger, 165.

24. Quoted in Salvatore, 152.

25. For Debs's imprisonment in Woodstock, see Ginger, 168–79.

26. Ibid., 177.

27. See "Liberty," Speech at Battery D, Chicago, on Debs's release from Woodstock jail, November 22, 1895, in Eugene V. Debs, *Writings and Speeches* (New York: Hermitage Press, 1948), 6–20.

28. See the essay "William Jennings Bryan: The Democrat as Revivalist," in Richard Hofstadter, *The American Political Tradition*.

29. Reprinted in Leon Fink, *Major Problems in the Gilded Age and the Progressive Era* (Lexington, Mass.: D.C. Heath, 1993), 176–80.

30. Quoted in Hofstadter, *American Political Tradition*, 245.

31. Hofstadter quotation in *American Political Tradition*, 250; Villard quotation, Ibid., 245.

32. Quoted in Ginger, 193.

33. *The Social Democrat*, March 17, 1898, quoted in Salvatore, 165.

34. Quoted in Salvatore, 192.

35. Ibid., 193–94.

36. Ibid., 218.

37. Ibid., 213.

38. For a description of the marriage, see Salvatore, 213–16.

39. Ibid., 242.

40. Ibid., 232.

41. See Ginger, 279–84.

5. "Stripped to the Buff"

1. Cited in Mark Sullivan, *Our Times*, vol. 4, *The War Begins, 1909–1914* (New York: Charles Scribner's Sons, 1932), 292–93.

2. Butt, *Taft and Roosevelt*, June 7, 1911, 672–73.

3. Letter from TR to Nicholas Longworth, June 19, 1911: in TR *Letters*, 7:290.

4. Finley Peter Dunne column in the *Kansas City Star*, November 6, 1910, cited in Mowry, *Theodore Roosevelt and the Progressive Movement*, 155.

5. Letter from TR to Henry Wallace, June 17, 1911: TR *Letters*, 300.

6. Letter from TR to Arthur Hamilton Lee, November 11, 1910: TR *Letters*, 163.

7. See Pringle, *Taft*, 658.

8. *New York Sun*, October 6, 20, 1911; see also Mowry, *Theodore Roosevelt and the Progressive Movement*, 184.

9. Ron Chernow, *The House of Morgan: An American Banking Dynasty and the Rise of Modern Finance* (New York: Atlantic Monthly Press, 1990), 122.

10. See Chernow, *House of Morgan*, 124–25.

11. Letter from Roosevelt to Attorney General Charles J. Bonaparte, November 4, 1907: *The Selected Letters of Theodore Roosevelt*, H. W. Brands, ed. (New York: Cooper Square Press, 2001), 457–58.

For a description of the Morgan settlement and the trip to Washington by Gary and Frick, see Chernow, *House of Morgan*, 126–28; Sullivan, *Our Times*, 462–65.

12. Pringle, *Theodore Roosevelt*, 445.

13. Letter from Roosevelt to James R. Garfield, October 31, 1911: TR *Letters*, 430.

14. Roosevelt, "The Trusts, the People, and the Square Deal," *The Outlook*, November 18, 1911, 649–56; see also Mowry, *Theodore Roosevelt and the Progressive Movement*, 191–92.

15. See John Morton Blum, *The Republican Roosevelt* (Cambridge, Mass.: Harvard University Press, 1993 [paper]), 116–21.

16. See Joseph Bucklin Bishop, *Theodore Roosevelt and His Time: Shown in His Own Letters* (New York: Charles Scribner's Sons, 1920), 1:184–85.

17. Letter from Roosevelt to William Bailey Howland, December 23, 1911: TR *Letters*, 466.

18. See David P. Thelen, *Robert LaFollette and the Insurgent Spirit* (Boston: Little, Brown, 1976), Intro. by Oscar Handlin and Pref. by the author, v–vii.

19. Ibid., 10–11.

20. Ibid., 25–26.

21. Ibid., 36.

22. Sullivan, *Our Times,* 473–74.

23. Wister, *Roosevelt: The Story of a Friendship* (New York: Macmillan, 1930), 300–01.

24. See Pringle, *Taft,* 768; see also *The Outlook.* "A Charter of Democracy," February 24, 1912.

25. Quoted in Sullivan, *Our Times,* 477.

26. *New York Times,* February 26, 1912.

6. "A Rope of Sand"

1. Butt, *Taft and Roosevelt,* 2:850.

2. Ibid., 2:846.

3. Manners, *T.R. and Will,* 210.

4. Butt, *Taft and Roosevelt,* 2:804.

5. Letter from White to Roosevelt, March 3, 1912, quoted in Sullivan, *Our Times,* 479–80.

6. Quoted in Manners, *T.R. and Will,* 216.

7. Sullivan, *Our Times,* 480–81.

8. *New York Times,* March 27, 1912; see also Mowry, *Theodore Roosevelt and the Progressive Movement,* 228.

9. *New York Times,* February 27, 1912.

10. Quoted in Pringle, *Taft,* 774.

11. *New York Times,* April 26, 1912.

12. Mowry, *Taft,* 780–81.

13. This incident was told to Taft's biographer Henry Pringle by Seibold himself; see Pringle, *Taft,* 781–82.

14. *Boston Post,* April 27, 1912.

15. *New York Times,* May 5, 1912.

16. See George Mowry, *Theodore Roosevelt and the Progressive Movement,* 132. A masterly explication of the 1912 Republican primaries can be found in Mowry's book.

17. See Manners, *T.R. and Will,* 219.

18. Quoted in Cooper, *The Warrior and the Priest,* 157.

19. Mowry, *Theodore Roosevelt and the Progressive Movement,* 234–35.

20. All figures for the primaries are found in John Allen Gable, *The Bull Moose Years: Theodore Roosevelt and the Progressive Party* (Port Washington, N.Y.: Kennikat Press, 1978), 14.

21. See Mowry, *Theodore Roosevelt and the Progressive Movement,* 236.

7. Standing at Armageddon

1. Quoted in Sullivan, *Our Times,* 498.

2. Quoted in fn. 12, Letter from Root to Roosevelt, February 12, 1912: TR *Letters,* 504.

3. Sullivan, *Our Times,* 505.

4. Poster reproduced in Sullivan, *Our Times,* 511.

5. "Mr. Dooley," by Finley Peter Dunne, *Chicago Tribune,* June 16, 1912.

6. See Gable, *The Bull Moose Years,* 14–15; also Mowry, *Theodore Roosevelt and the Progressive Movement,* 239–40.

7. See Manners, *T.R. and Will,* 235–38; Sullivan, *Our Times,* 505–07.

8. Broderick, *Progressivism at Risk,* 54; Mowry, *Theodore Roosevelt and the Progressive Movement,* 144.

9. Theodore Roosevelt, *Works,* 17:204–31; see also H. W. Brands, *T.R.: The Last Romantic* (New York: Basic Books, 1997), 715–16.

10. Quoted in Edmund Morris, *Theodore Rex* (New York: Random House, 2001), 13.

11. Quoted in Philip Jessup, *Elihu Root* (New York: Dodd, Mead, 1938), 2:202.

12. Quoted in Manners, *T.R. and Will,* 247.

13. Pringle, *Taft,* 806.

14. Ibid., 807; Sullivan, *Our Times,* 528–30.

15. Quoted in Manners, *T.R. and Will,* 258.

16. *New York Times,* June 20, 1912.

17. *New York Times,* June 21, 1912.

18. Mowry, *Theodore Roosevelt and the Progressive Movement,* 149.

19. *New York Times,* June 22, 1912.

20. Pringle, *Taft,* 809; Manners, *T.R. and Will,* 260–61.

21. *New York Times,* June 23, 1912.

22. Ibid.

23. Ibid.

8. The Fullness of Time

1. Quoted in Broderick, *Progressivism at Risk,* 59.

2. Woodrow Wilson to Mary Peck, April 23, 1911, quoted in Heckscher, *Woodrow Wilson,* 228.

3. See Cooper, *The Warrior and the Priest,* 172–74.

4. Quoted in Link, *The Road to the White House,* 279–80.

5. For the Nugent affair, see Link, *The Road to the White House,* 280–81.

6. Ibid., 307.

7. Ibid., 313–14; see also Heckscher, *Woodrow Wilson,* 238.

8. Quoted in Link, *The Road to the White House,* 318.

9. Both quotes from the *Newark Evening News,* April 6, 1911, and the *Trenton True American,* April 6, 1911, in Link, *The Road to the White House,* 318.

10. Quoted in Broderick, *Progressivism at Risk,* 76.

11. Heckscher, *Wilson,* 241; Link, *The Road to the White House,* 352–53; *New York Sun,* January 17, 1912.

12. Tumulty, *Woodrow Wilson As I Know Him,* 96.

13. Link, *The Road to the White House,* 356.

14. Tumulty, *Woodrow Wilson As I Know Him,* 97.

15. Letters printed in Tumulty, *Wilson As I Know Him,* 85–87.

16. The Hearst newspaper from which this quote is taken is the *New York American,* January 18, 1912. Both this quote and the excerpt from the letter from Taft to J. C. Hemphill, January 17, 1912, are cited in Link, *The Road to the White House,* 370.

17. Tumulty, *Woodrow Wilson As I Know Him*, 88.

18. Link, *The Road to the White House*, 373.

19. Ibid., 376.

20. Ibid., 381–82.

21. *Trenton True American*, April 5, 1912, quoted in Link, *The Road to the White House*, 385.

22. See Link, *The Road to the White House*, 386–87, 389.

23. See George and George, *Woodrow Wilson and Colonel House*, 75–76.

24. Ibid., 79–82.

25. James Chace and Caleb Carr, *America Invulnerable: The Quest for Absolute Security from 1812 to Star Wars* (New York: Summit Books, 1988), 155–56.

26. Quoted in George and George, *Woodrow Wilson and Colonel House*, 91.

27. Ibid., 93.

28. See James Chace and Caleb Carr, *America Invulnerable: The Quest for Absolute Security from 1812 to Stars Wars*, 155–56.

29 Quoted in George and George, *Woodrow Wilson and Colonel House*, 92–93.

30. Ibid., 99.

31. Ibid., 102.

32. Ibid., 105–06.

33. Broderick, *Progressivism at Risk*, 83–84.

34. Wilson to Mrs. Peck, June 9, 1912, quoted in Link, *The Road to the White House*, 430.

9. Baltimore

1. R. S. Baker, *Woodrow Wilson: Life and Letters* (London: Heinemann, 1932), vol. 3, *Governor 1910–1913*, 332.

2. Eleanor Wilson McAdoo, ed. *The Priceless Gift: The Love Letters of Woodrow Wilson and Ellen Axson Wilson* (New York: McGraw-Hill, 1962), 271.

3. Baker, *Woodrow Wilson*, 3:334.

4. Ibid., 3:335.

5. Ibid., 3:336.

6. Tumulty, *Woodrow Wilson As I Know Him*, 109.

7. McAdoo, *The Priceless Gift*, 271.

8. Baker, *Woodrow Wilson*, 3:336.

9. Tumulty, *Woodrow Wilson As I Know Him*, 113.

10. See David von Drehle, *Triangle: The Fire That Changed America* (New York: Atlantic Monthly Press, 2003), 24–31.

11. See Broderick, *Progressivism at Risk*, 88–89.

12. Baker, *Woodrow Wilson*, 3:327.

13. Ibid., 3:328–29.

14. *New York World*, June 26, 1912, quoted in Link, *The Road to the White House*, 435.

15. Ibid., 436.

16. From the *Proceedings of the Convention*, quoted in Link, *The Road to the White House*, 437.

17. Tumulty, *Wilson As I Know Him*, 115.

18. See Baker, *Woodrow Wilson*, fn. 3:341.

19. Ibid., 342–43; see also Link, *The Road to the White House,* 438–439.

20. *New York Times,* June 28, 1912; Baker, *Woodrow Wilson,* 343–44.

21. Quoted in Link, *The Road to the White House,* 443.

22. Quotations from Link, *The Road to the White House,* 444.

23. *New York Times,* June 28, 1912.

24. For nomination speeches, see the *New York Times,* June 28, 1912; see also Link, *The Road to the White House,* 445–46.

25. *New York Times,* June 29, 1912.

26 Baker, *Woodrow Wilson,* 349.

27. Link, *The Road to the White House,* 449–50.

28. Tumulty, *Wilson As I Know Him,* 119.

29. Broderick, *Progressivism at Risk,* 95; Baker, *Woodrow Wilson.* 3:352–53; William G. McAdoo, *Crowded Years* (Boston: Houghton Mifflin, 1931), 153–55; Tumulty, *Wilson As I Know Him,* 120–21.

30. Baker, *Woodrow Wilson,* 3:355–56.

31. Baker, *Woodrow Wilson,* fn. 1, 3:359. Newton D. Baker shared Senator Glass's view.

32. Link, *The Road to the White House,* 454.

33. See Broderick, *Progressivism at Risk,* 97.

34. *Baltimore Sun,* June 30, 1912.

35. Link, *The Road to the White House,* 440–41.

36. Ibid., 460.

37. Ibid., 461.

38. Ibid., 463–64.

39. Baker, *Woodrow Wilson,* 362.

40. *New York Times,* July 3, 1912; see also Broderick, *Progressivism at Risk,* 101.

41. *New York World,* July 5, 1912; see also Link, *The Road to the White House,* 470.

42. Ibid., 470.

43. Link, *The Road to the White House,* 471.

44. *New York Times,* July 17, 1912.

45. Quoted in Baker, *Woodrow Wilson,* 371–72.

46. *New York Times,* August 8, 1912.

10. The Indispensable Man

1. *New York Times,* August 6, 1912.

2. Ibid.

3. See Katherine Dalton, *Theodore Roosevelt: A Strenuous Life* (New York: Alfred A. Knopf, 2002), chap. 12, "A Progressive World Movement."

4. Roosevelt to Addams, undated telegram, in *Letters,* 595.

5. William Allen White, quoted in Gable, *The Bull Moose Years,* 76 (see White, 483).

6. Elting E. Morison, ed. *Letters of Theodore Roosevelt* (Cambridge, Mass.: Harvard University Press, 1954), fn. 594.

7. Fred D. Warren to Eugene Debs, August 8, 1912, in *Letters of Eugene V. Debs,* vol. 1, 1874–1912, J. Robert Constantine, ed. (Urbana, Ill.: University of Illinois Press, 1990), 535.

8. Dalton, *Theodore Roosevelt,* 393–95.

9. Quoted in Gable, *Bull Moose Years,* 60.

10. Quoted in Dalton, *Theodore Roosevelt,* 394.

11. See Gable, *Bull Moose Years,* 61–62.

12. Ibid., 62.

13. Letter from Roosevelt to Julian La Rose Harris, August 1, 1912, in *Letters,* 584–90.

14. *New York Times,* August 6, 1912.

15. Gable, *Bull Moose Years,* 82.

16. For Roosevelt's "Confession of Faith," see *New York Times,* August 7, 1912.

17. *New York Times,* August 8, 1912; Mary Elizabeth Lease had seconded the nomination of James B. Weaver at the People's Party convention in 1892 (Dalton, *Theodore Roosevelt,* fn. 92, p. 618).

18. Quoted in Gable, *Bull Moose Years,* 107.

19. *New York Times,* August 8, 1912.

20. *New York Times,* August 14, 1912.

11. To Make a Revolution: Debs and Haywood

1. Quoted in Salvatore, *Eugene Debs,* 206.

2. Ibid., 206.

3. Ginger, *The Bending Cross,* 215.

4. Haywood, William D., *Bill Haywood's Book: The Autobiography of William D. Haywood* (New York: International Publishers, 1929), 10–20.

5. Quoted in Melvyn Dubofsky, *"Big Bill" Haywood* (New York: St. Martin's, 1987), 17; for Haywood's early life, see also Dubofsky, chap. 2, "A Western Working-Class Life," Peter Carlson, *Roughneck: The Life and Times of Big Bill Haywood* (New York: W. W. Norton, 1963), chaps. 2, 3.

6. Ibid., 19.

7. Ibid., 20–21.

8. Quoted in Ginger, *The Bending Cross,* 216.

9. Ibid., 215–16.

10. Quoted in Dubofsky, *Haywood,* 30.

11. Ibid., 32.

12. Ibid., 33.

13. Quoted in Ginger, *Bending Cross,* 241.

14. For the story of Haywood's abduction, see Carlson, *Roughneck,* 92–96.

15. Quoted in Ginger, *Bending Cross,* 247.

16. Quoted in Carlson, *Roughneck,* 123.

17. Ibid., 124.

18. Quotations from the trial appear in Carlson, *Roughneck,* 123–35. On the Steunenberg assassination and trial, see also J. Anthony Lukas, *Big Trouble* (New York: Simon & Schuster/Touchstone, 1997).

19. See Dubofsky, *Haywood,* 53–57.

20. Ibid., 65.

21. Ibid., 70.

22. Quoted in Carlson, *Roughneck,* 190.

23. Quotes from Dubofsky, *Haywood,* 58–59.

24. Quoted in Salvatore, *Eugene V. Debs,* 252–53.

25. Ibid., 253.

26. Ibid., 254.

27. Quoted in Carlson, *Roughneck,* 196.

28. For Berger and Haywood citations, see Carlson, *Roughneck,* 198.

29. Quoted in Salvatore, *Eugene V. Debs,* 255.

30. Ibid., 258.

31. For the platform, see Broderick, *Progressivism at Risk,* 126.

32. See Salvatore, *Eugene V. Debs,* 260–61.

12. The New Freedom vs. the New Nationalism

1. Wilson to Mary Hulbert Peck, August 25, 1912, in Baker, *Life and Letters,* 3:390.

2. W. H. Taft to Helen Taft, July 22, 1912, quoted in Pringle, *Taft,* 817.

3. Eleanor Wilson McAdoo, *The Woodrow Wilsons* (New York: Macmillan Company, 1937), 172.

4. *New York Times,* August 29, 1912; see also Leonard Baker, *Brandeis and Frankfurter* (New York: Harper and Row, 1984), 85.

5. Baker, *Brandeis and Frankfurter,* 23.

6. Ibid., 24.

7. Ibid., 28.

8. Ibid., 29.

9. Ibid., 47–48.

10. Ibid.

11. See Dean Acheson, *Morning and Noon* (Boston: Houghton Mifflin, 1965), 47; see also David McLellan, *Dean Acheson: The State Department Years* (New York: Dodd, Mead, 1976), 16.

12. Baker, *Brandeis and Frankfurter,* 84.

13. Quoted in Link, *Wilson: The Road to the White House,* 489.

14. *New York Times,* September 3, 1912.

15. Quoted in Link, *Wilson: The Road to the White House,* 491.

16. Quoted in Link, *Wilson: The Road to the White House,* 492.

17. *New York Times,* September 3, 1912.

18. *New York Times,* September 10, 1912.

19. *New York Times,* September 15, 1912; see also Cooper, *The Warrior and the Priest,* 194–97; Gable, *The Bull Moose Years,* 124–25.

13. The Crusader

1. Quoted in Miller, *Theodore Roosevelt,* 528.

2. Ibid., 529.

3. Taft to Helen Taft, August 26, 1912, quoted in Pringle, *Taft,* 2:815.

4. Quoted in Pringle, *Taft,* 816.

5. Ibid., 818.

6. *New York Times,* August 13, 1912.

7. Quoted in the *New York Times,* September 30, 1912; see also Broderick, *Progressivism at Risk,* 156.

8. See Mowry, *Theodore Roosevelt and the Progressive Movement,* 176.

9. Gable, *The Bull Moose Years,* 11.

10. Broderick, *Progressivism at Risk,* 151.

11. Ibid., 152.

12. Gable, *The Bull Moose Years,* 112.

13. *New York Times,* September 6, 7, 1912; see also Broderick, *Progressivism at Risk,* 153.

14. *New York Times,* September 8, 1912.

15. *New York Times,* September 21, 1912.

16. See Broderick, *Progressivism at Risk,* 154

17. For the Wilson quotations, see Gable, *The Bull Moose Years,* 114.

18. George E. Mowry, "Election of 1912," 290, in *The Coming to Power: Critical Presidential Elections in American History,* Arthur M. Schlesinger Jr., ed. (New York: Chelsea House/McGraw-Hill, 1971); see also Gable, *The Bull Moose Years,* 114–15.

19. See Gable, *The Bull Moose Years,* 118–19.

20. For Harvey's editorial, see the *North American Review,* October 12, 1912; other quotations from Gable, *The Bull Moose Years,* 120; and from Mowry, *Theodore Roosevelt and the Progressive Movement,* 279–80.

21. Gable, *The Bull Moose Years,* 121.

22. Ibid., 121–22.

23. See Miller, *Theodore Roosevelt,* fn. 529.

24. Gable, *The Bull Moose Years,* 123.

25. See Mowry, *Theodore Roosevelt and the Progressive Movement,* 280; Roosevelt quote from Gable, *The Bull Moose Years,* 125.

14. The Moralist

1. House to Wilson, August 25, 1912, in *The Intimate Papers of Colonel House,* Charles Seymour, ed. (Boston: Houghton Mifflin, 1926), 1:68–69.

2. Ibid., 71.

3. Ibid., 73

4. Link, *The Road to the White House,* 494.

5. Ibid., 494–96.

6. *House Papers,* 74.

7. Ibid., 75–76.

8. Ibid., 76.

9. Ibid., 77.

10. See Link, *The Road to the White House,* 498.

11. Hoboken speech, September 21, 1912, in *The Papers of Woodrow Wilson,* Arthur Link, David W. Hirst, and John E. Little, eds. (Princeton: Princeton University Press, 1978), 1912, 25:215.

12. Quoted in Link, *The Road to the White House,* 499.

13. Ibid., 500.

14. Quoted from the *Raleigh News and Observer,* October 1, 1912, in Link, *The Road to the White House,* 501.

15. Both quotations in Link, *The Road to the White House,* 501–02.

16. From the *Trenton Evening Times,* July 31, 1912, quoted in Link, *The Road to the White House,* 502.

17. See Link, *The Road to the White House*, 502.

18. Exchange of letters between Villard and Wilson in Wilson *Papers*, August 14 and August 23, 1912, 25:26–27; 52–53.

19. Letter from Wilson to Bishop Alexander Walters of the African Zion Church, in Wilson *Papers*, October 21, 1912, 25:448–49; see also Link, 503–05.

20. These are the observations of William Bayard Hale, quoted in George and George, *Wilson and House*, 107.

21. Ibid., 108.

22. Quotations from Wilson's speeches in Minneapolis, see Link, *The Road to the White House*, 506-07.

23. Quoted in Baker, *Woodrow Wilson: Life and Letters*, 1910–1913, 392.

24. Quoted in Heckscher, *Woodrow Wilson*, 260.

25. *New York Times*, September 27, 1912.

26. *New York Times*, September 28, 1912; see also Link, *The Road to the White House*, 509.

15. The Authentic Conservative and the Red Prophet

1. *New York Times*, September 18, 1912.

2. Quoted from a letter from Taft to Delia Torrey, August 1, 1912, in Pringle, *Taft*, 2:823.

3. *New York Times*, August 2, 1912.

4. Ibid; see also Broderick, *Progressivism at Risk*, 164–65.

5. *New York Times*, October 2, 1912.

6. Broderick, *Progressivism at Risk*, 167–68.

7. *New York Times*, September 29, 1912.

8. *New York Times*, October 1, 1912; see also Broderick, *Progressivism at Risk*, 169–170.

9. See interview with Debs, *New York Times*, October 21, 1912.

10. Quoted in Salvatore, *Eugene V. Debs*, 263.

11. Ibid., 270.

12. Eugene V. Debs in the *International Socialist Review*, August 1912, quoted in Broderick, *Progressivism at Risk*, 172.

13. Quotation on Wilson and Roosevelt from the *National Ripsaw*, July 10, 22, 1912, in Broderick, 173.

14. Quoted in *National Ripsaw*, August 14, 1912, in Broderick, 175.

15. Berger speech in Congress, July 18, 1912, quoted in Broderick, 175.

16. Eugene V. Debs, "Speech of Acceptance," in *Debs*, Ronald Radosh, ed. (Englewood Cliffs, N.J.: Prentice-Hall, 1971), 58–59.

17. Arthur Schlesinger Jr., "Introduction" to the *Writings and Speeches of Eugene V. Debs* (New York: Hermitage Press, 1948), ix.

18. Radosh, ed., *Debs*, Elizabeth Gurley Flynn, "A Remembrance of an IWW Leader," 98. (When Flynn wrote this piece, she was an American Communist; this account is based on her acquaintance with Debs when she was fighting for the IWW.)

19. *New York Times*, September 30, 1912.

16. "To Kill a Bull Moose"

1. Wilson to Franklin P. Glass, September 6, 1912, quoted in Baker, *Life and Letters,* 400.

2. Link, ed., Wilson *Papers,* October 3, 1912, 327.

3. *New York Times,* October 9, 1912; see also Broderick, *Progressivism at Risk,* 185.

4. Ibid.

5. *New York Times,* October 6, 1912.

6. *New York Times,* October 7, 1912.

7. *Rocky Mountain News* of Denver, October 8, 1912, quoted in Link, *The Road to the White House,* 514.

8. See Link, *The Road to the White House,* 515.

9. Letter from Wilson to Mary Allen Hulbert (Peck), October 13, 1912, in Link, ed., Wilson *Papers,* 25:416.

10. Quoted in Dalton, *Theodore Roosevelt,* 403.

11. Manners, *T.R. and Will,* 278.

12. Ibid., 284.

13. The events surrounding the shooting of Roosevelt have been taken from the *New York Times,* October 15, 1912; see also Broderick, *Progressivism at Risk,* 189–92.

14. Quoted in Manners, *T.R. and Will,* 286.

15. Dalton, *Theodore Roosevelt,* 406.

16. For a full account of Mrs. Roosevelt receiving the news in New York City, see Sylvia Jukes Morris, *Edith Kermit Roosevelt: Portrait of a First Lady,* 385–87.

17. Quoted in Manners, *T.R. and Will,* 284.

18. *New York Times,* October 16, 1912.

19. Quoted in Morris, *Edith Kermit Roosevelt,* 388.

20. *New York Times,* October 17, 1912.

21. Quoted in Manners, *T.R. and Will,* 287.

22. *New York Times,* October 16, 1912.

23. Seymour, ed., *House Papers,* October 18, 78.

24. *New York Times,* October 21, 1912.

25. Link, *The Road to the White House,* 511.

26. Quoted in Broderick, *Progressivism at Risk,* 201.

27. See Manners, *T.R. and Will,* 289–90.

28. Quoted in Pringle, *Taft,* 839.

29. *New York Times,* October 31, 1912.

30. *New York Times,* November 1, 1912.

31. See Broderick, *Progressivism at Risk,* 207–08.

32. See Cooper, *The Warrior and the Priest,* 204–07.

33. Ibid., 219.

34. See George Mowry, "Election of 1912," in *The Coming to Power,* Arthur Schlesinger Jr., ed., 289–90.

17. The Ironies of Fate

1. For Wilson quotation and historian Walter LaFeber's characterization of Wilson as "the greatest military interventionist," see James Chace, "Woodrow Wilson," in *To the Best*

of My Ability: The American Presidents (New York: Dorling Kindersley, 2000), 196–205; see also Cooper, *The Warrior and the Priest,* 222.

2. See Dalton, *Theodore Roosevelt,* 440.

3. *New York Times,* January 13, 1914; see also Eric Goldman, *Rendezvous with Destiny: A History of Modern American Reform* (Chicago: Ivan R. Dee, 2001), 218–19.

4. See Cooper, *The Warrior and the Priest,* 227.

5. Ibid., 124–25.

6. Quoted in George and George, *Woodrow Wilson and Colonel House,* 125.

7. Quoted in the House Diary, November 22, 1915, in Charles Seymour, ed., *The Intimate Papers of Colonel House,* 124.

8. Quotation from Link can be found in Link, *The New Freedom,* 61–67.

9. *New York Times,* March 5, 1913.

10. Quoted in Dalton, *Theodore Roosevelt,* 414.

11. For the Brazilian expedition, see Theodore Roosevelt, *Through the Brazilian Wilderness* (New York: Charles Scribner's Sons, 1914); see also Dalton, *Theodore Roosevelt,* 429–39.

12. Gable, *The Bull Moose Years,* 223–24.

13. Letter from Roosevelt to William Allen White, November 7, 1914, in *The Letters of Theodore Roosevelt: The Days of Armageddon, 1914–1919,* 8:836–37.

14. See Dalton, *Theodore Roosevelt,* 443–44.

15. Roosevelt's Nobel Peace Prize speech can be found in Herman Hagedorn, ed., *The Works of Theodore Roosevelt* (New York: Charles Scribner's Sons, 1925), 17:274–77.

16. See the *New York Times,* September 27, October 4, 11, 18, November 1, 8, 15, 1914; see also, *Philadelphia North American,* November 8 and 15, 1914; *The Independent,* January 4, 1915; the *Outlook,* September 1914.

17. Blum, *The Republican Roosevelt,* 137.

18. Deep within the hold was a cargo of foodstuffs and contraband—4.2 million rounds of ammunition for Remington rifles, 1,250 cases of empty shrapnel shells, and eighteen cases of nonexplosive fuses. (Quoted in Paterson et al., *American Foreign Policy,* 2:257.)

19. Quoted in Heckscher, *Woodrow Wilson,* 354.

20. See "Election of 1916," by Link and Leary in *The Coming to Power,* 310.

21. Quotations from Arthur S. Link, *Campaigns for Progressivism and Peace, 1916–1917* (Princeton, N.J.: Princeton University Press, 1965), 44, 48.

22. Ibid., 94–95.

23. Quoted in Cooper, *The Warrior and the Priest,* 304.

24. Quoted in Gable, *The Bull Moose Years,* 247–48.

25. TR characterization of Hughes in a letter from TR to W. A. Wadsworth, June 23, 1916, in *Letters of Theodore Roosevelt,* 8:1078.

26. Quoted in Dalton, *Theodore Roosevelt,* 467.

27. Ibid., 471.

28. See Arthur Schlesinger Jr., ed., *The Coming to Power:* Arthur S. Link and William M. Leary Jr., "Election of 1916," 307.

29. See Link and Leary, "Election of 1916," in *The Coming to Power,* 319–20.

30. See *Theodore Roosevelt: Many-Sided American,* Natalie A. Naylor, Douglas Brinkley, and John Allen Gable, eds. (Interlaken, N.Y.: Heart of Lakes Publishing, 1992), John Milton Cooper, "If TR Had Gone Down with the *Titanic,*" 507–08.

31. See Salvatore, *Eugene V. Debs,* 275.

32. Ibid., 154.

33. Quoted in Ginger, *The Bending Cross*, 337.
34. Wilson "Peace without Victory" speech in Thomas Paterson and Dennis Merrill, *Major Problems in American Foreign Relations*, 4th ed. (Lexington, Mass.: D.C. Heath, 1995), 2:33–34.
35. Ibid., 272.
36. The Zimmermann telegram in Paterson and Merrill, *Major Problems in American Foreign Relations*, 4th ed., 33.
37. Quoted in Paterson et al., *American Foreign Policy: A History Since 1900*, 3rd ed., 273.
38. Quoted in Dalton, *Theodore Roosevelt*, 489. The Espionage Act was passed in 1917, the Sedition Act in 1918.
39. Ibid., 491.
40. See the Canton Speech in *Debs*, Ronald Radosh, ed., 66–78.
41. See Salvatore, *Eugene V. Debs*, 294–95.
42. Ibid., 295.
43. Quoted in Salvatore, *Eugene V. Debs*, 325.

18. Endgames

1. See John Morton Blum, *The Republican Roosevelt*, 141–42.
2. Cooper, *If TR Had Gone Down with the* Titanic, 503, 511.
3. TR Nobel Peace Prize Address, May 5, 1910, quoted in Cooper, *If TR Had Gone Down with the* Titanic, 511.
4. See Widenor, *Henry Cabot Lodge*, 276, fn. 36.
5. For an excellent discussion of the connection between power politics and idealism, see Widenor, *Henry Cabot Lodge*, 162–67.
6. TR to Lodge, *Letters*, Morison, ed., 6:135–36.
7. Quoted in Widenor, *Henry Cabot Lodge*, 166.
8. See John Milton Cooper, *Breaking the Heart of the World* (New York/Cambridge, U.K.: Cambridge University Press, 2001), 6–8.
9. For the encounter at the Blackstone, see Manners, *T.R. and Will*, 305.
10. Letter from TR to Taft, June 3, 1918, in *Letters*, Morison, ed., 8:1337.
11. John Milton Cooper, *The Warrior and the Priest*, 331–33.
12. Miller, *Theodore Roosevelt*, 562.
13. Quoted in Dalton, *Theodore Roosevelt*, 505.
14. *New York Times*, November 3, 1918; see also Dalton, *Theodore Roosevelt*, 510.
15. Quoted in Miller, 564.
16. Ibid., 565–66.
17. Quoted in Jukes, *Edith Kermit Roosevelt*, 433.
18. Memorandum, in *Letters*, Morison, ed., 1422.
19. See Paterson and Merrill, *Major Problems in American Foreign Relations*, 4th ed., 2:38–39.
20. Ibid., 213.
21. See John Maynard Keynes, *Essays and Sketches in Biography* (New York: Meridian Books, 1956), "The Council of Four, Paris 1919," 261.
22. See Paterson et al., *American Foreign Policy*, 3rd ed., 2:281–82.
23. Edith Wilson, *My Memoir*, 246.
24. Edwin A. Weinstein, *Woodrow Wilson: A Medical and Psychological Biography* (Princeton, N.J.: Princeton University Press, 1981), introduction, chapters 1, 9, 10.

25. Ibid., 316.

26. Ibid.

27. See Paterson et al., *American Foreign Policy,* 3rd ed., 2:286.

28. Ibid., 286.

29. Specifically, Lodge, with the help of Senator Porter J. McCumber, redrafted Article 10 as follows: "The United States assumes no obligation to preserve the territorial integrity or political independence of any country to interfere in controversies between nations . . . under the provision of Article 10 . . . unless in any particular case the Congress, which, under the Constitution, has the sole power to declare war or authorize the employment of the military and naval forces of the United States, shall by act or joint resolution so provide." Wilson immediately rejected the reservation. (See Auchincloss, *Woodrow Wilson,* 115.)

30. Weinstein, *Woodrow Wilson,* 353.

31. Cary Grayson, *Woodrow Wilson: An Intimate Memoir* (New York: Holt, Rinehart and Winston, 1959), 96.

32. Quoted in Edith Wilson, *My Memoir,* 283.

33. Cooper, *Breaking the Heart of the World,* 187–88.

34. Grayson, *Woodrow Wilson,* 99–100.

35. Ibid., 100.

36. Lodge to Root, quoted in Auchincloss, *Woodrow Wilson,* 119.

37. George and George, *Wilson and House,* 305–06.

38. Quoted in Paterson et al., *American Foreign Policy,* 3rd ed., 2:288.

39. Quoted in *To the Best of My Ability,* Morton Keller, "Warren G. Harding," 208.

40. Quoted in George and George, *Wilson and House,* 314.

41. Quoted in Heckscher, *Woodrow Wilson,* 645.

42. The interview with Arthur Link can be found in James Robert Carroll, *The Real Woodrow Wilson* (Bennington, Vt.: Images From the Past, 2001), 58–61.

43. Quoted in Heckscher, *Woodrow Wilson,* 663.

44. George and George, *Wilson and House,* 314.

45. Quoted in Pringle, *Taft,* 2:960.

46. Tumulty, *Woodrow Wilson As I Know Him,* 505.

47. For the release of Debs and his meeting with Harding, see Ginger, *The Bending Cross,* 414–15; Francis Russell, *In the Shadow of Blooming Grove: Warren G. Harding in His Times* (New York: McGraw-Hill, 1968), 462, 486–87; Salvatore, *Eugene V. Debs,* 328; Andrew Sinclair, *The Available Man: The Life Behind the Mask of Warren Gamaliel Harding* (New York: Macmillan, 1965), 225–28.

Epilogue: The Inheritors

1. See Arthur Schlesinger Jr., ed., *History of U.S. Political Parties: From Square Deal to New Deal* (New York: Chelsea House, 1973), vol. 8, 1910–1945, Michael Harrington, "The Socialist America, 1912–1925 (New Brunswick, N.J.: Rutgers University Press, 1984), 326.

2. Quoted in Arthur Schlesinger Jr.'s "introduction" to the *Writings and Speeches of Eugene V. Debs,* xiii.

3. Paterson et al., *American Foreign Policy,* v. 11, 3rd edition, 336.

4. Quoted in Eric Goldman, *Rendezvous with Destiny* (Chicago: Ivan R. Dee, 2001, reprinted from Alfred A. Knopf, 1952), 324.

5. Quoted in Cooper, *The Warrior and the Priest,* 351.

6. Goldman, *Rendezvous with Destiny,* 358.

7. Ibid., 367.

8. Cooper, *The Warrior and the Priest,* 352.

9. Ibid.

10. Paterson et al., *American Foreign Policy,* 3rd ed., 373–76.

11. Quoted in James Chace, "How Moral Can We Get?" *New York Times Magazine,* May 27, 1977.

12. See Cooper, *The Warrior and the Priest,* 361; see also Fareed Zakaria, "Our Way," *The New Yorker,* October 14 and 21, 2002, 78.

13. Quoted in Cooper, *The Warrior and the Priest,* 41.

BIBLIOGRAPHICAL NOTE

THE WORKS dedicated to the study of Theodore Roosevelt and Woodrow Wilson are too numerous to list, but there are certain works—aside from letters, diaries, and documents—that were especially valuable for me.

For Roosevelt, John Morton Blum's landmark study, *The Republican Roosevelt*; the detailed and wise biography, *Theodore Roosevelt: A Strenuous Life* by Kathleen Dalton; John Allen Gable's *The Bull Moose Years: Theodore Roosevelt and the Progressive Party*; and George E. Mowry's *Theodore Roosevelt and the Progressive Movement*. Other biographies that were most useful were H. W. Brands, *TR: The Last Romantic*; Nathan Miller, *Theodore Roosevelt: A Life*; Edmund Morris, *Theodore Rex*; Sylvia Jukes Morris, *Edith Kermit Roosevelt: Portrait of a First Lady*.

For Wilson, the multivolume study of the president by Arthur S. Link; August Heckscher's sympathetic, one-volume biography, *Woodrow Wilson*; Alexander L. George and Juliette George's personality study, *Woodrow Wilson and Colonel House*.

John Milton Cooper's *The Warrior and the Priest*, a comparative biography of Roosevelt and Wilson, is masterly in its judgments of the two men who helped create the modern presidency. William C. Widenor's controversial and intellectually engaging biography *Henry Cabot Lodge and the Search for an American Foreign Policy* expands our understanding of a major figure in U.S. foreign relations.

There are two classic biographies of Eugene V. Debs that are invaluable: Ray Ginger's *The Bending Cross*, and Nick Salvatore's *Eugene V. Debs: Citizen and Socialist*.

Henry Pringle's two-volume biography of William Howard Taft, published in 1939, still stands as indispensable.

Any study of the 1912 election will owe a debt to Francis L. Broderick's *Progressivism at Risk,* and to Richard Hofstadter's *The Age of Reform* and *The American Political Tradition.*

ACKNOWLEDGMENTS

ALICE MAYHEW, my editor at Simon & Schuster, has been unfailingly enthusiastic and committed to this project since its inception. Her editorial suggestions have been invaluable, especially her insistence on a strong narrative and a logical shape to the book. Roger Labrie's care and concern for the book have always buoyed me up. Suzanne Gluck at William Morris has been a steadfast advocate of my work.

I owe a great debt of gratitude to my good friend and colleague Mark Lytle, a distinguished American historian who has helped me through the minefields of the progressive era. Editorial suggestions from David Fromkin, Harvey Ginsberg, and Sidney Blumenthal have been, as always, cautionary and wise. Excellent research assistance was provided by Rob Ponce, John Steinmetz, Rijin Sahakian, and especially by Jonathan Cristol. Sarah Chace, Rebecca Chace, and Zoe Chace have been unfailingly supportive of this work.

The librarians at the Stevenson Library of Bard College were always ready and willing to assist me. The Tamiment Institute, Bobst Library, New York University, was most useful for research on Eugene V. Debs and the Socialist Party.

Conversations with Caleb Carr made it possible to begin this long journey through the election and consequences of 1912.

Above all, I am deeply grateful to Joan Bingham for her unflagging dedication and indispensable editorial advice. She did everything to give me the time and energy to think through and complete this book. Her commitment was beyond measure.

INDEX

Abernathy, Bud, 23, 75
Abernathy, Temple, 23
Acheson, Dean, 194
Adams, Henry, 26, 107
Adams, John, 5
Adams, Steve, 176–77
Addams, Jane, 162, 167–68
AFL. *See* American Federation of Labor (AFL)
African Americans
    Addams on, 167–68
    AFL on, 169
    Debs on, 71, 75
    Democratic Party on, 101, 163, 164–65
    Gompers on, 75
    Haywood on, 183
    House on, 137–38
    LaFollette on, 101
    lynching of, 163, 164, 214
    Progressive Party and, 161, 163
    at Republican convention, 161
    Roosevelt on, 43, 163–65, 264
    voting rights of, 7, 101, 164
    Wilson on, 43, 213–15, 243–44
African Game Trails (Roosevelt), 13
agrarianism, 83, 142, 162. *See also* farmers
Aldrich, Nelson W., 16–17, 18, 19, 29, 30, 31, 32, 33, 55, 56, 202
Allen, Henry J., 121
Altgeld, John Peter, 78
American Association of Foreign Language Newspapers, 213
American Federation of Labor (AFL), 75, 79, 83, 90, 159, 169, 171–72, 173, 174, 176, 181, 182, 277, 278

American Railway Union (ARU), 74, 76, 77, 78, 79, 82–83, 85
American Tobacco Company, 32
Amos, James, 265
Appeal to Reason, 88, 89, 90, 176, 177
Arthur, Chester A., 122
ARU. *See* American Railway Union (ARU)
Atlantic Charter, 281
Autobiography (Roosevelt), 59, 246
Axson, Edward, 45
Axson, Ellen, 44–45. *See also* Wilson, Ellen
Axson, Stockton, 45, 133

Baker, George F., 96, 97
Baker, Newton D., 150
balance of power, 2, 255, 266, 268
Ballinger, Richard, 15, 16
Baltimore Sun, 144–45
Bankhead, John, 151, 156, 157–58
Bankhead, William, 151
banking system, 158, 186, 195, 244
Barnes, J. Mahlon, 186
Barrymore, Ethel, 177–78
Baruch, Bernard, 204
Belmont, August, 75, 146, 148, 150, 151, 173
Benson, Allan, 254–55
Berger, Victor, 81, 86, 170, 174, 183, 184, 223
Bettrich, Mary Marguerite, 69
Beveridge, Albert J., 16, 162, 165–66, 168, 234
bimetallism, 84, 135. *See also* currency reform; free silver issue
blacks. *See* African Americans

Blum, John Morton, 248
Bolitho, William, 2
Bonaparte, Charles, 162
Bones, Helen, 250
Borah, William E., 112, 116, 178
bossism, political
    LaFollette on, 101, 102
    in New Jersey, 127, 128
    reformers on, 7, 146–47
    Roosevelt on, 109, 118
    Taft and, 109, 111
    Wilson on, 41, 62, 126, 142, 147, 159,
        211, 212
Boyce, Ed, 170, 171–72, 173
Brandeis, Louis D., 192–96, 197, 203,
        205, 206, 216, 243
Brotherhood of Locomotive Firemen, 72,
        73, 74–75, 79, 83
Brown, John, 57
Brownsville riot, 164
Bryan, William Jennings
    in 1896, 254
    in 1908, 90, 239
    Clark and, 135, 139, 140–41, 142,
        143, 144, 145, 155–56
    in Congress, 84
    on currency reform, 84
    on democracy, 148
    in Democratic Party, 40, 84, 125, 128,
        148–49, 150–51, 152
    Murphy on, 147
    as newspaper columnist, 148
    populism of, 40, 43, 83, 84–85
    progressivism of, 148, 150, 153, 158
    on Republican national convention,
        144
    on Roosevelt, 144
    as secretary of state, 248, 249
    speeches of, 84
    on Taft, 144
    white supremacy of, 84
    Wilson and, 129–30, 131–32, 134–35,
        139–41, 143, 144, 145, 146, 155,
        157, 228
Bull Moosers, 117, 118, 162, 163
Bureau of Corporations, 32
Bush, George W., 8
business, big. *See also* capitalism, indus-
    trial

    on African Americans, 75
    Brandeis on, 194, 197
    Clark on, 155–56
    Debs on, 7–8, 81, 85
    LaFollette on, 101, 102
    newspapers and journals on, 130
    People's Party on, 83
    progressives on, 102
    Roosevelt on, 7, 8, 17, 18, 51, 57, 59,
        99, 103, 105, 109, 111, 167, 192,
        196–97, 206, 237–38
    Taft on, 8, 95, 167
    Wilson on, 7, 8, 51, 52, 62, 126, 132,
        147, 158, 192, 196, 216, 217, 244,
        283
Butler, Nicholas Murray, 236
Butt, Archibald Willingham
    on New York State Republican conven-
        tion, 56
    Roosevelt/Taft relationship and,
        21–22, 23, 35, 36, 93–94, 107, 108
    Taft and, 19, 28, 29, 30–31, 60

campaign contributions and spending, 18,
        163
Cannon, "Uncle" Joe, 17, 18, 19, 29, 30,
        31, 33, 55, 56
capitalism, industrial. *See also* business,
        big
    Boyce on, 172
    Debs on, 67–68, 70, 73, 82, 85, 86,
        223, 225, 278
    Gompers on, 75
    Haywood on, 182
    IWW on, 169
    Lawrence strike against, 180
    Roosevelt on, 196, 197
    Socialist Democratic Party on, 86
    Wobblies on, 180
Carnegie, Andrew, 37, 100, 204
Carnegie Steel Corporation, 74
Carter, Jimmy, 8
censorship, 257
Chernow, Ron, 96, 97
child labor, 7, 57, 167, 186, 203, 224, 232
Churchill, Winston, 281, 282
Circle for Negro War Relief, 264
Civil War, 137, 239
Clark, James Beauchamp "Champ"

Bryan and, 135, 139, 140–41, 142, 143, 144, 145, 155–56
as Democratic Speaker of the House, 125, 159
Hearst on, 134, 136, 139, 147
Murphy and, 149
as presidential nominee, 151, 152, 153, 154, 157, 158
Wilson and, 159, 229
Clayton Anti-Trust Act, 244
Clemenceau, Georges, 2, 266, 267, 273–74
Cleveland, Grover, 77, 78, 80, 135
Clinton, William J., 8
coal strike of 1902, 18
Cochems, Harry, 230, 231–32
Coeur d'Alene strike, 175
Cold War, 282
Collier's magazine, 205, 206, 234
Colorado Fuel and Iron Company, 206
Committee to Defend America by Aiding the Allies, 281
Communist Party, 5, 277
competition. *See also* Sherman Anti-Trust Act
Croly on, 58
Debs on, 81
FDR on, 280
Jefferson on, 58
small business and, 31
Taft on, 95
TR on, 167, 206
U.S. Steel and, 98
Wilson on, 7, 192, 195, 197, 203, 216, 217, 244, 283
Congress, U.S. *See also* Senate, U.S.
in 1908, 32
in 1910, 6, 34, 52, 94
in 1918, 2, 261
in 1938, 281
Berger in, 183, 223
on blacks, 43, 214
Bryan in, 84
Clark in, 139
conservatives in, 32
Debs and, 255
Democratic Party and, 2, 239, 246, 281
FDR and, 280

on forest reserves, 15
LaFollette in, 101, 103
progressives in, 32, 103, 239
Republicans in, 2, 6, 18, 32, 94, 246, 261, 267
on Sherman Anti-Trust Act, 98
Taft and, 32
on tariffs, 17, 33, 34
TR and, 18, 29, 32, 265
Underwood in, 147
Versailles Treaty and, 268–69, 302n29
Wilson and, 214, 244, 246, 270
on World War I, 256
Congress of Industrial Organizations (CIO), 278
conservation, 7, 14–15, 17, 18, 59–60, 163, 207
conservative(s)
Aldrich as, 29, 31
Berger as, 223
Cannon as, 29, 31
in Congress, 32
in Democratic Party, 41, 131, 132, 216, 243
Harmon as, 150
in Republican Party, 17, 31, 32, 55–56, 95, 113, 119, 122, 144
Roosevelt and, 7, 105
in Socialist Party of America, 173, 184, 185, 186, 254, 277
on Supreme Court, 280
Taft and, 25, 32, 55, 56, 66, 95, 219, 220
Underwood and, 141, 147, 150
on unions, 169
Wilson and, 41, 51, 132, 134, 145, 216
Constitution, U.S.
Debs on, 5, 258
on executive power, 33
First Amendment, 5, 258
judiciary on, 105
martial law and, 173
Nineteenth Amendment, 265
Versailles Treaty and, 302n29
contract, freedom of, 51. *See also* Sherman Anti-Trust Act
Cooper, John Milton, 281
corruption. *See also* bossism, political
in New York primary elections, 109

corruption (*cont'd*)
   Roosevelt on, 32, 109
   in Tammany Hall, 146
   Wilson on, 51, 62, 126
Cortelyou, George, 96
Courier-Journal (Louisville), 205
Cowles, Anna "Bamie," 22, 28, 234
Cox, James M., 272
Cripple Creek strike, 173
Crisis, 214
Croly, Herbert, 58–59
currency reform, 18, 84–85, 186. *See also*
   bimetallism; free silver issue

Daniels, Josephus, 131, 213–14
Darrow, Clarence, 70, 80, 177–79, 259,
   274
Das Kapital (Marx), 81
Debs, Eugene Victor, 66–90
   in 1916, 254
   on African Americans, 71, 75
   arrest, conviction, and imprisonment
      of, 3, 5–6, 79–81, 257–59, 274–75
   Berger and, 183, 185–86
   on big business, 7–8, 74, 81, 85
   campaigning by, 89–90, 222–25, 236
   on capitalism, 67–68, 70, 73, 82, 85,
      86, 223, 225, 278
   conservatives on, 173
   on Constitution, 5, 258
   death of, 278
   Democratic Party and, 72, 80, 222
   early life of, 68–73
   Haywood and, 176, 177, 179–80,
      183–84, 185, 186, 222
   Hillquit and, 183, 185–86
   on labor movement, 7–8, 72–90, 169,
      170, 174, 179, 181, 185, 186–87,
      222, 278
   marriage of, 73–74, 88–89
   on Moyers, 176, 177
   New York Times on, 77, 90, 225
   on Pettibone, 176, 177
   Populist Party and, 83, 85, 222–23
   on presidency, 6
   on Progressive Party, 222, 223
   on railroads, 70–71, 72–73, 74–75,
      76–80, 177
   Rebellion led by, 77–79

   Roosevelt and, 90, 176, 199, 203–4,
      223, 224, 225, 235
   in Socialist Party, 5–6, 7, 66, 67, 74,
      81, 83, 87, 88, 89, 169, 170, 172,
      173, 179, 183–84, 185–87,
      222–25, 238, 239, 277–78
   speeches of, 5–6, 66–68, 82, 83, 86,
      87, 88, 89, 135, 163, 168–70, 172,
      255, 257, 258, 277
   Supreme Court on, 3, 80
   Taft on, 219, 225
   votes for, in 1912 election, 7, 238, 239
   Wilson and, 5, 222, 223, 224, 225, 275
   on World War I, 3, 255
Debs, Jean Daniel, 68–69, 70, 87
Debs, Kate, 73–74, 81, 87, 88–89, 90
Debs, Mary Marguerite "Daisy," 69, 70, 71
Debs, Theodore, 70, 72, 78, 81, 87–88,
   89, 90
democracy
   Bryan on, 148
   Croly on, 58–59
   Debs on, 81
   direct, 102, 103, 141
   Jefferson on, 59
   representative, 103
Democratic National Committee, 144,
   159, 204, 210, 212
Democratic Party
   in 1890, 102
   in 1896, 40, 83, 84
   in 1897, 65
   in 1900, 40, 84
   in 1908, 84, 90
   in 1910, 34, 50–53, 60, 61–65, 94,
      128
   in 1911, 103
   in 1916, 250, 251, 254, 255
   in 1918, 2
   in 1920, 272
   in 1938, 281
   on African Americans, 101, 163,
      164–65
   Brandeis on, 194
   Bryan in, 40, 84, 125, 128, 148–49,
      150–51, 152
   Congress and, 2, 239, 246, 281
   conservatives in, 41, 131, 132, 216,
      243

Debs and, 72, 80, 222
House in, 138
on immigrants, 213
Murphy in, 146
national convention of, 146–52, 153
in New Jersey, 39, 41, 50–53, 126,
    127, 128, 212
in New York, 156, 211
populism in, 40, 83, 135
progressivism in, 52, 129, 132, 134,
    144, 167, 202, 207, 211, 251, 252
Republican split and, 125
Roosevelt and, 104, 165
Senate and, 239
in South, 129, 131, 163–65, 201,
    213–14, 243, 281
special interests in, 165
Taft on, 221
on Versailles Treaty, 271
Wall Street and, 150
Wilson and, 7, 39, 40, 41, 50–51, 61,
    62–63, 142, 143, 158, 160, 191,
    195–96, 243
Dix, John H., 210, 211, 212
Dodge, Cleveland, 159
Dolliver, Jonathan P., 16, 17
draft, military, 261
DuBois, W. E. B., 163, 264
Dunne, Finley Peter, 17, 116

Edison, Thomas Alva, 205
eight-hour day issue, 18, 74, 76, 163, 172,
    232
Eliot, Charles William, 47, 168
Emerson, Ralph Waldo, 236
Employers' Liability and Safety Appliance
    Laws, 18
environment, 7, 14–15, 17, 59–60
Espionage Act, 3, 5, 257, 301n38

Farmer-Labor Party, 277
farmers
    debt of, 83–84
    progressivism and, 100, 162
    Roosevelt and, 31, 207
    on tariffs, 31, 32, 84, 207
    Wilson on, 135
Federalists, 58
Federal Reserve Act, 244

Federal Trade Commission, 244
First National Bank, 96
Fitzgerald, John F., 158
Fitzgerald, John J., 158
Flinn, William "Bill," 119, 162
Flood, Hal, 151
Frankfurter, Felix, 118
free silver issue, 40, 83, 84, 85, 139. *See
    also* bimetallism; currency reform
free speech, 67, 180, 258
Frick, Henry Clay, 98, 100

Gable, John, 166
Galt, Edith Bolling, 46, 250–51. *See also*
    Wilson, Edith
Garfield, James A., 122, 232
Garfield, James R., 14, 15, 98, 103, 162
Gary, Elbert, 97, 98
General Managers Association, 77, 78, 79,
    80
George, Lloyd, 2, 266, 268
George Washington (U.S. steamship), 1
Gibbons, James Cardinal, 93, 148
Gladstone, William Ewart, 44
Glass, Carter, 155
Gompers, Samuel "Sam," 75, 77, 78–79,
    159, 171, 172, 173, 174, 176
Gooding, Frank, 175
Gorky, Maxim, 176
Gould, Jay, 74
Grant, Ulysses S., 23, 122
Grayson, Carey, 46–47, 269, 270, 273
Great Depression, 185, 247, 278, 279
greenbackers, 135
Gregory, S. S., 80
Grey, Edward, 12

Hamilton, Alexander, 8, 58–59, 66, 197,
    283
Hanna, Mark Alonzo, 24–25, 75
Hapgood, Norman, 205, 234
Hardie, Keir, 81, 180
Harding, Warren Gamaliel, 122, 272–73,
    274–75, 279
Harmon, Judson, 125, 134, 139, 145, 146,
    147, 149–50, 152, 153, 158
Harper and Brothers, 40
Harper's Weekly, 40, 130, 132, 133
Harris, Julian LaRose, 164

Harrison, Benjamin, 25–26, 122
Harvey, George, 40–41, 50–51, 52, 64,
    128, 129, 130, 132–34, 140, 192,
    204–5
Hay, John, 26
Hayes, Rutherford B., 122
Haywood, Henrietta, 177
Haywood, Nevada Jane, 171, 177
Haywood, Vernie, 177
Haywood, William "Big Bill"
    abduction, imprisonment, and trial of,
        175–76, 177–79
    Debs and, 183–84, 186, 222
    early life of, 170–71
    as head of IWW, 169–70, 179, 180,
        181–82, 184, 224
    as Socialist, 254, 277
    on Western Federation of Miners exec-
        utive board, 172, 173–75
Hearst, William Randolph, 134, 136, 139,
    147, 156–57
Heckscher, August, 46
Hepburn Act, 18
Herron, Helen, 26. *See also* Taft, Nellie
Hibben, John Grier, 48–49, 137
Hillis, Charles, 220, 221
Hillquit, Morris, 86, 170, 182, 183
History of the American People (Wilson),
    135–36, 213
H.M.S. *Prince of Wales* (British battle-
    ship), 281
Hofstadter, Richard, 53, 84
Holmes, Oliver Wendell, 193
Homestead strike, 74
Hoover, Herbert, 279
Hopkins, John, 79
hours, factory, 7, 18, 99, 203
House, Edward Mandell
    on Clark-Murphy coalition, 149, 212
    early life of, 137–38
    Philip Dru, Administrator by, 139
    Wilson and, 137, 139–41, 142,
        209–10, 212, 235, 245, 250, 251,
        265, 267–68, 271
House of Representatives, U.S., 32, 94,
    125, 159
Hughes, Charles Evans, 55, 252, 253–54,
    261
Hughes, William, 212, 213

Hull House, 162
Hulman, Herman, 72
Hundred Days (1933), 279

Idaho Daily Statesman, 178
immigrants
    AFL on, 169
    in Lawrence, MA textile mill strike,
        180–81
    living and working conditions of, 7
    in Louisville, KY, 192–93
    at Republican convention, 161
    Socialism and, 87, 183
    Tammany Hall and, 147
    Wilson on, 135–36, 142, 213, 215
income tax, 18, 57, 102, 158, 244
individualism
    Debs on, 87
    Jefferson on, 58, 59
    Taft on, 220
Industrial Workers of the World (IWW),
    169, 170, 173–74, 179, 180, 181,
    182, 184, 224
industry
    expansion of, 7, 25, 31
    on free coinage of silver, 40
    progressives on, 100
    working class and, 33
inflation, 272
insurance, 72, 163, 167, 186. *See also*
    workmen's compensation
International Socialist Review, 184, 185
Interstate Commerce Act, 220
Interstate Commerce Commission, 18,
    57, 99, 206
isolationism, 282
IWW. *See* Industrial Workers of the World
    (IWW)

Jackson, Andrew, 148
Jackson Day dinner, 131–32, 139
James, Henry, 40
James, Ollie M., 149, 151
Jefferson, Thomas, 8, 58, 59, 66, 148,
    194, 196, 244, 283
Jim Crow laws, 244
Johnson, Hiram, 120, 122, 162, 168, 201,
    229, 253
Johnson, Jack, 202

Johnson, Lyndon B., 8
Joline, Adrian, 131, 132, 140
Journal (Atlanta), 201
Juarès, Jean, 180

Kaiserin Augusta Victoria (steamship), 21
Kautsky, Karl, 81
Kelley, Florence, 162
Kellor, Frances, 162
Kennan, George, 248
Kennedy, John F., 8, 158
Kern, John W., 148, 149
Keynes, John Maynard, 266
Khaki election, 266
King, Edward, 97
Knox, Frank, 281

labor movement. *See also specific labor
     unions; specific strikes*
    Debs on, 7–8, 72–90, 169, 174, 179,
         185, 186–87, 222, 278
    farmers on, 207
    Gompers on, 171
    Haywood on, 173, 177, 182
    Roosevelt on, 57, 163, 232
    Socialists on, 183
    strikes by, 173
    Wilson on, 51, 52, 62, 135, 172–73,
         216
LaFollette, Belle, 101
LaFollette, Mary, 104
LaFollette, Robert Marion "Bob," 100,
     101–5, 112, 113, 122, 277
Lambert, Alexander, 233
land reform, Socialists on, 186
Langdell, Christopher Columbus, 193
Lawrence strike of textile workers,
     180–81, 182, 185, 225
League of Nations, 20–21, 49, 265, 266,
     267–68, 271, 272, 273, 274, 279,
     282
League to Enforce Peace, 263
Lenin, Vladimir Ilyich, 180
Life of Gladstone (Morley), 152
Lincoln, Abraham, 4, 19, 81, 89, 112, 122,
     141, 187, 194, 235, 239, 252, 262,
     275
Link, Arthur, 128, 147, 214, 245, 273
Lippman, Walter, 184

Lodge, Henry Cabot
    during Harrison administration, 26
    on judiciary, 105
    on military power, 262, 268–69
    Roosevelt and, 14, 15, 17, 18–19, 21,
         22, 34, 35, 36, 56, 105
    as senator, 261, 262, 268–69, 271,
         273, 302n29
    Taft aided by, 112
    on Versailles Treaty, 268–69, 271,
         302n29
    Wilson and, 5, 49, 269, 271, 273,
         302n29
London, Jack, 176
Longworth, Alice Roosevelt, 21, 22, 28,
     200, 234
Longworth, Nicholas "Nick," 21, 28, 200
Louisville Courier-Journal, 128
Lusitania (British steamship), 249,
     300n18
Luxemburg, Rosa, 180

Mack, Norman E., 144, 148
Magazine, The, 72, 75
Mann Act, 220
Marshall, Thomas, 5, 152, 156, 158, 273
Martin, Elbert, 230–31
Martine, James E., 63, 64–65
Marx, Karl, 81
Marxists, 180
McAdoo, William Gibbs, 129, 137, 144,
     154, 192, 210, 211, 212, 250
McCombs, William, 129, 137, 144,
     145–46, 154, 155, 156, 158,
     191–92, 210, 212
McCorkle, Walter, 129
McCumber, Porter J., 302n29
McDonald, Jesse, 175
McKinley, William, 25, 85, 122, 231, 232,
     233–34, 272
McParland, James, 174, 175, 176, 177,
     178
meatpacking industry, 18
Metzel, Kate, 73. *See also* Debs, Kate
Mine Owners Association, 178
Minor, Nevada Jane, 171
monopolists, monopolies
    Brandeis on, 194
    Debs on, 74

monopolists, monopolies, (*cont'd*)
  farmers on, 84, 207
  FDR on, 280
  LaFollette on, 103
  progressives on, 100
  Taft on, 95–96
  TR on, 99, 103, 206
  U.S. Steel and, 98
  Wilson on, 192, 195, 217, 227
Moore and Schley, 97, 98
morality, moralism
  Debs on, 67, 74
  of Populists, 85
  Roosevelt on, 105, 113, 248, 262
  of Taft, 122
  Wilson on, 51, 64, 66, 137, 215, 243, 245, 270
Morgan, J. Pierpont, 18, 40, 75, 96–97, 99, 100, 133, 150, 173, 194, 204
Mowry, George, 32, 112
Moyer, Charles, 173, 174–76, 177, 178, 179
Munsey, Frank, 109, 120–21, 163, 204
Murphy, Charles "Charlie," 143, 144, 146, 149, 151, 153, 155, 210, 211, 212
Murphy, John, 233
Murray, "Alfalfa Bill," 153

National Association for the Advancement of Colored People (NAACP), 167, 214, 264
National City Bank, 96
National Civic Federation, 75
National German-American League, 205
National Immigration League of New York, 136
National Progressive Republican League, 100, 103
National Recovery Act (NRA), 280
natural resources, 7, 59–60, 86
New Jersey Federation of Labor, 136
New Republic, The, 58
News and Observer (Raleigh), 131
New York Age, 214
New York Evening Post, 130, 214
New York Stock Exchange, 96, 97
New York Sun, 40, 41, 130, 131, 132
New York Times
  on Belmont, 151
  on Beveridge, 165–66
  on Debs, 72, 77, 80, 90, 222, 225
  on election of 1916, 253
  Ochs at, 41
  on Progressive Party convention, 161
  on Roosevelt, 35–36, 94, 166, 202
  on Taft, 35–36, 94
  on Wilson, 65, 227
New York World, 111, 130, 131, 148, 149, 223, 236
Nobel Peace Prize, 20, 248, 262
Norris, George, 112
North American Review, 40, 204–5
Norton, Charles, 36
Nugent, James R., 61, 127, 128, 129

Ochs, Adolph S., 41
Olney, Richard, 77
Orchard, Harry, 174–75, 176, 177, 178, 179
Outlook, The, 57, 99, 100, 116

Page, Walter Hines, 129
Paine, Thomas, 5
Palmer, A. Mitchell, 5, 258, 275
Palmer raids, 258
Panic of 1893, 76, 102
Panic of 1907, 96–98, 100
Parker, Alton B., 144, 148–49
Parker, John M., 163
paternalism
  Cleveland on, 77
  of Roosevelt, 66, 207
  of Wilson, 126, 196
patronage
  by Clark, 157
  by Sullivan, 157
  by Taft, 33, 109, 110
  in Tammany Hall, 147
  by Wilson, 243–44
Payne, Sereno, 17
Payne-Aldrich tariff bill, 17, 33, 34
Peck, Mary Allen Hulbert, 46–47, 126, 130, 137, 142, 143, 159, 191, 229, 245, 250
Pendergast, William A., 122, 167
pensions, 163, 167
People's Party, 83
Perkins, George, 98, 109, 120–21, 163, 204

Pettibone, George, 174–76, 179
Philip Dru, Administrator (House), 139
Pinchot, Gifford, 14–15, 16, 17, 18, 19, 34, 35, 103, 163
Pinkerton Detective Agency, 174
population, expansion of, 7
Populists, Populist Party
 Bryan on, 40, 43, 83, 84–85
 Debs and, 83, 85, 222–23
 progressivism and, 58, 162–63
 White on, 162
 Wilson on, 135
President Grant (U.S. steamship), 16
primary elections, 63, 109, 110, 112, 113, 126, 141, 142
Princeton University
 Joline a trustee of, 131
 Wilson as professor and president of, 6, 39, 41, 44, 45, 47–50, 51, 61, 65, 66, 133, 213, 245
 on Wilson's run for U.S. president, 52, 63, 133
Progressive Bulletin, 205
Progressive National Committee, 252
Progressive Party. *See also* progressivism, progressive(s)
 in 1914, 247
 in 1916, 251, 252
 African Americans and, 161, 163
 Brandeis on, 205
 campaign of, 204–7
 Debs on, 222, 223
 on governmental power, 197
 national convention of, 161–63, 165–68
 Roosevelt in, 118, 120–21, 143, 166–68, 237–39, 246
 Socialists and, 277
progressivism, progressive(s), 3, 80, 100.
  See also Progressive Party
 in 1910, 94
 in 1911, 103
 Addams as, 167
 Aldrich on, 33
 on big business, 100, 102
 Bryan and, 148, 150, 153, 158
 Clark on, 125, 139, 150, 153
 in Congress, 32, 103, 239
 conservatives and, 8

 in Democratic Party, 52, 60, 129, 132, 134, 144, 167, 202, 207, 211, 251, 252
 farmers and, 100, 162
 Hughes as, 252
 James on, 149
 Johnson as, 253
 LaFollette on, 100, 104
 in New Jersey, 52, 53, 60, 61, 127
 Parker as, 163
 Populist strain of, 58, 162–63
 Republican Party and, 32, 34, 113, 135, 207, 209, 254
 Roosevelt and, 6, 32, 41, 112, 163, 201
 on Root, 28
 Socialists and, 277
 Taft and, 32, 95, 108, 221–22
 Tumulty as, 53
 Wilson and, 61, 126, 129, 130–31, 134–35, 145, 149, 150, 158, 195–96, 203, 204, 223, 227, 238, 251
Prohibition, 137
Promise of American Life, The (Croly), 58
Providence Journal, 202
public works, 84
Pullman, George, 76
Pullman strike, 74, 76–79, 85, 89, 172, 177
Pure Food and Drug Act, 18, 220
Pyne, Moses Taylor, 48, 49, 50, 51

racism, 135–36, 213–14, 243–44. *See also* African Americans
railroad(s). *See also* transportation; *specific strikes; specific unions*
 Brandeis on, 194
 Chicago, Burlington and Quincy, 74
 Debs on, 70–71, 72–73, 74–75, 76–80
 farmers and, 84
 Missouri, Kansas, and Texas, 131
 Northern Securities and, 18, 99
 Roosevelt on, 18, 32
 Vandalia, 73
Reagan, Ronald, 8
Record, George, 62
Reparations Commission, 267
Republican National Committee, 25, 116, 117, 119, 122, 204, 220, 253, 265

Republican Party
  in 1908, 17, 32, 63, 89
  in 1910, 34, 55–56, 94
  in 1911, 103
  in 1914, 247
  in 1916, 252, 253, 254, 255
  in 1938, 281
  Brandeis in, 194
  in Congress, 2, 6, 18, 32, 94, 246, 261, 267
  conservatives in, 17, 31, 32, 55–56, 95, 113, 119, 122, 144
  FDR and, 282
  Hanna in, 25
  on Harrison, 26
  LaFollette in, 100, 101
  national convention of, 115–23, 144, 161
  in New Jersey, 63, 127, 128
  in New York State, 36, 55–56, 60
  progressives and, 32, 34, 113, 135, 207, 209, 254
  Root on, 119
  in South, 164
  special interests in, 165
  split in, 3, 8, 34, 55–56, 109, 115, 125, 143, 200, 209, 221, 222
  Taft in, 100, 219
  on Tammany Hall, 210
  on tariffs, 17, 31, 32, 33, 34, 158, 243
  TR and, 6–7, 17, 19, 55–56, 60, 104, 105, 109, 112, 118, 238–39, 254, 263, 264, 272
  on Versailles Treaty, 271
  Wilson and, 127, 143, 209, 213, 238, 272
Republican Roosevelt, The (Blum), 248
Richardson, Edmund, 175, 178, 179
Rockefeller, John D., 18, 75, 100, 173, 206
Rockefeller, John D. Jr., 33
Roosevelt, Alice Lee, 14
Roosevelt, Archie, 5, 22, 256, 257
Roosevelt, Corinne, 4
Roosevelt, Edith, 4, 11, 13, 15, 21, 22, 27–28, 94, 115, 117, 166, 233–34, 265
Roosevelt, Eleanor, 211
Roosevelt, Ethel, 11, 15, 233

Roosevelt, Franklin Delano
  executive power used by, 240
  New Deal of, 8, 278, 279, 280
  on nomination for president, 168
  Stimson and, 60
  on Tammany Hall, 211, 212
  third term of, 231
  TR and, 279–80, 281
  unionism and, 185
  as vice presidential nominee, 272
  Wilson and, 278–79, 280–81, 282–83
Roosevelt, Kermit, 11, 12, 13, 15, 22, 117, 247, 256
Roosevelt, Laura, 233
Roosevelt, Nicholas, 199
Roosevelt, Philip, 229
Roosevelt, Quentin, 4, 22, 256, 264
Roosevelt, Ted, 13, 22, 233, 256
Roosevelt, Theodore "Teddy"
  in 1916, 251–52
  in 1920, 3
  in Africa, 11, 12, 13–14, 15
  on African Americans, 43, 163–65, 264
  assassination attempt on, 229–35
  Autobiography by, 59, 246
  on big business, 7, 8, 17, 18, 51, 57, 59, 99, 100, 103, 105, 109, 111, 167, 192, 194, 196–97, 203, 206, 237–38
  Brazilian expedition of, 4, 246–47
  Bryan on, 144
  Bull Moosers and, 117, 118, 162, 163
  campaigning by, 109–13, 200–202, 203–4, 229, 237–38, 240, 247
  "Charter for Democracy" of, 105
  Clark and, 147
  Collier's on, 205
  Croly's effect on, 58
  Debs and, 90, 176, 199, 203–4, 223, 224, 225, 235
  Democratic Party and, 104, 165
  on environment, 14–15, 17
  European trip of, 15–16, 20–21, 36–37
  FDR and, 278, 279–80, 281, 282–83
  Female Brain Trust of, 162
  on Harrison, 26
  Harvey on, 204–5
  House on, 139

on Hughes, 253

illness and death of, 4, 264–65

immigrants on, 213

on judiciary, 57, 105, 110

Knox and, 281

LaFollette and, 100, 103–4

Lodge and, 14, 15, 17, 18–19, 21, 22, 34, 35, 36, 56, 105

on modern art, 246

on Morgan, 96

on National Progressive Republican League, 103

New Nationalism of, 7, 57, 66, 113, 164, 192, 196–97, 202, 203, 240, 279

New York Times on, 35–36, 94, 166, 202

New York welcome to, 21–23

Nobel Peace Prize won by, 20, 248, 262

Parker defeated by, 144

personality of, 6–7, 11, 13, 16, 20, 27, 245

on Pinchot, 14, 15, 16, 17

on presidency, 6, 8, 19, 33, 35, 100, 104, 106, 239–40, 283

Progressive Party of, 118, 120–21, 143, 166–68, 237–39, 246

on reform, 7, 17–18, 31–32, 57, 104, 105, 163, 167, 232, 247, 265

Republican Party and, 6–7, 17, 19, 55–56, 60, 104, 105, 109, 112, 118, 238–39, 254, 263, 264, 272

on Root, 119

on Sherman Anti-Trust Act, 95

speeches of, 20–21, 105, 110, 111, 112, 117, 118, 120, 123, 166–67, 201, 203, 229, 231, 232, 233, 237–38, 247, 248, 262, 264

Stimson and, 279, 281

Taft, Nellie on, 26

Taft and, 3, 6, 8, 11–13, 14, 15, 17, 18–20, 21–22, 23, 26, 29–30, 34–36, 37, 55–56, 57, 60, 93–94, 95, 98–99, 100, 104, 107–13, 115–16, 117, 118, 119–20, 121, 123, 164, 199–200, 201, 219, 220, 221, 234–35, 236–37, 263

on tariff revision, 17, 31, 32, 57, 203, 206

Through the Brazilian Wilderness by, 247

Underwood and, 147

on U.S. Steel, 94, 97–99

on wages, 99, 167, 206, 229, 232

on war, 239–40

western tour of, 56, 57–58, 60

White on, 281

Wilson and, 3, 4, 65–66, 126, 160, 191, 192, 195, 196–97, 203, 205, 206, 207, 213, 215–16, 217, 227, 235, 244, 248, 256–57, 261, 263

on women, 163, 229, 232, 237

World War I and, 248, 249, 253, 261, 263

Root, Clara, 28

Root, Elihu, 24, 28, 105, 108, 115, 118–19, 120, 121, 200, 219, 262, 263, 271

Rough Riders, 22–23, 116

Rublee, George, 163

Russell, Lillian, 205

Russian Revolution, 277

Russo-Japanese War, 20

Ryan, Thomas Fortune, 40, 41, 128, 133, 135, 146, 148, 150–51, 157

S. S. *Hamburg* (steamship), 29

safety, workplace, 18, 163, 186

Salvatore, Nick, 71

Sanger, Margaret, 184

Schiff, Jacob, 18, 63, 204

Schlesinger, Arthur Jr., 223

Schrank, John, 231

Second International, 180

Sedition Act, 3, 257, 301n38

segregation, 243

Seibold, Louis, 111, 236

Seidel, Emil, 186, 225

self-determination, 244, 265, 266–67, 281

Senate, U.S. *See also* Congress, U.S.

Aldrich in, 17, 18, 29, 33, 202

Cannon in, 17, 18, 19, 29

Democrats and, 239

election of, 52, 63–65, 158, 244

FDR and, 282

on League of Nations, 274

Republicans in, 32, 94

on Sedition Act, 257

Senate, U.S. (*cont'd*)
  Smith in, 63
  Socialists on, 186
  on tariff revision, 33
  on Versailles Treaty, 267, 269, 271
Shaw, George Bernard, 274
Sherman, James S. "Sunny Jim," 55, 56, 60, 122, 235–36
Sherman Anti-Trust Act, 31–32, 77, 95, 98, 99, 220, 244
Sinclair, Upton, 177, 274
six-day week, Roosevelt on, 163
Smith, James Jr. "Jim," 41, 50–51, 52, 53, 61–62, 63, 64, 65, 127, 128, 129, 212–13
Social Democracy of America, 85
Social Democratic Herald, 174
Socialist Democratic Party, 85–86
Socialist Party of America
  in 1904, 67
  in 1908, 67, 68, 89
  in 1916, 239, 254–55, 259
  in 1918, 257
  in 1920, 239, 259
  Berger in, 81, 183, 184, 185–86, 223
  Communists and, 277
  conservatives in, 173, 184, 185, 186, 254, 277
  Debs in, 5–6, 7, 66, 67, 74, 81, 83, 87, 88, 89, 169, 170, 172, 173, 179, 183–84, 185–87, 222–25, 238, 239, 277–78
  Gompers on, 75
  Haywood in, 179, 180, 181–84, 185, 186
  Hillquit in, 182, 183, 185–86
  national convention of, 170, 181–87
  Thomas in, 278
  Western Federation of Miners and, 170, 172
  Wilson's crackdown on, 258
  on World War I, 254
Socialist Party of New York, 184
Socialists
  expulsion of, 258
  on presidency, 186
  Taft on, 220
Southern Society of New York, 129

Spanish-American War, 22
special interests
  Beveridge on, 165–66
  Hamilton and, 59
  Wilson on, 62, 66, 243
Spring-Rice, Cecil, 26
Standard Oil Company, 18, 32
states' rights, 40, 196, 203, 237
Steffens, Lincoln, 103, 177, 274
Steunenberg, Frank, 174–75
Stevens, Edwin S., 41
Stillman, James, 96, 97
Stimson, Henry L., 60, 94, 279, 281
Straus, Oscar, 162
strikes, labor. *See also specific strikes*
  at Cripple Creek, 173
  Debs on, 73, 74, 81, 185
  nonviolence in, 180
  Wilson on, 135
suffrage, 7, 101, 162, 163, 164, 168, 186, 194, 201, 265
Sugar Trust, 32
Sullivan, Mark, 13, 103, 120
Sullivan, Roger, 156, 157, 159
Sulzer, William, 212
Supreme Court, U.S.
  Brandeis on, 192, 194
  conservatives on, 280
  on Debs, 3, 80
  FDR discussing, 280
  on Haywood, Moyer, and Pettibone, 176
  Holmes on, 193
  Hughes on, 252
  on National Recovery Act, 280
  Socialists on, 186
  Taft on, 6, 23, 26, 274
  TR discussing, 57

Taft, Bob, 263
Taft, Charles "Charlie," 25, 26, 30, 35, 220, 263
Taft, Helen, 36
Taft, Nellie, 12, 21, 26, 27, 28–29, 30–31, 35, 36, 37, 107, 219, 221
Taft, Robert A., 221
Taft, William Howard
  in 1908, 27, 90
  on African Americans, 164

on big business, 8, 95–96, 99, 104,
111, 167, 235
Bryan on, 144
Butt and, 19, 21–22, 23, 28, 29,
30–31, 35, 36, 60, 93–94, 107, 108
campaigning by, 110–13, 200, 204,
219–22, 235–37
conservatives and, 25, 32, 55, 56, 66,
95, 219, 220
on Debs, 219, 225
early life of, 23–24
as governor-general of Philippines, 24
Hanna and, 24–25
House and, 139
Hughes and, 252
on League of Nations, 272
on League to Enforce Peace, 263
Lee on, 95
legal career of, 3, 6, 23, 24, 25, 26, 274
Lodge and, 112
marriage of, 12, 26, 27, 28–29, 30–31,
35, 36
on McKinley, 25
on military force, 262
New York Times on, 35–36, 94
on Pinchot, 14, 15, 18
on presidency, 6, 11–12, 23, 26, 27,
29, 33–34
Progressive Party and, 32, 95, 108,
221–22
in Republican Party, 100, 219
Roosevelt and, 3, 6, 8, 11–13, 14, 15,
17, 18–20, 21–22, 23, 26, 29–30,
34–36, 37, 55–56, 57, 60, 93–94,
95, 98–99, 100, 104, 107–13,
115–16, 117, 118, 119–20, 121,
123, 164, 199–200, 201, 219, 220,
221, 234–35, 236–37, 263
Root on, 119
on Socialists, 220
speeches of, 95, 108, 111, 112, 219,
220, 221–22, 235
on tariff revision, 17, 18, 30, 31, 33–34
vote tally, in 1912 election, 238
weight problem of, 23, 24, 35, 107–8
Wilson and, 191, 200, 213, 216, 219,
220, 235
World War I and, 263

Taggart, Thomas, 156
Tammany Hall, 146–47, 149, 150, 153,
155, 210, 211, 212, 225
tariff revision
Congress on, 17, 33, 34
farmers on, 31, 32, 84, 207
Payne-Aldrich tariff bill on, 17, 32, 33,
34
Republican Party on, 17, 31, 32, 33,
34, 158, 243
Roosevelt on, 17, 31, 32, 57, 203, 206
Taft on, 18, 30, 31
Wilson on, 158, 192, 195, 228
taxes, 18, 57, 102, 158, 244
Tennessee Coal and Iron Company, 95,
96, 97–99
Terrell, Scurry, 229, 230, 231
Thelen, David, 102
Thomas, Norman, 278
Thomas, Ransom H., 96
Through the Brazilian Wilderness (Roo-
sevelt), 247
transportation. *See also* railroad(s)
Brandeis on, 193–94
Populists on, 84
Socialists on, 186
Truman, Harry S, 8
Trust Company of America, 96
trusts, financial. *See also* business, big;
Sherman Anti-Trust Act
in 1907, 96
Brandeis on, 194
Morgan on, 97
Roosevelt on, 17, 18, 99, 100, 167,
192, 194, 203, 206
Ryan and, 135
Taft on, 99, 111, 235
tariffs and, 31
Wilson on, 51, 132, 158, 160, 216,
217, 228, 244
Tumulty, Joseph "Joe," 53, 63, 131–32,
133, 134, 137, 144, 145, 146, 153,
154, 254, 271, 275

Uncle Remus's Home Magazine, 164
Underwood, Oscar, 125, 134, 139, 141,
144, 145, 147, 150, 151, 152, 156,
157–58

Underwood-Simmons tariff, 244
unemployment, 84, 135, 163, 167, 272
unions. *See* labor movement
United Auto Workers, 278
United Nations, 282
United States Steel Corporation, 94,
    95–96, 97–99, 100, 104, 227
United Textile Workers of America, 181
unit rule, 149–50, 157
utilities, Wilson on, 52, 126

Vanderbilt, Cornelius, 22
Versailles conference and Treaty, 1, 137,
    265–69, 270, 271, 273–74, 302n29
Viereck, George Silvester, 205–6
Villard, Oswald Garrison, 85, 214–15

Wabash strike, 74
wages
    during depression, 76
    Gompers on, 171
    Gould on, 74
    Roosevelt on, 99, 167, 206, 229, 232
    Wilson on, 203, 206
Wagner-Connery Act, 280
Waldron, J. Milton, 214–15
Wallace, Henry C., 94
Warren, Fred, 88, 89, 163, 176
Warren, Samuel D. Jr., 193
Washington, Booker T., 43, 164, 165
Washington, George, 5, 148, 262
Watterson, "Marse Henry," 128, 133, 134,
    135, 205
wealth
    Croly on, 58
    Debs on, 68
    FDR on, 279
    progressives on, 100
    TR on, 279–80
    Wilson on, 51, 61
Wells, Bulkeley, 173
West, Andrew, 47–48, 49–50
Western Federation of Miners (WFM),
    169, 170, 171, 173, 174, 179
Western Labor Union, 172
WFM. *See* Western Federation of Miners
    (WFM)
Wharton, Edith, 20, 264
White, Henry, 108

White, William Allen, 12, 16, 162–63,
    205, 247, 252, 274, 281
white supremacy, 84, 213–14
Wickersham, George, 30
Wilhelm II, Kaiser, 16, 36–37
Willkie, Wendell, 281
Wilson, Edith, 1–2, 3, 43, 46, 251, 268,
    269, 270, 271, 273
Wilson, Edmund, 48
Wilson, Eleanor "Nellie," 129, 143, 145,
    153
Wilson, Ellen, 45–47, 130, 144, 145, 154,
    159, 214, 250
Wilson, Jessie, 153
Wilson, Joseph Ruggles, 41–43
Wilson, Margaret, 42, 152–53, 159
Wilson, Thomas Woodrow
    on African Americans, 43, 213–15,
        243–44
    Baker and, 150
    on big business, 7, 8, 51, 52, 61, 62,
        126, 132, 147, 158, 160, 192,
        195, 196, 216, 217, 227, 228,
        244, 283
    on bossism, 41, 62, 126, 142, 147,
        159, 211, 212
    Brandeis and, 192, 194–96
    Bryan and, 129–30, 131–32, 134–35,
        139–41, 143, 144, 145, 146, 155,
        157, 228
    campaigning by, 61–63, 128–42, 203,
        204, 209–17, 227–29, 238
    on competition, 7, 192, 195, 197, 203,
        216, 217, 244, 283
    Congress and, 214, 244, 246, 270
    conservatives and, 41, 51, 132, 134,
        145, 216
    death of, 274
    Debs and, 5, 222, 223, 224, 225, 275
    Democratic Party and, 7, 39, 40, 41,
        50–51, 61, 62–63, 142, 143, 158,
        160, 191, 195–96, 243
    early life of, 41–44
    on European trip, 1–2, 3–4
    FDR and, 278–79, 280–81, 282–83
    foreign policy of, 243, 255, 262, 271
    Fourteen Points of, 265, 266–67, 281
    as governor of New Jersey, 6, 63, 125,
        126

Harvey and, 40–41, 50–52, 132–34
History of the American People by,
    135–36, 213
House and, 137, 139–41, 142,
    209–10, 212, 235, 245, 250, 251,
    265, 267–68, 271
illness of, 45, 268, 269, 270–71, 273
on immigrants, 135–36, 142, 213, 215
on James, 149
on labor movement, 51, 52, 62, 135,
    172–73, 216
Lodge and, 5, 268–69, 273, 302n29
marriages of, 44–45
Murphy and, 147, 210, 211, 212
New Freedom of, 7, 192, 195, 196,
    203, 227, 243, 244, 251, 280
in New Jersey governorship campaign,
    60–63
New York Times on, 65, 227
on Parker, 145
Peck and, 46–47, 126, 130, 137, 142,
    143, 159, 191, 229, 245, 250
political beginnings of, 39–41, 44–45
prejudice of, 135–36, 245
on presidency, 6, 8, 128–29, 142, 283
as president, 1–4, 152–60, 238, 239,
    243–46, 249–51, 253–54
at Princeton University, 6, 39, 41, 44,
    45, 47–50, 51, 61, 65, 66, 133,
    213, 245
progressives and, 61, 126, 129,
    130–31, 134–35, 145, 149, 150,
    158, 195–96, 203, 204, 223, 227,
    238, 251
on reform, 7, 62, 126, 195, 203, 206,
    238, 244
Republican Party and, 127, 143, 209,
    213, 238, 272
Smith and, 51, 52, 53, 61–62, 63,
    64–65, 212–13
on Socialist Party, 258
Southern votes for, 165, 201
on special interests, 62, 66, 243
speeches of, 5, 39–40, 51, 52–53,

61–63, 65, 66, 126, 132, 138, 141,
    142, 203, 211, 215–16, 228, 229,
    235, 265, 269–70, 274
Sullivan and, 157
Taft and, 191, 200, 213, 219, 220, 235
on tariff revision, 158, 192, 195, 228
TR and, 3, 4, 65–66, 126, 160, 191,
    192, 195, 196–97, 203, 205, 206,
    207, 213, 215–16, 217, 227, 235,
    244, 248, 256–57, 261, 263
on Underwood, 147
on Versailles Treaty, 1, 137, 265–69,
    270, 271, 273–74
during World War I, 137, 243, 249,
    251, 255, 256
Winthrop, John, 87
Wister, Owen, 104
Wobblies, 169, 180, 182. *See also* Indus-
    trial Workers of the World (IWW)
women
    Mann Act and, 220
    at Progressive Party convention,
        161–62, 167–68
    Roosevelt on, 163, 229, 232, 237
    Socialist Democratic Party on, 86
    voting rights of, 7, 162, 163, 168, 186,
        194, 265
Woodruff, "Tiny Tim," 162
workmen's compensation, 126
World's Week, 129
World War I, 255–56
    Benson on, 255
    conclusion of, 1–2, 264
    Debs on, 3, 255
    Roosevelt and, 248, 249, 253, 261, 263
    Socialists on, 254
    Taft and, 263
    Wilson during, 137, 243, 249, 251,
        255, 256
World War II, 281, 282
Wyman, Isaac, 50

Zerbst, Fred, 258–59
Zimmermann, Arthur, 256

ABOUT THE AUTHOR

JAMES CHACE was the Paul W. Williams Professor of Government and Public Law at Bard College, and Director of the Bard/New York Program on Globalization and International Affairs. The former managing editor of *Foreign Affairs,* and editor of *World Policy Journal,* he is the author of eight previous books, most recently *Acheson: The Secretary of State Who Created the American World* (Simon & Schuster, 1998), named the "Best Book of 1998" by the American Academy of Diplomacy. He passed away in October 2004.